BRANDON
LIPCHIK

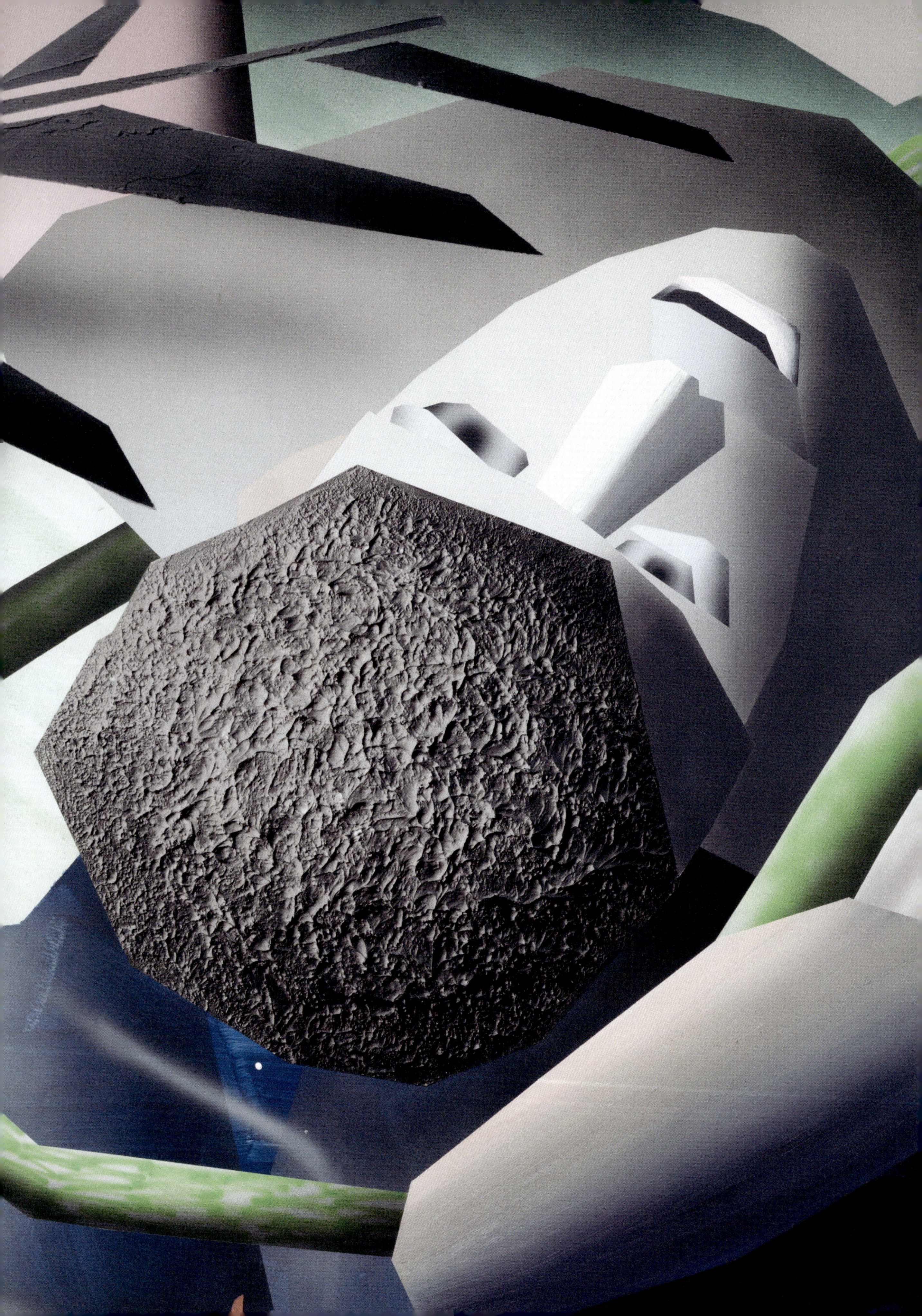

BRANDON LIPCHIK

Moonbeams of Allegory

Edited by · Herausgegeben von
Amely Deiss & Tamara Reitz, Kunstpalais, Stadt Erlangen

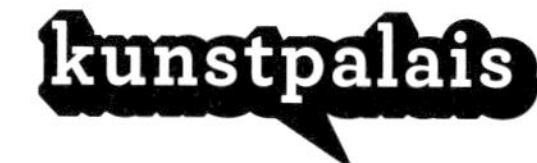

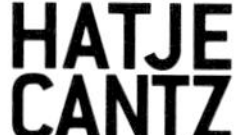

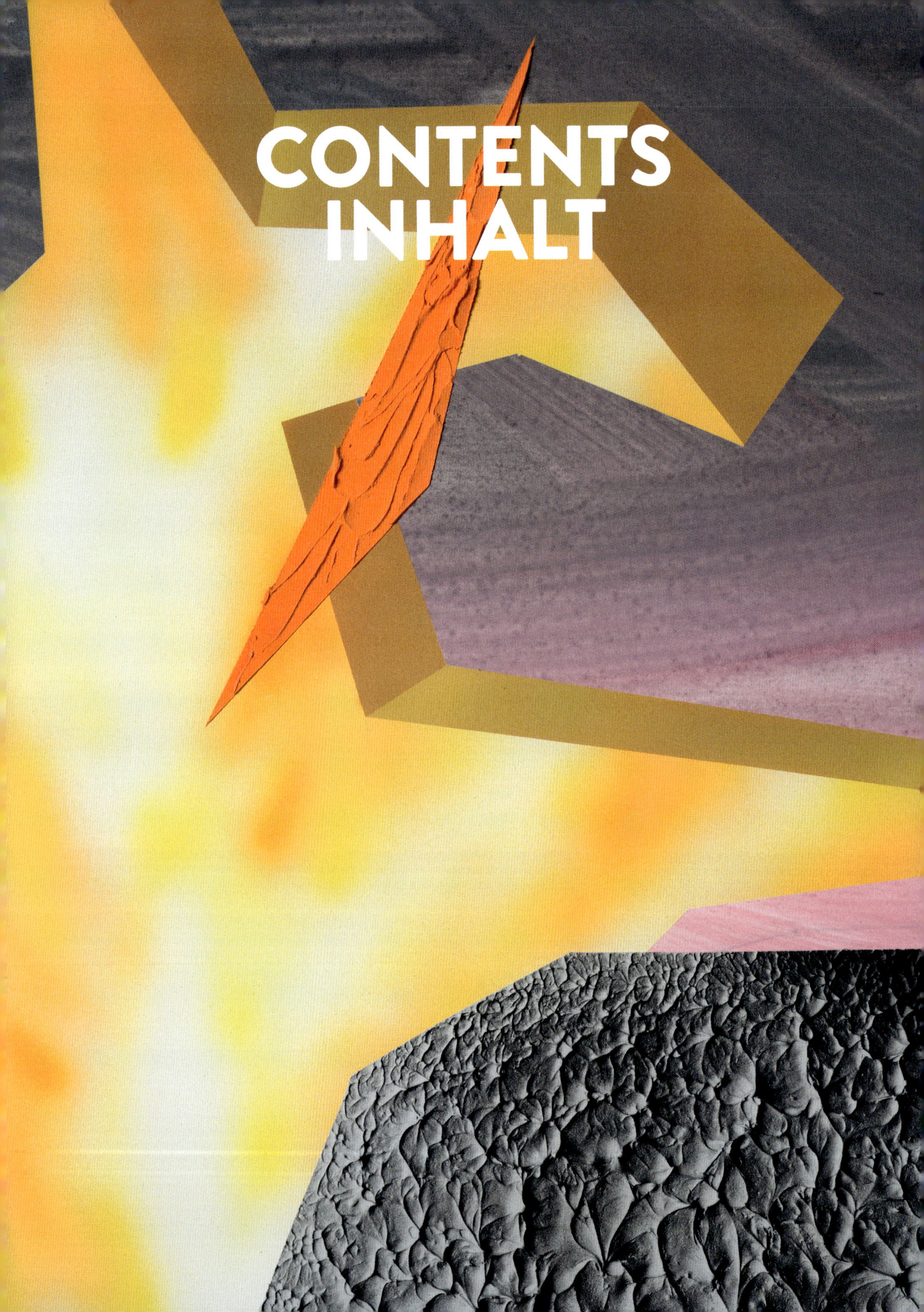

CONTENTS
INHALT

WORKS
ARBEITEN

TEXTS
TEXTE

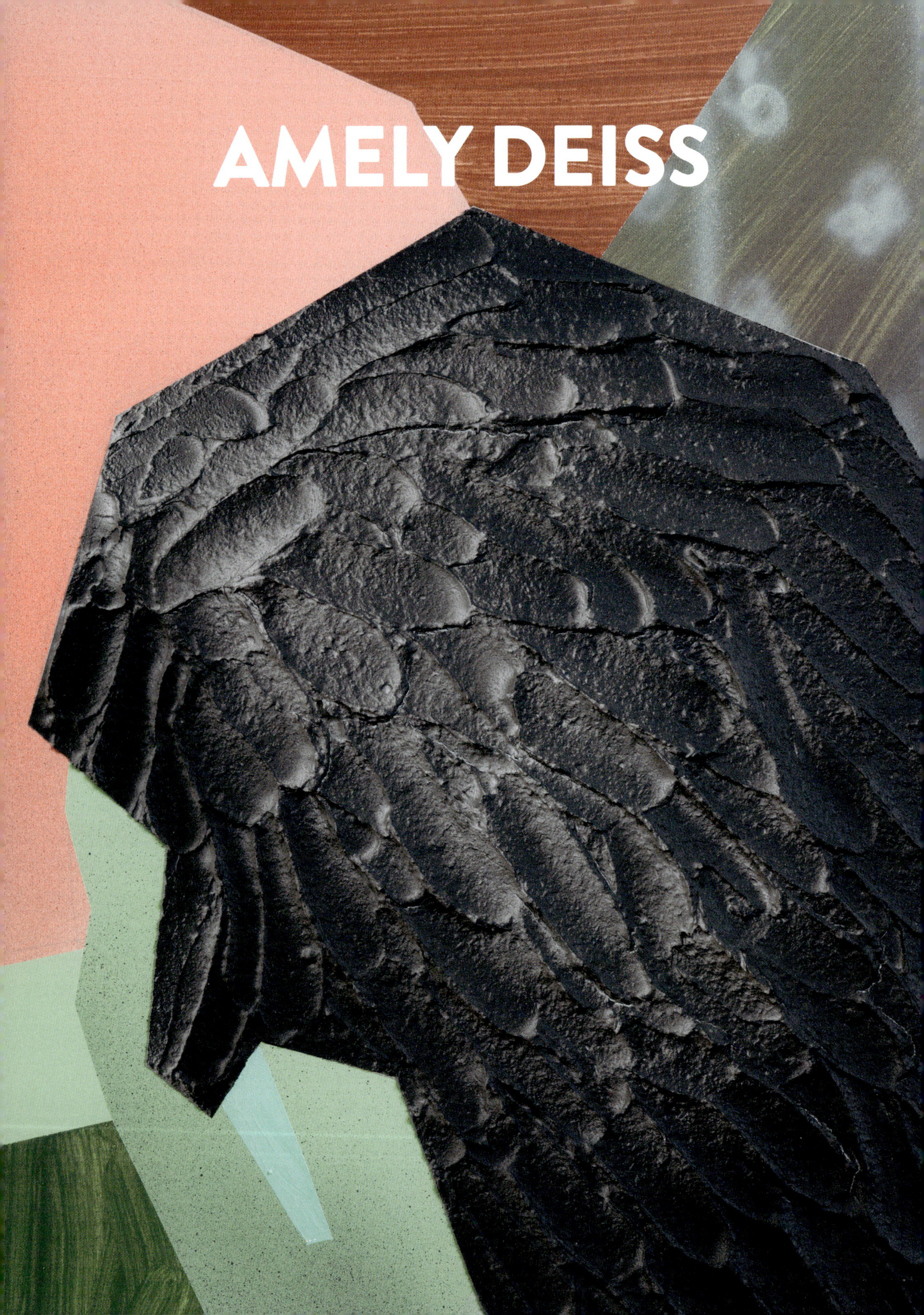
AMELY DEISS

THE MAGIC PULL

The picture is glowing. It seems to produce light from within itself, in green and neon yellow, in bright turquoise—and yet it must be night, because somewhere far back in Brandon Lipchik's *Looking through yellow light* (2022) **[▸ P. 66/67]**, you can see the moon in the darkness. In an expressive gesture, a somehow sunken figure holds a twisted hand protectively in front of their face and is looking through their fingers, out of the picture, framed by light—or rather by color, which the artist has turned into light. The figure is looking past us, with their left hand resting on a thick branch that cuts through the foreground of the painting and seems to reach into our world. We come close to this figure, very close while at the same time being ignored. The figure seems too captivated by what is happening. But what is actually happening? The painter deliberately shows us only part of it—we can follow the figure's gaze into the light—but what they actually see is left to our imagination. It is as if we were looking at someone looking at a screen and trying to read in their face what they are seeing. Indeed, as is often the case in Brandon Lipchik's work, the glow of the whole image is reminiscent of a computer screen at night. At the same time, *Looking through yellow light* also brings to mind mysterious natural phenomena such as the green glow of the aurora borealis.

All is quiet.

In *Fallen Angel* (2021) **[▸ P. 122]**, which feels like the counterpart to *Looking through yellow light* and might be my other favorite painting by Brandon Lipchik, the protagonist also holds his spread fingers at head height but this time in a fighting stance. Edged flames flicker in the background. Pointed long leaves and stalks reach out from the edge of the painting towards the figure like enemy weapons. Flowing red washes around the figure's lower body like a glowing stream of lava. Here, too, we do not see what the figure is reacting to.

All is in commotion.

I am reminded of the thrilling gloom and dizzying disorientation that I used to feel when I entered computer game worlds like *Alone in the Dark*. One turn of the cursor too far and the ground is pulled out from under my feet as I try to navigate the hero, constructed from polygonal shapes, through a house full of puzzles. Inserting the right object or applying the right technique makes the enemy dissolve into a pearly swarm of spherical bubbles.

Lipchik's heroes are frozen in a perfect pose, as the absolute center of the composition. Moving and unmoving at the same time.

The angular appearance of the figures, reminiscent of computer game graphics of the 1980s and 1990s, also distinctively comes into play in the riding figure on *La Guerre des Chiens* (2022) **[▸ P. 98/99]**. For in this work, Lipchik lets us enter into his world a little further, via VR technology and scenes programmed by the artist himself, which he creates as three-dimensional continuations of his painting. VR glasses transport us right into the scene: we can move around in it, look around in all directions, see everything up close—and try to find out what the naked figure on horseback and the fighting dogs are all about, whose world seems to be limited by the edge of the low plinth.

The enigmatic motifs are so captivating that you can easily forget to pay full attention to the color and look closely at how Lipchik composes them: the almost self-luminous violet of the human body, the animals in blue, red and khaki and, last but not least, the colors of the mysteriously divided sky—a star-spotted deep dark blue and pink-banded turquoise. Colors that you have probably never seen united like this before or at least have not found beautiful in this combination. And yet they are. Very much so! Above all, they are at least as exciting and sophisticated as the combination of motifs, symbols and references and just as thrilling as the paintings' narrative. Lipchik is a master of colors—and of textures. The flakiness and thinning out at the edges of the airbrush next to perfect, smooth and sharply contrasting surfaces, monochrome or with color gradients, surfaces on which individual brushstrokes can be discerned, or the dense, thick accumulation of color that in Lipchik's work makes hair, for example, almost physically tangible. The artist fearlessly lets them collide, puts them together like pieces of a jigsaw that only make sense in this one way. Lipchik contrasts the imitation of materials—as the old masters did to perfection in still lifes with the iridescence of a glass, the softness of a fur, of the plump skin of a fruit—with a whole new variety of surfaces. A composition in which the surfaces and parts are not mimetic, but rather stand on their own merits.

It is not surprising then that my Kunstpalais colleagues and I have long felt magically drawn to these paintings. Fortunately for us, Brandon Lipchik accepted our invitation to stage a solo exhibition at Kunstpalais, and it was a great joy for us to organize the first large institutional solo show for and with him.

This beautiful book has been produced on the occasion. It is the artist's first comprehensive catalog, with much to see: the works presented here go back to paintings that were created in 2019. They take viewers from pastel-colored still lifes, via sun-drenched, turquoise pool scenes, to the mysterious scenes of Lipchik's present paintings. As we, the viewers, confront one mystery, a new one opens up. Lipchik's works evoke so many associations, feelings and memories that one likes to contemplate them by oneself. However, at the same time, company is wanted to help us discover them. Therefore, in this book, three different authors take us by the hand:

Tamara Reitz, the exhibition's curator, looks at Lipchik's latest series of works, which is also the starting point for our Kunstpalais exhibition. Accompanied by Robert Frost, Marcel Duchamp and VR glasses, she takes us into a nocturnal wilderness as the new setting for Lipchik's works. In his essay, journalist and art critic Oliver Koerner von Gustorf discusses early works, reflects on artistic models, perception of bodies and cinematic counterparts, while Kristian Vistrup Madsen lets Brandon Lipchik himself have his say in an engaging interview, which covers Americana and Berlin, loneliness and the escapism of painting.

Florian Frohnholzer and Thomas Pruss from the Sofarobotnik graphic design office have lovingly designed this book and managed to make the materiality of the works as intensely perceptible as possible. The nonchronological sequence of the paintings opens up completely new encounters within the different groups of works.

Tamara Reitz as curator of the exhibition and editor of the catalog has immersed herself in Brandon Lipchik's art. She has managed this large-scale project in all its details—tirelessly, imaginatively and with enthusiasm for the artist's work— and the entire team at Kunstpalais has made sure that this exhibition with all its special features became a reality.

I would like to take this opportunity to thank them all very much!

Finally, very special thanks go to Brandon Lipchik. We are absolutely delighted to have been able to create this book and this exhibition together with him!

Whatever it is about Brandon Lipchik's art that appeals to you so much that you are now holding this book in your hand, be it the mysteriously calm or the wild narrative, the darkness or the glow, the art-historical, literary, cinematic references or the aesthetic echoes of computer games of past decades and the digital world of more recent times, be it color, form, material or movement—one element alone will be enough to magically pull you in and open your eyes to all the other fascinating aspects in a whirling frenzy. Fortunately, we have Brandon Lipchik's works here in front of us on the most beautiful paper and we are just as fortunate that we certainly cannot get them out of our heads either.

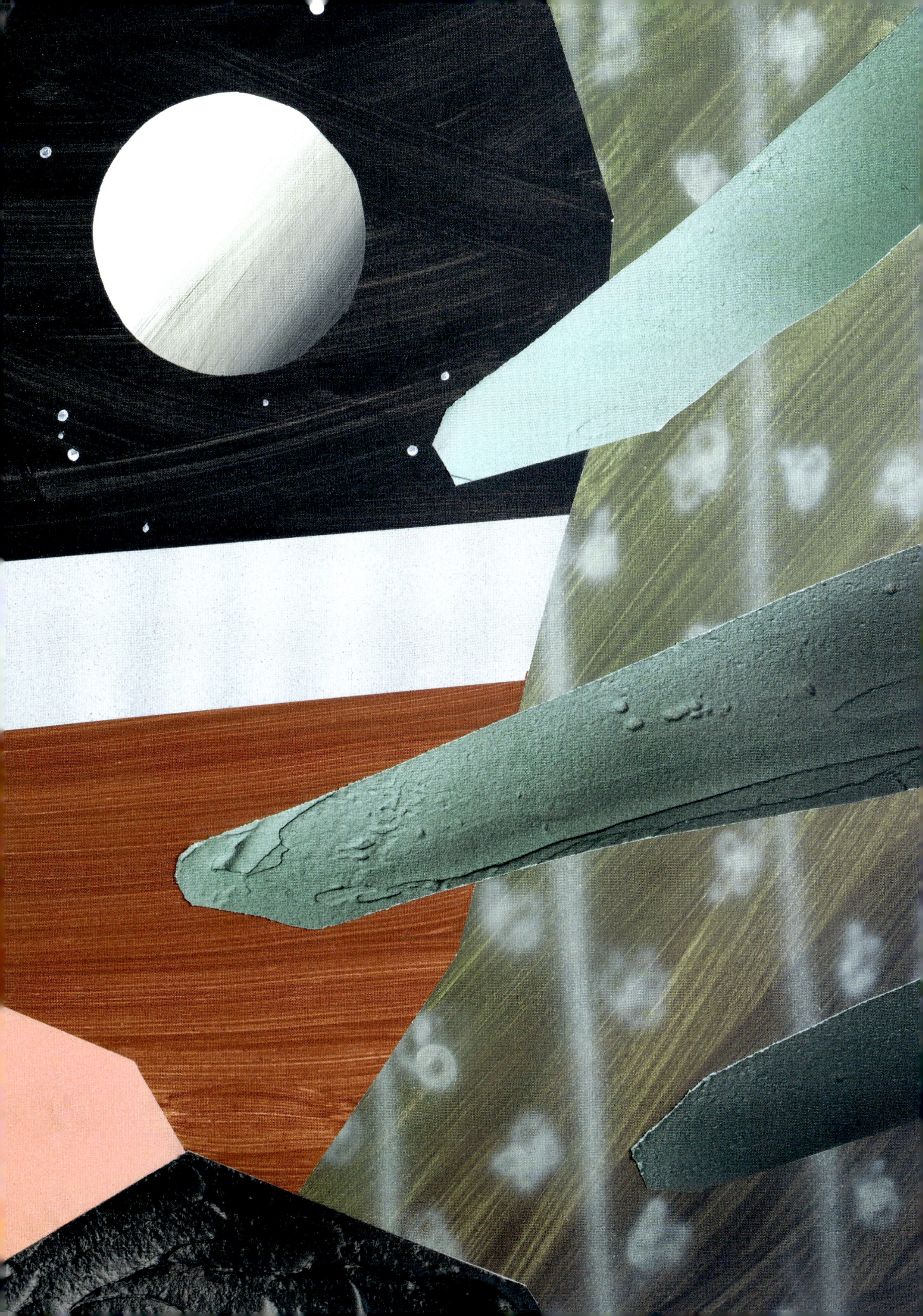

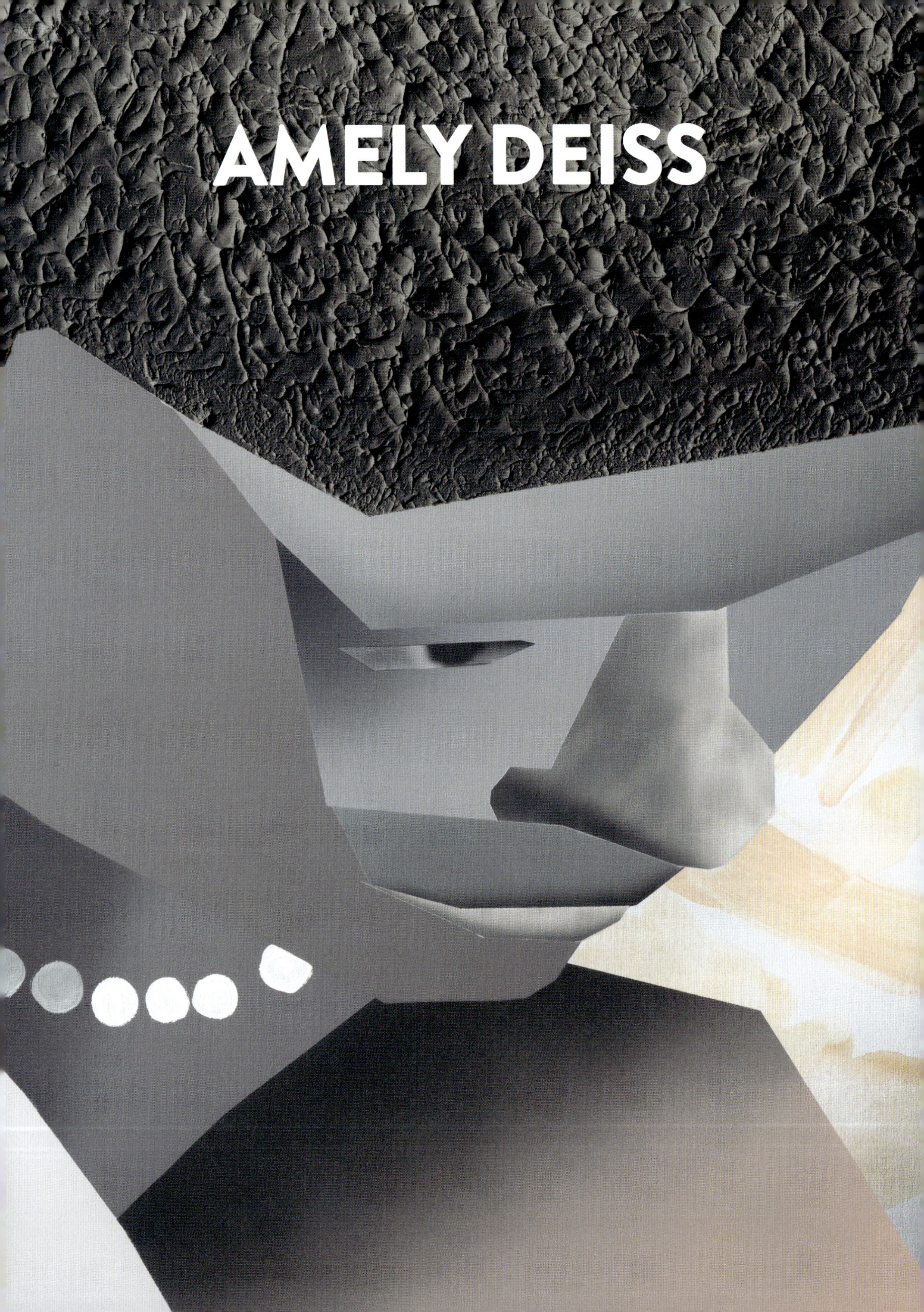
AMELY DEISS

IM MAGISCHEN SOG

Das Bild leuchtet. Es scheint geradezu aus sich heraus Licht zu produzieren, in Grün und in Neongelb, in hellem Türkis – und doch ist es wohl Nacht, denn irgendwo weit hinten auf Brandon Lipchiks *Looking through yellow light* (2022) **[▸ S. 66/67]** steht der Mond im Dunkeln. In expressiver Geste hält sich die irgendwie versunkene Figur eine verdrehte Hand schützend vors Gesicht. Blickt durch die Finger, aus dem Bild heraus, eingerahmt durch Licht – beziehungsweise durch Farbe, die der Künstler zu Licht gemacht hat. Blickt an uns vorbei. Die linke Hand der Figur liegt auf einem dicken Ast, der den Vordergrund des Bildes durchschneidet und in unsere Welt hineinzuragen scheint. Wir kommen ihr nah, dieser Figur, sehr nah – während sie selbst uns ignoriert. Zu gefesselt scheint sie von dem zu sein, was da gerade passiert. Aber was ist das eigentlich? Der Maler zeigt uns absichtsvoll nur einen Teil davon – wir können dem Blick der Figur ins Licht folgen – doch was sie tatsächlich sieht, bleibt unserer Vorstellung überlassen. So als sähe man jemanden von gegenüber auf einen Bildschirm schauen und versuche, in seinem Gesicht abzulesen, was er gerade sieht. Und tatsächlich, wie häufiger in den Werken Brandon Lipchiks, erinnert das Leuchten des ganzen Bildes an den nächtlichen Schein des Computerbildschirms. Gleichzeitig denkt man bei *Looking through yellow light* aber auch an geheimnisvolle Naturphänomene wie das grüne Leuchten des Polarlichts.

Alles ist ruhig.

Auf dem gefühlten Pendant zu diesem Bild, vielleicht meinem anderen Lieblingsbild von Brandon Lipchik, *Fallen Angel* (2021) **[▸ S. 122]**, hält der Protagonist ebenfalls die gespreizten Finger auf Kopfhöhe – diesmal jedoch in kämpferischer Haltung. Im Hintergrund züngeln kantige Flammen. Spitze lange Blätter und Halme streben vom Bildrand aus auf die Figur zu wie gegnerische Waffen. Fließendes Rot umspült als glühender Lavastrom den Unterkörper der Figur. Auch hier sehen wir nicht, worauf die Figur reagiert.

Alles ist in Aufruhr.

Ich fühle mich an die aufregende Düsternis und die schwindelerregende Orientierungslosigkeit erinnert, die mich früher beim Eintritt in Computerspielwelten wie *Alone in the Dark* umfangen haben. Eine Cursordrehung zu weit, und es zieht mir den Boden unter den Füßen weg, während ich versuche, den aus polygonen Formen konstruierten Helden durch ein Haus voller Rätsel zu navigieren. Das richtige Objekt eingesetzt oder die richtige Technik angewandt und der Gegner löst sich in einen perlenden Schwarm kugelrunder Blasen auf.

Die lipchikschen Held*innen sind in perfekter Pose erstarrt, als absolutes Zentrum der Komposition. Bewegt und unbewegt zugleich.

Die kantige, an Computerspielgrafiken der 1980er und 1990er erinnernde Erscheinung der Figuren kommt auch bei der reitenden Figur auf *La Guerre des Chiens* (2022) **[▸ S. 98/99]** auf besondere Weise zum Tragen. Denn unter anderem bei dieser Arbeit lässt uns Lipchik gleich noch ein weiteres Stück hinein in seine Welt: über die Technik der Virtual Reality und die vom Künstler selbst programmierten Szenerien, die er als dreidimensionale Fortführung seiner Malerei anlegt. Eine VR-Brille befördert uns mitten in die Szenerie: Wir können uns darin bewegen, uns in alle Richtungen umschauen, alles aus nächster Nähe betrachten – und versuchen herauszufinden, was es mit der nackten, reitenden Figur und den kämpfenden Hunden auf sich hat, deren Welt durch den Rand der niedrigen Plinthe begrenzt zu sein scheint.

Die Rätselhaftigkeit der Motive ist so vereinnahmend, dass man darüber leicht vergessen kann, sich den Farben mit voller Aufmerksamkeit zu widmen. Sich genau anzuschauen, wie Lipchik sie komponiert: das geradezu selbstleuchtende Violett des menschlichen Körpers, die Tiere in Blau, Rot und Khaki und nicht zuletzt die Farben des auf rätselhafte Weise geteilten Himmels: sternengetupftes tiefdunkles Dunkelblau und pink gebändertes Türkis. Farben, die man so wahrscheinlich noch nie vereint gesehen hat – oder in der Kombination zumindest nicht schön gefunden hat. Und doch sind sie es. Und wie! Und vor allem mindestens ebenso spannungsreich und raffiniert wie die Kombination der Motive, Symbole und Verweise. Ebenso spannend wie die Bilderzählung an sich. Lipchik ist ein Meister der Farben. Und der Texturen! Das Flockige, sich an den Rändern Ausdünnende des Airbrush neben perfekten, glatten und scharf gegeneinander abgetrennten Flächen, monochrom oder mit Farbverlauf, Flächen, auf denen einzelne Pinselstriche zu erkennen sind – oder eben die dichte, dicke Anhäufung von Farbe, die bei Lipchik beispielsweise Haar fast körperlich erlebbar macht. Der Künstler lässt sie unerschrocken aneinanderstoßen, setzt sie zusammen wie Teile eines Puzzles, die nur auf diese eine Weise Sinn ergeben. Dem Imitieren von Stofflichkeiten, wie sie alte Meister in Stillleben zur Perfektion trieben – hier das Schillern eines Glases, hier die Weichheit eines Pelzes, dort die pralle Schale einer Frucht –, setzt Lipchik eine ganz neue Vielfalt an Oberflächen entgegen. Eine Komposition, in der die Oberflächen und Partien eben nicht mimetisch sind, sondern vielmehr in ihrem Wert für sich stehen.

Kein Wunder also, dass meine Kolleg*innen aus dem Kunstpalais und ich uns schon lange magisch angezogen fühlten von dieser Malerei. Der Einladung zur Einzelausstellung, die wir daraufhin aussprachen, ist Brandon Lipchik zu unserem Glück gerne gefolgt, so dass wir nun mit Freude die erste große institutionelle Soloshow für und mit ihm ausrichten durften.

Und vor allem ist zu diesem Anlass dieses schöne Buch entstanden – der erste umfangreiche Katalog des Künstlers. Entsprechend viel gibt es zu sehen: Die abgebildeten Werke reichen bis 2019 als Entstehungsjahr zurück und führen die Betrachter*innen entlang pastellfarbener Stillleben über sonnenüberflutete, türkisleuchtende Poolszenen hin zu den mysteriösen Szenerien der lipchikschen Jetztzeit. Während wir uns als Betrachter*innen dem einen Rätsel stellen, tut sich ein neues auf. Lipchiks Werke rufen so viele Assoziationen, Gefühle und Erinnerungen auf, dass man gerne alleine sein mag mit den Bildern und ihrer Betrachtung – sich gleichzeitig aber auch Begleitung wünscht, die beim Entdecken hilft. Und so nehmen uns in diesem Buch gleich drei unterschiedliche Autor*innen mit ihren Texten an die Hand:

Die Kuratorin der Ausstellung, Tamara Reitz, schaut sich mit uns die jüngste Werkserie Lipchiks an, die auch Ausgangspunkt für die Ausstellung im Kunstpalais ist. Mit Robert Frost, Marcel Duchamp und VR-Brille führt sie uns in die nächtliche Wildnis, dem neuen Schauplatz der lipchikschen Werke. Journalist und Kunstkritiker Oliver Koerner von Gustorf schlägt in seinem Essay einen Bogen zu den frühen Arbeiten, denkt über künstlerische Vorbilder, Wahrnehmung von Körpern und filmische Pendants nach. Und Kristian Vistrup Madsen lässt in seinem unterhaltsamen Interview Brandon Lipchik selbst zu Wort kommen – und spricht mit ihm über Americana und Berlin, über die Einsamkeit und den Eskapismus beim Malen.

Florian Frohnholzer und Thomas Pruss vom Grafikbüro Sofarobotnik haben es mit der liebevollen Gestaltung dieses Buchs geschafft, die Materialität der Werke maximal intensiv spürbar zu machen und eröffnen in der nicht chronologischen Abfolge der Bilder ganz neue Begegnungen innerhalb der unterschiedlichen Werkgruppen.

Tamara Reitz als Kuratorin der Ausstellung und Redakteurin des Katalogs hat sich Brandon Lipchiks Kunst umfassend angenommen und unermüdlich, ideenreich und mit Begeisterung für das Werk dieses große Projekt in all seinen Details ausgearbeitet. Und das Team des Kunstpalais hat mit vereinten Kräften daran gearbeitet, dass die Ausstellung mit all ihren Besonderheiten Wirklichkeit wird.

Ihnen allen sei an dieser Stelle aufs Herzlichste gedankt! Ganz besonderer Dank gilt schließlich Brandon Lipchik selbst. Wir freuen uns unglaublich, dass wir mit ihm gemeinsam dieses Buch und diese Ausstellung entstehen lassen konnten!

Was auch immer es ist, was Sie selbst an Brandon Lipchiks Kunst so angesprochen hat, dass Sie jetzt dieses Buch in der Hand halten – sei es das mysteriös Ruhige oder die wilde Narration, die Dunkelheit oder das Leuchten, die kunsthistorischen, literarischen, filmischen Bezüge oder die ästhetischen Anklänge an Computerspiele vergangener Jahrzehnte und das Digitale neuerer Zeiten, sei es Farbe, Form, Material oder Bewegung: Schon dieses eine Element wird ausreichen, um Sie im magischen Sog mit sich hinabzuziehen und Ihnen in einem wirbelnden Rausch die Augen für all die anderen faszinierenden Aspekte zu öffnen.

Zum Glück haben wir Brandon Lipchiks Arbeiten hier auf schönstem Papier vor uns – doch auch aus dem Kopf gehen sie uns mit Sicherheit nicht mehr. Zum Glück.

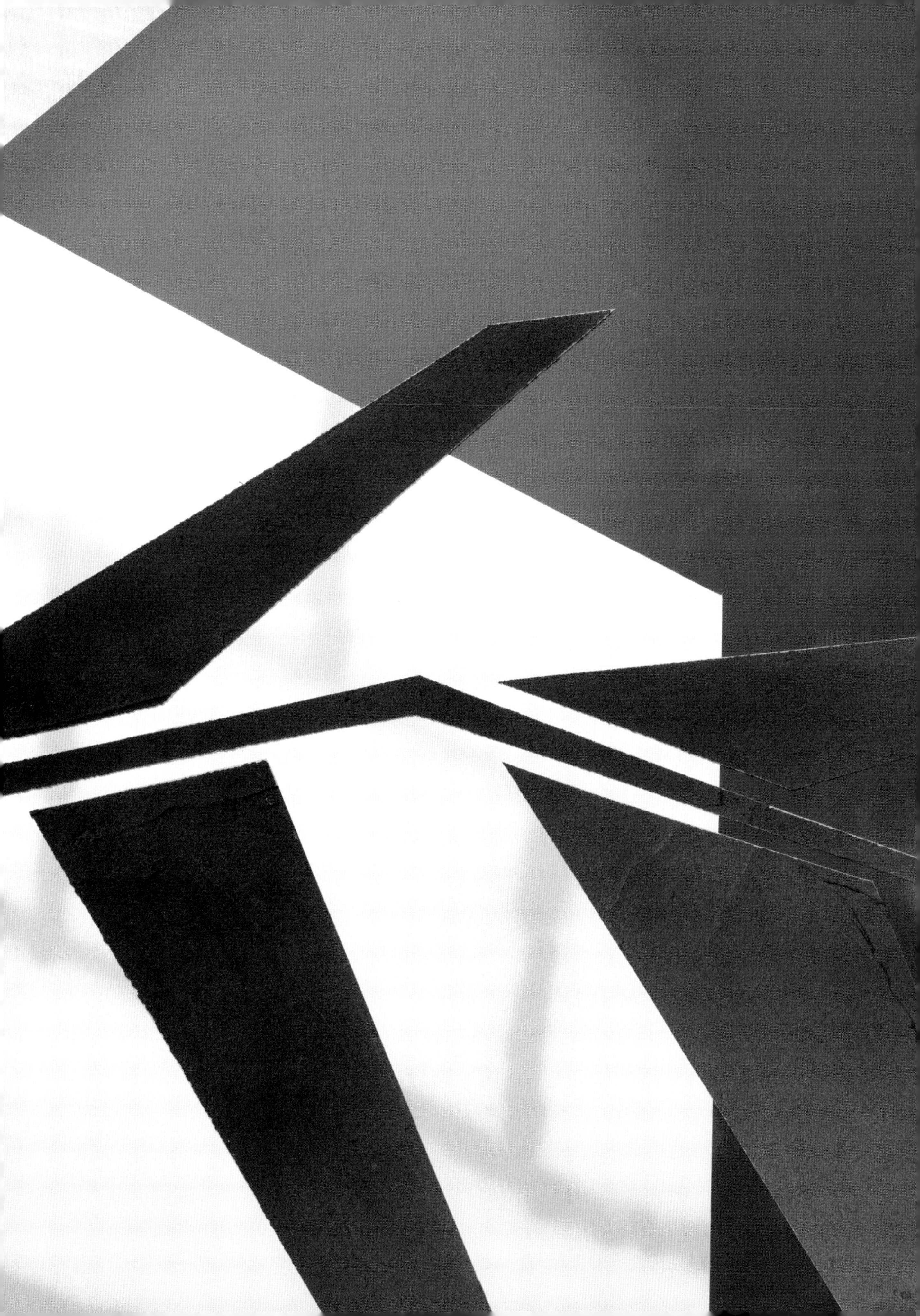

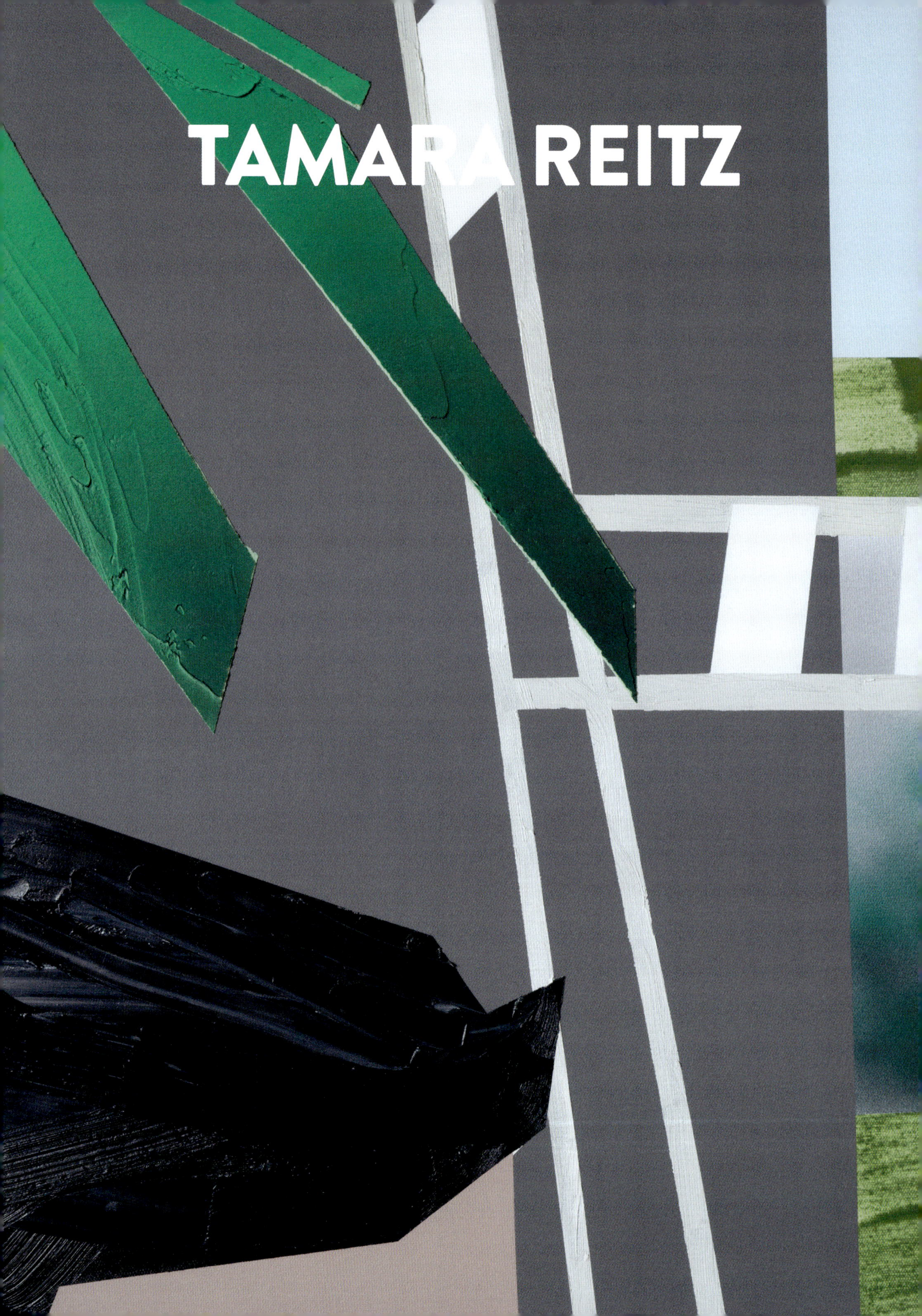
TAMARA REITZ

A MIDNIGHT DREAM

The woods are lovely, dark and deep,
But I have promises to keep,
And miles to go before I sleep,
And miles to go before I sleep.
— Robert Frost[1]

Uncanny. That was the first thought that popped into my head when I looked at the painting. An adjective I hadn't actually associated with Brandon Lipchik's work before. After all, the artist's earlier works were characterized by pastel-toned lightness and contemporary poolscapes in poppy colors, where his naked avatar-like figures romped in and around swimming pools or lounged on the perfect lawns of fenced-in suburban gardens. This new scene by contrast first struck me as uncomfortable and oppressive, even outright disturbing.

But its psychological depth and all the art-historical, literary, and pop-cultural references that cropped up in Lipchik's painting *A beauty and the beast* (2022) **[▶ P.78/79]** eventually mesmerized me. The title already reveals what it's apparently about—namely, the eponymous folk tale, which was most famously adapted into Walt Disney's animated film *Beauty and the Beast* (1991). However, one probably wouldn't describe the Disney version about the beautiful Belle and the prince who has been transformed into a beast as dark and eerie or even erotic. The focus of Lipchik's composition, on the other hand, is—quite explicitly—a sexual act between human and beast. But unlike in the fairy tale, the humanoid here isn't identifiable as a woman, but rather a figure without specific sexual traits. There is, however, at least one thing clear at the center of the composition: the erect penis of a distinctly inhuman figure who is otherwise only dimly discernible. In a nocturnal landscape with a rosé-colored full moon in the distant, jet-black starry sky, the creature throws itself at a naked figure lying on their back in a green lawn to the left. Its mouth wide with relish revealing pointed teeth, the creature clutches its human counterpart, who turns their face away from the viewer. The figure's feelings about the situation are only revealed in the reflection that appears in the hand mirror they're holding up. They catch sight of their own reflection: their mouth gaping in shock or pleasure, eyes opened wide. The drama of the depiction is further intensified by spotlights along the image's lower edge and an indeterminate orange light source shining down diagonally from above. They illuminate the action, staging it as if on a theater stage or a dance floor while exposing us—the viewers—as voyeurs of this wild and uncomfortably erotic scene.

By embedding the depiction in an unfamiliar, dreamlike forest landscape, this and other paintings in the exhibition *Moonbeams of Allegory* recall the surreal landscape paintings of the naïve artist Henri Rousseau, whose *Belle et la Bête* (1908, Beauty and the Beast) Lipchik is clearly quoting. Whereas the previous paintings were set in the fenced gardens of American suburbs with meticulous lawns and square swimming pools emblematic of civilizational order, *A beauty and the beast* suggests a new direction. The characters have left behind the orderly confines of suburbia and undertake clandestine erotic adventures in a remote and untamed nature. In fact, nature increasingly becomes the protagonist itself. We encounter more and more animal figures, werewolf-like creatures, and paradisiacal birds interacting with the anonymous avatars, and even unpopulated landscape paintings where nature stands on its own for the first time in Lipchik's work. Draped ornamental plants have been replaced by tree trunks, gnarled branches, and conifers dominated by a dark blue-green palette with accents in pink, yellow, and purple.

Lipchik creates this surreal wilderness using 3D design software, making it the setting for eerie narratives and legends. However, the artist's digital working methods aren't limited to the renderings that serve as sketches for his analog paintings; he goes a step further and even allows viewers to virtually immerse themselves in his images. The act between human beauty and animalistic beast as well as the painting's dark atmosphere can thus be experienced on a further immersive level. With the help of VR glasses, viewers find themselves in the virtual version of the painting and in front of the same rectangular platform that serves as the presentation surface for the group of figures. Before the flat stage set of a forest surrounded by deciduous trees and fern-like vegetation, the viewer inevitably becomes a clear witness to the events. Frozen in motion, Lipchik's figures look like exhibits in a virtual diorama. The analog ancestors of such stagings have been popular since the 19th century, especially in the museum context. Against the backdrop of colonialism, such exhibits brought the visitors of natural history museums closer to foreign and exotic life worlds. It is known, for example, that Rousseau's jungle paintings were partly informed by the flora and fauna in the dioramas of the *Jardin des Plantes* in Paris. The defenseless naked body in a natural landscape as well as the explicit, almost pornographic eroticism confronting the viewer in Lipchik's work also brings to mind one of the most famous dioramas in art history, Marcel Duchamp's *Etant Donnés: 1° la chute d'eau, 2° le gaz d'éclairage …* (1946–1966, *Given: 1. The Waterfall, 2. The Illuminating Gas …*). One of Duchamp's last pieces, which he worked on for two decades, it practically forces the viewer into the role of a voyeur and confronts them with the disturbing eroticism of the situation. In the installation, the viewer peers through peepholes in an aged wooden door onto a scene constructed in a kind of showcase behind it. Through an opening in a brick wall behind the door, a nude female body appears with her legs spread, lying in a pile of dry brushwood and foliage against the backdrop of a vivid forest landscape with a waterfall. Phallus-like, the faceless stranger holds up a gas lamp in her left hand. The division of Duchamp's diorama-like assemblage into multiple layers as well as the forceful staging of the viewers as prurient onlookers resonates with Lipchik's VR installation. Unlike Duchamp, however, he doesn't have us look through a binocular door, but allows us to observe, even enter the situation through VR glasses. What Duchamp's and Lipchik's works share is a marked interest in the act of looking and playing with perspectives. Both artists' works are imbued with erotic energy and the uneasy feeling of directly witnessing something forbidden or secret.

Although the VR glasses in Lipchik's work let users move around the pictorial space, while in Duchamp's work they inevitably remain behind the wooden door, intimate proximity to the action in both is only ever superficially suggested. In fact, the angular aesthetics of the inanimate group of figures on the stage-like platform have a primarily distancing effect on the virtual "visitors." Despite the VR glasses, viewers do not become part of the action nor can they participate in it. Instead, they inevitably remain in the position of spectators. Indeed, the sign centrally placed in front of the stage underlines the viewers' passive role and brings Lipchik's work closer to the sublime display of natural history dioramas and museum displays. Unlike an information panel in a museum, however, the text on the display is not a scientific explanation, but a poem by the artist that can be read as a commentary on the fictional scene depicted and reveals the artist's feelings. With stanza and verse numbers as well as poignantly quoted words, Lipchik's text clearly refers to one of the most popular works by the American poet Robert Frost: *Stopping by the woods on a snowy evening* (1922). The four stanzas recount the thoughts of someone driving a horse-drawn sleigh who suddenly stops in the middle of nature, far from any civilization, to admire the snowfall and the beauty of the forest at night. In the last stanza, however, he remembers the obligations he still has to fulfill and the long distance to be covered before he can sleep. Lipchik's poem adapts Frost's nature poem and transforms it into a poetic commentary on his work *A beauty and the beast*. Frost's poem is about being attracted to the forest's somber beauty, the contrast between civilization and nature, the desire for peace of mind, and the urge to simply leave one's everyday duties behind. As a symbol of untamed nature and irrationality, the forest becomes a place of longing that promises unbridled freedom, a place without control and prohibitions. At the same time, the driver in the poem is aware that he cannot escape his obligations—an inner conflict between irrational subconscious and rational behavior, between libidinal drives and control, which can also be seen in the complex of works around *A beauty and the beast*.

Animalistic, instinctive love, the nocturnal forest as the site of fantastic erotic events, the magical power of the moon, the turning away from the order of urban civilization, and theatrical staging—all these aspects of Lipchik's *A beauty and the beast* can also be found in another literary masterpiece: Shakespeare's five-act comedy *A Midsummer Night's Dream* (c. 1595), which isn't only about the errant ways of love, but also unbridled desire. In this popular comedy, the human protagonists are temporarily transported out of their everyday lives to the alternative world of the forest, where duties and order are forgotten. "Their civilized ego seems to be stripped away—they continually change partners abruptly, desire turns into disgust and vice versa; ... the enchanted forest ... can be seen as a metaphor for the dream state in which the polymorphous drives of the id, freed from the strict control of the waking ego, give us pleasure and terror."[2] One of the plot lines even thematizes the erotic relationship between the beautiful fairy queen Titania and the weaver Nick Bottom, who has been transformed into a donkey. As in *A Midsummer Night's Dream*, nightmare and fantasy are tied together in Lipchik's latest work. Moreover, Shakespeare's play is also about the illusion of theater, about thematizing staging as staging. This self-referentiality also resonates with Lipchik's work when he presents his narratives on rendered digital stages, which emphasizes the viewers' position as such.

As in Frost's poem and Shakespeare's comedy, the narratives in Lipchik's latest works take place at night or in twilight, which further heightens the eerie, mystically charged atmosphere of the depictions. The moon shines in nocturnal or twilit skies: sometimes more, sometimes less fully, hovering directly above the figures or far off in the distance, but it invariably shows up in every painting. Rarely, however, does it function as a natural light source in the image. The dramatic illumination of the scenes comes from the beams of spotlights in a wide variety of colors, which capture the action obliquely from above or below. In some paintings, the stage spotlights can even be found in the image. Like part of the imaginary fourth wall at the front of a proscenium stage, they separate the stage action from the viewers and thus reinforce the perception of the act as a performance. The artist's theatrical lighting effects, as well as affect-laden scenes, are reminiscent not least of a master of these two disciplines: Caravaggio. Lipchik, however, translates the dramatic lighting into his own personal contemporary language of color and form. Whereas Caravaggio's lighting is logically comprehensible, the highlights and strong shadows in Lipchik's work are often hard to place, almost surreal. Although the figure in *A beauty and the beast* is illuminated by a spotlight at the bottom of the picture, it remains in darkness. A pond-like water surface in *Forest Stage* (2022) **[▶ P. 44/45]**, on the other hand, magically glows from within without any clearly discernible light source. The darkly dramatic use of light also evokes the films of American artist and director David Lynch, who is known for his portentous use of light and shadow as an expression of the uncanny. In addition to references to art history and American film, Lipchik's use of artificial light in his latest works also testifies to the influence of the place they were made in, namely Berlin. The stark color contrasts of blue-black darkness and garish color accents of green, blue, and red in some paintings conjure images of flashing beams of light synonymous with the dance floors of Berlin's nightclubs. The sky, divided into light and dark, hints at the blurring of day and night in the vibrant club scene. The ever-present moon heralds a larger context that points beyond the narratives depicted.

Under the cover of night in a forest landscape, Lipchik presents another narrative with gloomy origins. Gazing at his muscular body, pronounced six-pack, and penis, we encounter an emphatically masculine figure in the painting *Crucified Sebastian* (2022). Tied to a stake, his arms are crossed behind his back and his body is covered in arrows, allowing us to identify the figure as Saint Sebastian. According to legend, the beautiful young soldier was to be killed with arrows for publicly professing the Christian faith. Sebastian, however, survived the firing squad of archers. Since then, he has been invoked as a patron saint for a variety of causes. For Lipchik, he seems central as the patron of the queer community. Lipchik again relocates the scene of martyrdom to a nocturnal stage illuminated by spotlights. While the scene may initially appear historical or timeless, the white tennis socks and shorts of the torturers squatting at the bottom of the image lend it a contemporary touch. In his dream world, it even becomes possible to positively rewrite or continue traditional narratives. Thus, in *Sebastian's revenge* (2022) [▶ P. 77], the artist gives the saint the opportunity to take revenge on his tormentors. Here, two figures who previously enjoyed the sight of their victim being tortured now flee into the woods with their buttocks bared. This time, they themselves are pursued by arrows as retribution for the iniquities they committed in *Crucified Sebastian*.

The uncanny feeling that takes hold of you when you first look at the painting *A beauty and the beast*, that jolts your subconscious, inexplicably repelling and attracting you at once, defines the paintings, VR installations, and poems in Lipchik's exhibition *Moonbeams of Allegory*. Yet this oppressive mood is also repeatedly broken by casual and clearly humorous moments. Thus, the artist's latest works present themselves like the acts of a play, like the fantastic, erotic dreams of a Shakespearean comedy, where reality and illusion are blurred, where fantasy and nightmare are tied together. Artificial forest landscapes paired with the neon-colored light shows of Berlin nightclubs form the backdrop of fantastic narratives and become the unifying element in the artist's mysterious night pieces. As in Robert Frost's popular poem, a frightening yet restful nocturnal nature becomes a place of longing and a projection surface for wishes and dark desires.

1 4th stanza from Robert Frost, "Stopping by Woods on a Snowy Evening," in: Robert Frost, *Promises to Keep – Poems*, 1922, 9th ed., Munich 2011.

2 Alan Posener, *William Shakespeare*, 2016, 3rd Ed. (eBook), Hamburg 2016, chapter 2.2., paragraph 3.

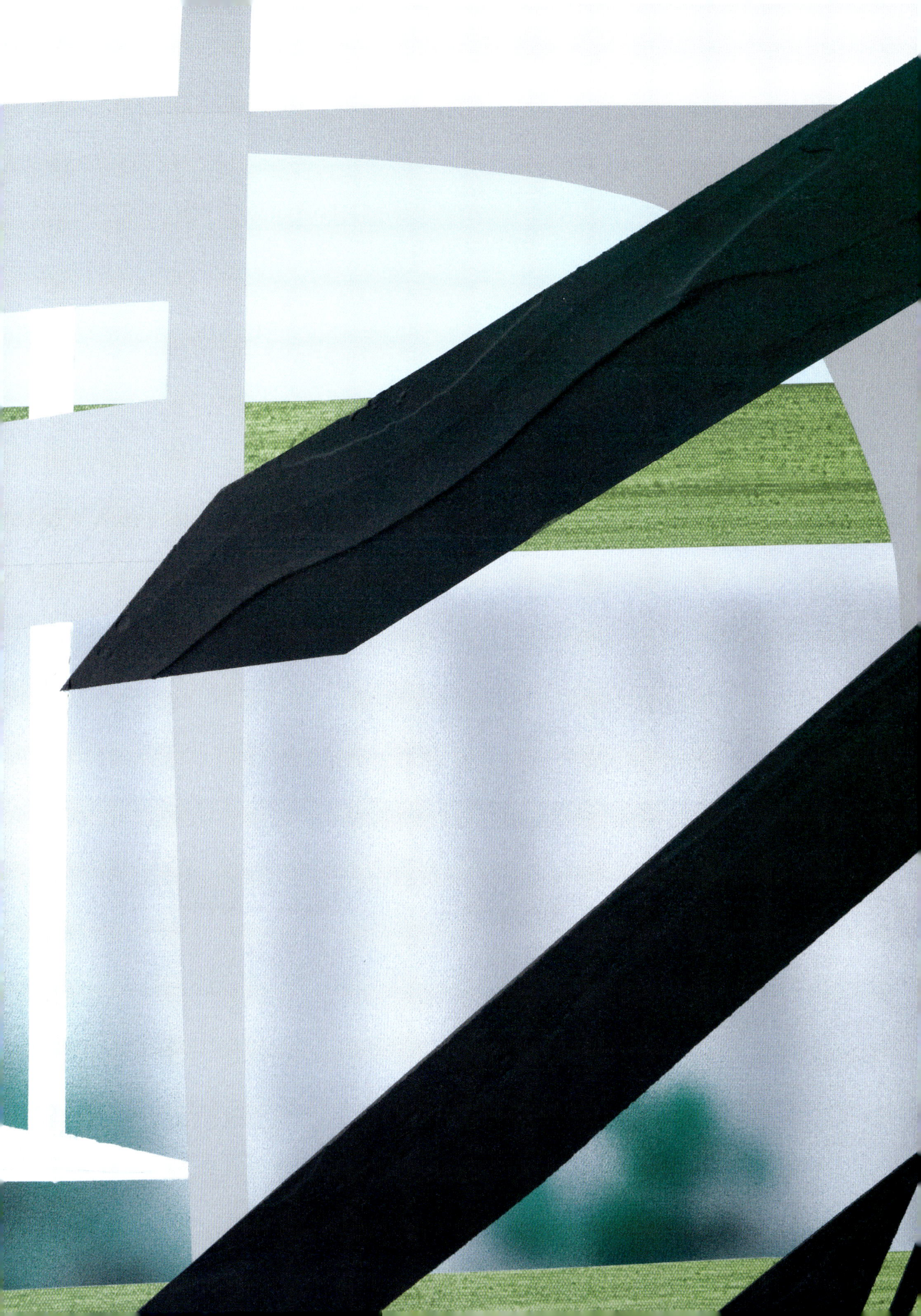

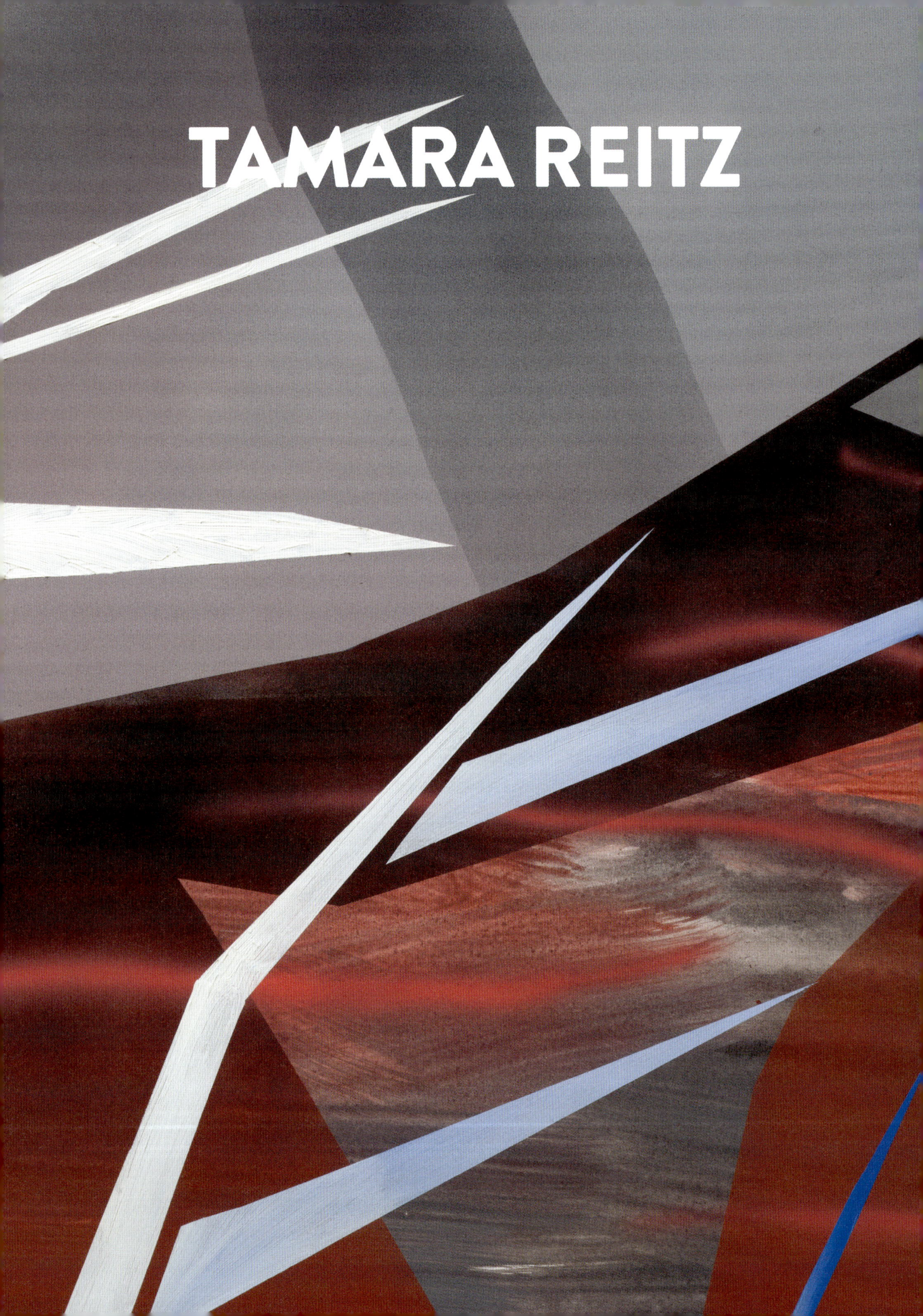
TAMARA REITZ

EIN MITTERNACHTS-TRAUM

Der Wald ist lieblich, dunkel, tief,
doch ich muss tun, was ich versprach,
und Meilen gehn bevor ich schlaf,
und Meilen gehn bevor ich schlaf.
— Robert Frost[1]

Unheimlich. Das war der erste Gedanke, der mir beim Betrachten des Gemäldes durch den Kopf schoss. Ein Adjektiv, das ich bislang eigentlich nicht mit dem Werk Brandon Lipchiks in Verbindung gebracht hatte. Waren die früheren Arbeiten des Künstlers doch geprägt von pastellfarbener Leichtigkeit und von zeitgenössischen Poollandschaften in poppigen Farben, wo sich seine nackten, avatarartigen Figuren in und um Schwimmbecken tummelten und sich auf den perfekten Rasenflächen von umzäunten Vorstadtgärten räkelten. Im Vergleich dazu erschien mir diese neue Szene zunächst unangenehm beklemmend, ja sogar verstörend.

Mit seiner psychologischen Tiefe und den sich aufdrängenden kunsthistorischen, literarischen und popkulturellen Bezügen zog mich Lipchiks Gemälde *A beauty and the beast* (2022) [▶ S. 78/79] aber auch sofort in seinen Bann. Der Titel verrät, worum es augenscheinlich geht. Nämlich um das gleichnamige Volksmärchen – als dessen heute wohl populärste Adaption sicherlich Walt Disneys Zeichentrickfilm *Beauty and the Beast* (1991) gelten darf. Als düster und unheimlich oder gar erotisch würde man die Disney-Version um die schöne Belle und den in ein Biest verwunschenen Prinzen jedoch vermutlich nicht bezeichnen. Im Zentrum von Lipchiks Komposition hingegen steht – ganz explizit – der sexuelle Akt zwischen Mensch und Tier. Anders als im Märchen handelt es sich bei der menschlichen Figur jedoch nicht eindeutig um eine Frau, sondern um eine Figur ohne spezifische Geschlechtsmerkmale. An zentraler Stelle der Komposition hingegen: der erigierte Penis einer nur schemenhaft ausmachbaren, aber eindeutig unmenschlichen Gestalt. In nächtlicher Landschaft mit einem am fernen, tiefschwarzen Sternenhimmel stehenden roséfarbenen Vollmond stürzt sie sich auf eine nackte, rücklinks auf grünem Rasen liegende Figur. Mit lustvoll aufgerissenem Maul und spitzen Zähnen umklammert die Kreatur ihr menschliches Gegenüber, das sein Gesicht von den Betrachter*innen abwendet. Was die Figur in der Situation empfindet, verrät nur ihr Spiegelbild, das in dem von ihr emporgehaltenen Handspiegel erscheint. Mit vor Schreck oder Lust geöffnetem Mund und geweiteten Augen erblickt sich die Figur darin selbst. Die Dramatik der Darstellung wird durch Scheinwerfer am unteren Bildrand und einer unbestimmten orangefarbenen Lichtquelle von schräg oben zusätzlich verstärkt. Sie leuchten das Geschehen aus, präsentieren es wie auf der Bühne eines Theaters oder einer Tanzfläche und enttarnen uns – die Betrachter*innen – als Voyeur*innen dieser wilden und unangenehm erotischen Szene.

Durch das Einbetten der Darstellung in eine unbekannte, traumartige Waldlandschaft erinnern dieses und andere Gemälde der Ausstellung *Moonbeams of Allegory* nicht zuletzt an die surrealen und naiven Landschaftsgemälde des Malers Henri Rousseau, dessen Werk *Belle et la Bête* (1908, *Die Schöne und das Biest*) Lipchik sogar ganz konkret zitiert. Waren die Schauplätze seiner bisherigen Gemälde die umzäunten Gärten amerikanischer Vororte mit ihren akkuraten Rasenflächen, wo quadratische Swimmingpools sinnbildlich für die Ordnung der Zivilisation standen, deutet sich in *A beauty and the beast* eine neue Richtung an. Die Figuren haben die begrenzenden Mauern der ordentlichen Vorstädte hinter sich gelassen und stürzen sich in klandestine und erotische Abenteuer in abgelegener, ungezähmter Natur. Tatsächlich wird die Natur zunehmend selbst zur Protagonistin. Vermehrt begegnen wir Tierfiguren, werwolfähnlichen Gestalten und paradiesischen Vögeln, die mit den anonymen Avataren in Aktion treten, und sogar menschenleeren Landschaftsgemälden, in denen bei Lipchik die Natur erstmals ganz für sich steht. Die drapierten Ziergewächse wurden abgelöst von Baumstämmen, knorrigen Ästen und Nadelbäumen. Dominiert von einer dunklen, blau-grünen Farbigkeit mit rosafarbenen, gelben und lila Akzenten.

Diese unwirkliche Wildnis schafft Lipchik mithilfe von 3D-Design-Software und lässt sie zum Schauplatz von schaurigen Narrativen und Legenden werden. Die digitalen Arbeitsprozesse des Künstlers beschränken sich jedoch nicht auf Renderings, die er als Entwürfe für seine analogen Gemälde verwendet, er geht noch einen Schritt weiter und ermöglicht den Betrachter*innen sogar das virtuelle Eintauchen in seine Bilder. So lässt sich der Akt zwischen menschlicher Schönheit und animalischer Bestie sowie die düstere Atmosphäre des Gemäldes auf einer weiteren, immersiven Ebene erleben: Mithilfe einer VR-Brille finden sich die Betrachtenden in der virtuellen Version des Gemäldes und vor eben jener rechteckigen Plattform wieder, die als Präsentationsfläche der Figurengruppe dient. Umgeben von Laubbäumen und farnähnlicher Vegetation und vor dem flachen Bühnenbild eines Waldes werden sie noch eindeutiger und unweigerlicher zu Zeug*innen des Geschehens. In der Bewegung erstarrt erscheinen Lipchiks Figuren dabei auf ihrer Bühne wie Exponate in einem virtuellen Diorama. Die analogen Vorfahren dieser Inszenierungen kennt man seit dem 19. Jahrhundert vor allem aus dem musealen Kontext. Hier brachten sie den Besucher*innen von naturwissenschaftlichen Sammlungen vor dem Hintergrund des Kolonialismus fremde und exotische Lebenswelten näher. So ist bekannt, dass Rousseau seine Kenntnis von Flora und Fauna für seine Dschungelbilder teilweise den Dioramen des *Jardin des Plantes* in Paris entnahm. Der ausgelieferte nackte Körper in einer Naturlandschaft, die explizite, fast pornografische Erotik, mit der man als Betrachter*in bei Lipchik konfrontiert wird, lässt aber zugleich auch an eines der bekanntesten Dioramen der Kunstgeschichte denken, an Marcel Duchamps *Etant Donnés: 1° la chute d'eau, 2° le gaz d'éclairage …* (1946–1966, dt. *Gegeben sei: 1. Der Wasserfall, 2. Das Leuchtgas …*). Auch diese Arbeit – Duchamps letzte, an der er zwei Jahrzehnte arbeitete – zwingt die Betrachtenden geradezu hinein in die Rolle von Voyeur*innen und konfrontiert sie mit der beunruhigenden Erotik der Situation. In Duchamps Installation erspähen die Betrachtenden durch Gucklöcher in einer gealterten Holztür den szenischen Aufbau in einer Art Schaukasten dahinter: Im Durchbruch einer hinter der Tür befindlichen Backsteinwand erscheint mit gespreizten Beinen ein nackter Frauenkörper, in einer Anhäufung von trockenem Reisig und Laub liegend vor der Kulisse einer lebendigen Waldlandschaft mit Wasserfall. Phallusgleich hält die gesichtslose Unbekannte in ihrer linken Hand eine Gaslampe empor. Der in mehrfachen Ebenen unterteilte Aufbau von Duchamps dioramaartiger Assemblage sowie die nachdrückliche Inszenierung der Betrachtenden als Schaulustige ähnelt der VR-Installation Lipchiks. Er lässt uns jedoch nicht wie Duchamp durch eine binokulare Tür blicken, sondern ermöglicht das Beobachten, ja sogar Betreten der Situation durch eine VR-Brille. Was Duchamps und Lipchiks Arbeiten verbindet, ist ein ausgeprägtes Interesse am Akt des Schauens und am Spiel mit Perspektiven. Die Werke beider Künstler sind durchdrungen von erotischer Energie und dem unbehaglichen Gefühl, unmittelbar Zeug*in von etwas Verbotenem oder Geheimem zu werden.

Obwohl die Nutzer*innen bei Lipchik sich mithilfe der VR-Brille sogar innerhalb des Bildraumes bewegen können, während sie bei Duchamp unweigerlich hinter der hölzernen Tür verbleiben, wird nur vordergründig auch eine intime Nähe zum Geschehen suggeriert. Tatsächlich wirkt die unbelebte Figurengruppe in ihrer kantigen Ästhetik und die bühnenartige Plattform distanzierend auf die virtuellen „Besucher*innen". Trotz der VR-Brille werden sie nicht zum Teil des Geschehens und können auch nicht aktiv daran partizipieren, sondern verbleiben unweigerlich in der Position von Zuschauer*innen. Ja das zentral vor der Bühne platzierte Hinweisschild unterstreicht die passive Rolle der Betrachtenden geradezu und rückt Lipchiks Arbeit wieder näher an die erhabene Zurschaustellung von naturwissenschaftlichen Dioramen und musealen Displays heran. Anders als bei einer Informationstafel im Museum handelt es sich bei dem Text auf dem Aufsteller jedoch nicht um eine wissenschaftliche Erklärung, sondern um ein Gedicht des Künstlers, das als Kommentar zum dargestellten fiktiven Geschehen gelesen werden kann und die Gefühle des Künstlers offenbart. Mit Strophen- und Verszahl sowie mit pointierten Wortzitaten bezieht sich Lipchik mit seinem Text ganz klar auf eines der populärsten Werke des amerikanischen Poeten Robert Frost: *Stopping by the woods on a snowy evening* (1922, *Rast am Wald an einem verschneiten Abend*). In vier Strophen geht es hier um den Fahrer eines Pferdeschlittens, der mitten in der Natur fern von jeder Zivilisation plötzlich stoppt, um den Schneefall und die Schönheit des nächtlichen Waldes zu bewundern. In der letzten Strophe erinnert er sich jedoch an seine Verpflichtungen, denen er nachkommen muss, und an den langen Weg, der noch zurückzulegen ist, bevor er schlafen kann. Lipchik adaptiert in seinem Gedicht die Naturlyrik Frosts und verwandelt sie in einen poetischen Kommentar zu seinem Werk *A beauty and the beast*. In Frosts Gedicht geht es um die Anziehung der düsteren Schönheit des Waldes, um den Kontrast zwischen Zivilisation und Natur, um den Wunsch nach Seelenfrieden und dem Drang, seine Alltagspflichten einfach hinter sich zu lassen. Der Wald als Symbol für ungezähmte Natur und Irrationalität wird zum Sehnsuchtsort, der Freiheit und Ungebundenheit verspricht, einem Ort ohne Kontrolle und Verbote. Gleichzeitig ist dem Fahrer im Gedicht bewusst, dass er seinen Verpflichtungen nicht entgehen kann – ein innerer Konflikt zwischen irrationalem Unterbewusstsein und rationalem Verhalten, zwischen triebhaftem Verhalten und Kontrolle, der sich auch in Lipchiks Werkkomplex *A beauty and the beast* erkennen lässt.

Die animalische, triebgesteuerte Liebe, der nächtliche Wald als Ort erotischer und fantastischer Geschehnisse, die magische Macht des Mondes, die Abkehr von der Ordnung der städtischen Zivilisation, die theaterähnliche Inszenierung hat Lipchiks *A beauty and the beast* mit einem weiteren literarischen Kunststück gemein: In Shakespeares Komödie *Ein Sommernachtstraum* (um 1595) geht es in fünf Akten nicht nur um die Irrungen der Liebe, sondern auch um zügelloses Begehren. In diesem populären Lustspiel werden die menschlichen Protagonist*innen für gewisse Zeit aus ihrer Alltagswelt in die alternative Welt des Waldes versetzt, in der Pflichten und Ordnung vergessen werden. „[I]hr zivilisiertes Ich scheint abgestreift – wiederholt abrupt wechseln sie die Partner, schlägt Begehren in Abscheu um und umgekehrt; […] Der Zauberwald […] kann als Metapher für den Traumzustand gelten, in dem die polymorphen Triebregungen des Es, von der strengen Kontrolle des wachen Ich befreit, uns Lust und Schrecken bereiten.“[2] Einer der Handlungsstränge thematisiert sogar das erotische Verhältnis zwischen der schönen Feenkönigin Titania und den in einen Esel verwandelten Weber Zettel. Wie im Sommernachtstraum liegen auch in Lipchiks neuesten Werken Alptraum und Wunschtraum nah beieinander. Darüber hinaus geht es in Shakespeares Stück auch um die Illusion des Theaters, um die Thematisierung der Inszenierung als Inszenierung. Diese Selbstreferenzialität klingt auch bei Lipchik an, wenn er seine Narrative auf gerenderten oder digitalen Bühnen präsentiert und den Betrachter*innen so ihre Position als solche verdeutlicht.

Wie in Frosts Gedicht und Shakespeares Komödie spielen sich die Narrative in Lipchiks neuesten Arbeiten in der Nacht oder im Dämmerlicht ab, was die unheimlich-mystische aufgeladene Atmosphäre der Darstellungen noch zusätzlich steigert. Am nächtlichen oder halbdunklen Himmel scheint der Mond: mal mehr, mal weniger voll, unmittelbar über den Figuren schwebend oder in weiter Ferne, aber ausnahmslos in jedem Gemälde. Selten bildet er jedoch die natürliche Lichtquelle im Bild. Für die dramatische Ausleuchtung der Szenen sorgen die Lichtkegel von Scheinwerfern in den unterschiedlichsten Farben, die das Geschehen von schräg oben oder unten erfassen. In einigen Gemälden findet man die Bühnenstrahler sogar direkt im Bild. Wie ein Teil der imaginären vierten Wand am vorderen Rand einer Guckkastenbühne grenzen sie Bühnengeschehen und Betrachter*innen voneinander ab und verstärken so die Wahrnehmung des Aktes als Darbietung. Die theatralischen Lichteffekte des Künstlers, aber auch die affektgeladenen Szenen lassen nicht zuletzt an einen Meister dieser beiden Disziplinen denken: Caravaggio. Die dramatische Lichtführung überträgt Lipchik jedoch in seine ganz persönliche, zeitgenössische Farb- und Formsprache. Ist die Belichtung bei Caravaggio logisch nachvollziehbar, erscheinen die Schlaglichter und starken Schatten bei Lipchik häufig nicht klar zuordenbar, fast surreal. Obwohl die Gestalt in *A beauty and the beast* von einem am unteren Bildrand befindlichen Scheinwerfer angestrahlt wird, bleibt sie im Dunkeln. Eine teichähnliche Wasserfläche in *Forest Stage* (2022) [▸ S. 44/45] hingegen erstrahlt auf magische Art und Weise von innen heraus, ohne dass eine konkrete Lichtquelle auszumachen wäre. Der düster-dramatische Lichteinsatz erinnert zugleich an die Filme des amerikanischen Künstler-Regisseurs David Lynch, der für seinen bedeutungsschweren Licht- und Schatteneinsatz als Ausdruck des Unheimlichen bekannt ist. Neben Bezügen zur Kunstgeschichte und zum amerikanischen Film lässt sich in Lipchiks Einsatz von künstlichem Licht auch der Einfluss Berlins als Entstehungsort dieser neuesten Arbeiten erkennen. Die starken Farbkontraste aus schwarzblauer Dunkelheit und grellen Farbakzenten aus Grün, Blau und Rot in einigen Gemälden rufen Bilder von den tanzenden Strahlen der Lichtorgeln auf den Dancefloors des Berliner Nachtlebens hervor. Im hell und dunkel geteilten Himmel deutet sich das Verschwimmen von Tages- und Nachtzeiten in der vibrierenden Clubszene an. Der immer präsente Mond kündet dabei von einem größeren Sinnzusammenhang, der über die dargestellten Narrative hinausweist.

Unter dem Deckmantel der Nacht und erneut vor dem Hintergrund einer Waldlandschaft präsentiert Lipchik eine weitere, im Ursprung düstere Erzählung. Mit ihrem muskulösen Körper, dem ausgeprägtem Sixpack und dem Penis begegnen wir im Gemälde *Crucified Sebastian* (2022) einer nachdrücklich männlich gestalteten Figur. Der Pfahl, an den sie mit hinter dem Rücken gekreuzten Armen gebunden ist, und ihr von Pfeilen überzogener Körper lassen sie uns als den heiligen Sebastian identifizieren. Weil er sich öffentlich zum christlichen Glauben bekannte, sollte der schöne, junge Soldat der Legende nach mit Pfeilen getötet werden. Den Beschuss durch Bogenschützen überlebte Sebastian jedoch. Seither wird er für vielseitige Belange als Patron angerufen. Für Lipchik zentral scheint er als Patron der queeren Community. Die Szene des Martyriums verlegt Lipchik erneut auf eine nächtliche Bühne, erhellt von Scheinwerferlicht. Mag die Szenerie zunächst historisch oder zeitlos erscheinen, verleihen die weißen Tennissocken und Shorts der am unteren Bildrand hockenden Peiniger ihr zeitgenössische Aktualität. In seiner Traumwelt wird es sogar möglich, traditionelle Erzählungen positiv umzuschreiben oder fortzusetzen. So gibt der Künstler in *Sebastian's revenge* (2022) [▸ S. 77] dem Heiligen die Möglichkeit, sich an seinen Peinigern zu rächen. Mit entblößten Hintern flüchten zwei Figuren, die sich zuvor scheinbar am Anblick ihres gefolterten Opfers ergötzten, in den Wald. Diesmal selbst verfolgt von den Pfeilen ihrer in *Crucified Sebastian* begangenen Schandtat.

Das unheimliche Gefühl, das einen beim ersten Blick auf das Gemälde *A beauty and the beast* ergreift, das am Unterbewusstsein rüttelt und einen auf scheinbar unerklärliche Weise abstößt und anzieht zugleich, bestimmt die Gemälde, VR-Installationen und Gedichte in Lipchiks Ausstellung *Moonbeams of Allegory*. Immer wieder wird diese beklemmende Stimmung jedoch auch durch lockere, eindeutig humorvolle Momente gebrochen. So präsentieren sich die neusten Arbeiten des Künstlers wie die Akte eines Theaterstücks, wie der fantastisch-erotische Traum in einer Shakespeare-Komödie, wo Realität und Illusion miteinander verschwimmen und wo Wunsch- und Alptraum ganz dicht beieinander liegen. Künstliche Waldlandschaften gepaart mit den neonfarbenen Lichtspielen Berliner Nachtclubs bilden die Kulisse fantastischer Narrative und werden zum verbindenden Element in den geheimnisvollen Nachtstücken des Künstlers. Eine ängstigende, aber zugleich Erholung verheißende nächtliche Natur wird so wie in Robert Frosts populärem Gedicht zum Sehnsuchtsort und zur Projektionsfläche von Wünschen und dunklen Begierden.

1 4. Strophe aus Robert Frost, „Rast am Wald an einem verschneiten Abend" („Stopping by Woods on a Snowy Evening"), in: Robert Frost, *Promises to keep – Poems/Gedichte*, 1922, 9. Aufl., München 2011.

2 Alan Posener, *William Shakespeare*, 2016, 3. Aufl. (eBook), Hamburg 2016, Kap. 2.2., Abs. 3.

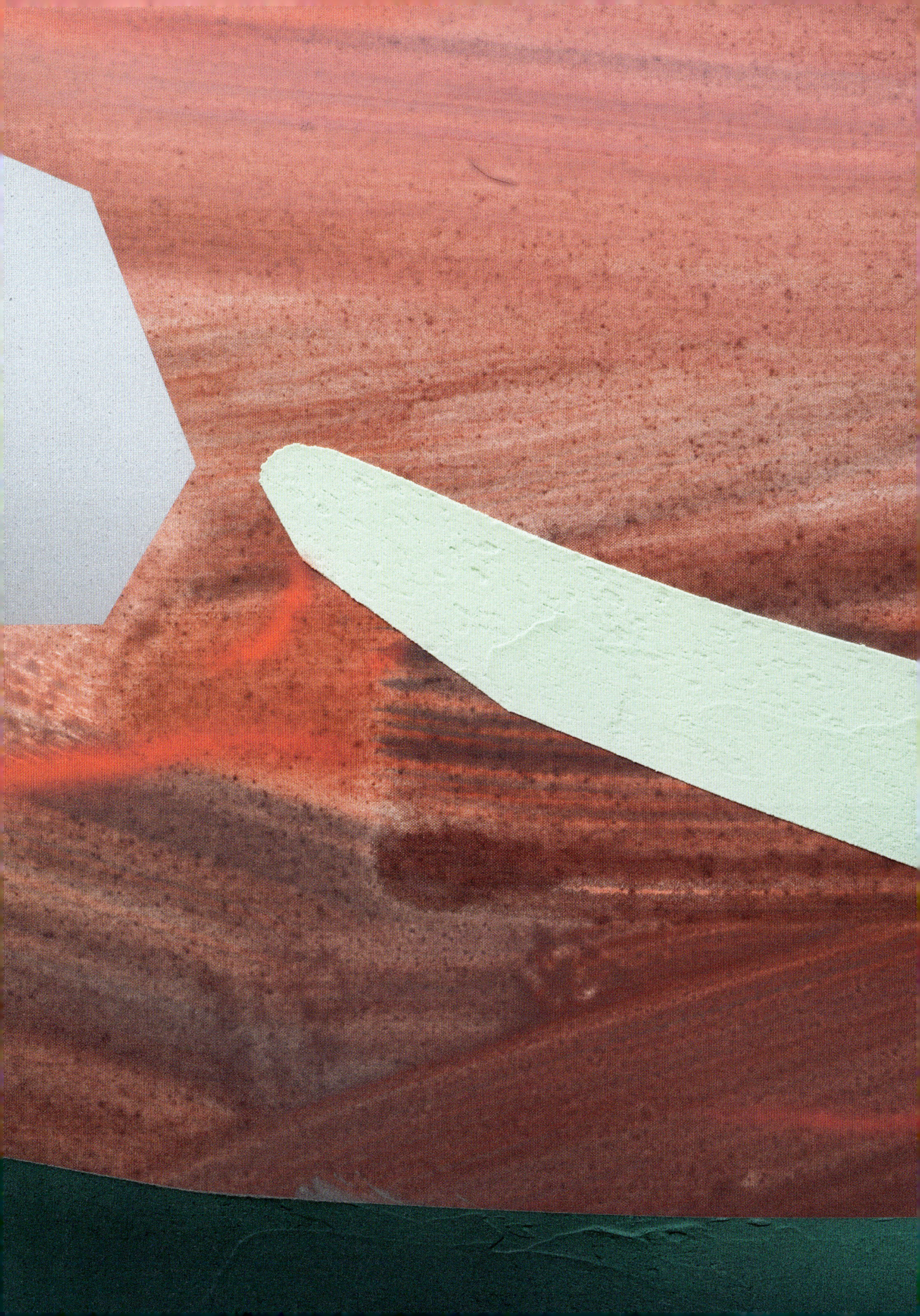

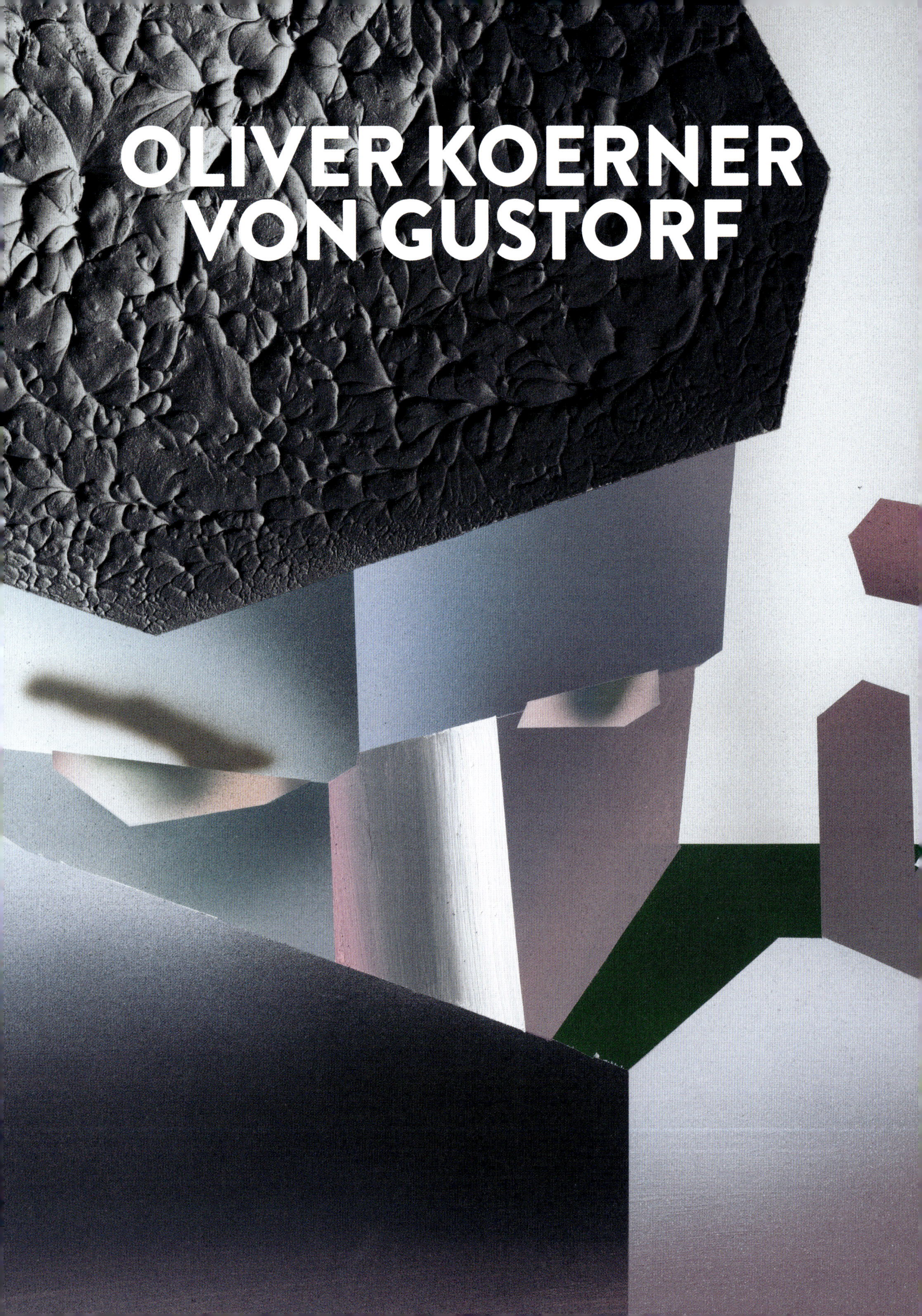
OLIVER KOERNER
VON GUSTORF

MOON BATHING IN THE END TIMES

Brandon Lipchik's Romantic Materialism

1. WHITE LOTUS

All those hot, fragmented bodies bathing in the moonlight on Brandon Lipchik's recent paintings. Like Ophelia in John Everett Millais' famous painting, they float pale in swimming pools, entwined with plastic tubes, like vines, snakes, or endlessly long cocks showering them with chlorinated water. They look up to the night sky, cuddled up in their artificially shimmering skins, lounging in jacuzzis on the lawn, dancing on pedestals, taking selfies, fucking, studying their reflections. The whole world's a reflection, a dream. Maybe that light shining on them, green, purple, blue isn't moonlight at all, but spotlights, strange stars hanging heavy in the firmament. Maybe they aren't bodies either, but avatars, architectures, surfaces, materials morphed together that merely recall bodies while reconfiguring into something else as soon as you look away, into chunky, razor-sharp sheets, shards, shadows.

Despite whatever "mysticism" or "eroticism" these bodily architectures might exude, they convey a sense of normalization, functionality, something washable. This might be due to the rendering software Lipchik uses to composite his images. He then projects them onto canvas, using airbrush, tape, and brushes to materialize the digital image as painting. Lipchik creates his world with the same means used to create 3D visualizations for games, exhibition stands, stores, garages. The combination of industrial advertising methods with "artistic" or "authentic" gestures, of the functional with the sacred, reflects a global cultural landscape that functions much the same. There's this promise of a "once-in-a-lifetime experience," of absolute uniqueness and originality, of love, beauty, inner and outer adventure, yet it is delivered within a matrix of total homogenization and commercialization.

All dreams are customized for you, baby: millions travel to Disneyland, yet it's an unmatched experience for each individual. Millions cavort on Grindr, TikTok, Instagram, and Tinder, posing the same poses, photographing the same beards, nipples, tattoos, negligees, cooking the same food, making the same memes, captioning their clips with Harry Styles' *As it Was*, pumping up their biceps and asses, baking cupcakes, or building tiny houses. They all use the same filters, but surely theirs was unique, and of course there's someone completely different out there, waiting just for them. Not without cheek, Lipchik's pool and garden landscapes recall American suburbs, of resorts like those in the U.S. television series *The White Lotus* (2021), where various exotic or romantic "themes" are played out in the architecture and interior design down to the entertainment program. The Art Deco wallpaper is digital, the palm trees flown in, the Moroccan tiles punched out of plastic, the employees under minimum wage. Everything in this modular world of experiences can be taken down, folded up, seasonally updated, fired as needed. Likewise, consumers' bodies are turned into construction sites for events, pimped out with diets, wellness and training, injected, suctioned, sanded, cut, dyed.

The body is a capitalist body. And thus Lipchik's paintings run through the possible permutations of commercialized and industrial color palettes, formal languages, and symbols. The browns and espressos, the dull greens and grays he used in his mystical paintings like

Howling Snake (2020) [▸ P. 114] in his exhibition *Visions of Song* at the Robert Grunenberg Gallery in Berlin could just as easily be found in mid-century boutique hotels with faux Eames furniture, while the stylized tree branch structures recall Nordic designer cups. Already there it became unmistakably clear what Lipchik would elaborate in his more recent paintings. He shows how prefabricated even the most extreme inventions of our selves are, how limited the rehearsed, performative gestures of our Instagrammable lives—lives in which we grow increasingly addicted to sharing everything, branding ourselves as products, highlighting our unique selling points. In the fast-paced, young art scene that is, of course, increasingly marketing itself on Instagram, a year seems like an eon. For example, the paintings Lipchik produced in his mid-twenties after graduating from the Rhode Island School of Design and Brown University are already part of his "early work." At the same time, there is also a certain compulsion for attention in the marketplace that is not openly talked about. Just as young art is now supposed to arouse immediate, almost erotic attraction, to be smart, attractive, and hot like high-end design, so too must the artists. The work, the biography, the artist's own appearance, their aesthetic and conceptual strategies must all be desirable; they have to "look good".

2. A BIGGER SPLASH

Lipchik worked as a model in his student days and was represented by one of the biggest, most influential agencies worldwide. He grew up, so to speak, with the visual vocabulary of looks and poses—the entanglement of fashion, art history, pop culture, and eroticism. The images created between 2018 and 2019 have a paradoxically sexualized charge. Lipchik digitally deconstructs male bodies, spaces, landscapes, decorative objects, and fauna, breaking them down into rudimentary abstract forms. Yet his practice is quite different from Avery Singer, the godmother of post-internet painting who was already working with rendering programs and airbrushes in the early 2010s and influenced subsequent generations. In her paintings like *The Studio Visit* (2012)—arguably her most famous—she thematized her role and life as an artist, the mediation and marketing of art, and the discrepancy between the rituals of contemporary painting and digital image production. What was fascinating about Singer was that her paintings contrasted the banal democratic aesthetics of games and rendering programs with the highly masculine modern pathos of Constructivism, Futurism, and Cubism. Under new auspices, Singer picked up on the formal debates as well as aesthetic and conceptual strategies of U.S. women painters such as Laura Owens, Amy Sillman, and Charlene van Heyl, who have decisively shaped the discourse on painting in the U.S. over the last two decades.

Even though he uses the visual language of so-called post-digital painting, Lipchik, who is six years younger, operates from a completely different position. In *Windows Into Exile*, he decidedly eschews the discourses of current painting and the operating system of art, even though he is influenced by them: "At university I became really interested in Julie Mehretu's work. I really fell in love with her process of sourcing information from architectural plans and real life structures and taking visual information from that and incorporating it into a rendering to make abstraction. I was attracted to her use of digital tools to create. Obviously everyone with a computer has access to such technology so I felt it was just another tool in the artist's belt to create."[1] Lipchik taps into a very different agenda in his digital-analog painting: the hyper-sensitive gay aesthetic, the queer codes of café society, and the later jet set of the 1960s and 1970s. He works with themes of interior design, decor, craft, illustration. The title of the exhibition alludes to the novel *The Exile of Capri* (1959) by French writer Roger Peyrefitte, based on the life of Baron Jacques d'Adelswärd-Fersen (1880–1923). In 1903, the Parisian aristocrat was convicted of pederastic relations with Parisian schoolboys and declared *persona non grata* in the city's salons. He went into exile on Capri, where he lived with his longtime younger boyfriend Nino Cesarini in an exquisitely furnished Art Nouveau villa, Villa Lysis, named after Plato's dialogue on friendship and homosexual love. Above the entrance, Fersen had painted the Latin inscription AMORI ET DOLORI SACRUM (dedicated to love and suffering). In 1923 he took his own life with an overdose of cocaine.

One of the topoi of the incipient modernism from the end of the 19th century onwards was the gay or dandy who creates a decadent fantasy world for himself in self-imposed isolation or exile, one where he wastes away and usually dies. A pioneering work here was Joris-Karl Huysman's cult book *Against Nature* published in 1884, in which the eccentric young aristocrat Jean Floressas Des Esseintes retreats to his exquisitely designed villa to die. In one of the novel's key scenes, he glues diamonds to the shell of a live giant tortoise so it would match the carpet. The animal perishes from this will to style. Oscar Wilde's novel *The Portrait of Dorian Gray* (1890) and Thomas Mann's *Death in Venice* (1911) further immortalized this motif in mass culture. This topos involves a broader set of themes: artificiality, absolute aesthetic sensibility, literally acting *against nature*. That is, against biological sex, against procreation, against aging, against the compulsion to subordinate oneself to life and the society that considers itself "natural". The avatars that populate Lipchik's painting operate precisely within this thematic complex. The programmatic inability to live and the fascination with death have something radically emancipatory and liberating about them.

In *Windows Into Exile*, Lipchik, who also visited Fersen's villa in Capri, deconstructs not only the bourgeois aesthetics of the baron and his contemporaries, like the photographer Wilhelm Plüschow, which were based on antiquity and classicism. He also responds to the fact that the desire was for boys and young men from the working class and peasant families. Lipchik constructs semi-abstract interiors that are completely devoid of time and class, a tremendously physical, seductive, sculptural trompe l'oeil painting. He makes the canvas look like a digital construction site, as if it were cobbled together from Photoshop layers, with three-dimensional forms emerging from their depths: the muscles of an upper arm, green leaves cut as if from woodchip wallpaper, hair swirls, tools like hammers and saws, amphorae, Polaroids, iron fences, nipples, hard and plastic as the candy in the store. At the same time, his avatars are decadent or romantic, like the figures in 19th century symbolist painting, literature, and music. Of course, Lipchik plays with the aesthetics of New Wave and prep-culture in Luca Guadagnino's *Call Me By Your Name* (2017), even invoking the infamous peach. But that, too, is a nod to a decadent, hedonistic era. He sexualizes the surface without restraint—with airbrushed tulips that sit on the paintings like lipstick imprints on Kleenex tissues, with plastic, minty, yellow, pink puddles of paint that drift on the canvas like sperm or liquid varnish. Like the pasty streaks of paint he sculpts from plaster, they recall the way Laura Owens gives her paintings a sculptural touch and satirizes expressive, affect-laden gestures.

But Lipchik doesn't need this conceptual distance; he unabashedly uses the artificial splashes, smears, and blooms like seductive decorative elements. His Capri series spells out a nostalgic alphabet of homosexual taste. It includes Cocteau and Cecil Beaton as well as David Hockney's pool paintings and the melancholy jet-set glamour of the Hockney film *A Bigger Splash* (1973). And unlike, say, Avery Singer, who uses painting robots and digital printing to create a conceptual distance from the ingenious touch of the brush on canvas in her perfectly photo-realistic paintings, Lipchik takes an inverse, more outsider approach here. Whenever he's asked why he has to paint his digital images on canvas at all, he always replies that this physical contact is extremely important, that painting has an almost sexual component for him. He takes the route of digital image production to arrive at a queer painting that is extremely physical without becoming macho. Just as David Hockney arrived at digital painting on his iPad in his later work, Lipchik goes through the digital to arrive at something analog—an extremely sensual, painterly form with sculptural features.

"I think I felt a connection with Hockney after seeing his paintings and this narrative around pools," Lipchik says, "because the pool was a symbol that I understood in Americana. I think it stands for prosperity, leisure, American dreams and Hollywood fantasies that you see in film over and over again. I shared similar experiences growing up in suburbia—different from Hollywood but in a similar vein. The pool was also the place where I started to discover the depths of my own sexuality. And the theme continued on."[2] One of Lipchik's all-time favorite paintings is Hockney's 1972 *Portrait of an Artist (Pool with Two Figures)*, which also plays a central role in the Hockney biopic *A Bigger Splash* (1973). It shows Hockney's lover Peter Schlesinger standing poolside in a mountain landscape, gazing down at a figure floating in the water. The angular shapes of the pool, tiles, and flagstones create a web of horizontal and vertical lines enmeshing both figures. Interestingly, Lipchik's painting does something similar to what Hockney so masterfully exemplifies here: he combines the two genres of portraiture and landscape painting. Hockney's painting was made during a traumatic period of separation from Schlesinger. It is a montage of different temporal and spatial levels, composed of photographs, re-enacted scenes, and a shooting with Schlesinger, which Hockney paints together. *Portrait of an Artist* (*Pool with Two Figures*) thus thematizes the blurring of external and internal experience, physical and emotional distance, performativity and authenticity, the distorted, fragmented, mediatized perception of bodies, places, feelings—themes that also dominate Lipchik's painting.

Hockney then took this multi-perspectival visual narrative further in the early 1980s with his Polaroid works. These portraits or landscapes are composed of up to 120 Polaroids arranged in a grid, each showing a different perspective. When Hockney photographed a person next to a table with a bouquet of flowers on it, he would move around the person, the table, and bouquet of flowers, taking close-ups of details such as blossoms or shoes, then move away again for other shots. You could say he circles subjects and objects, moving through space like a drone continuously taking pictures. In the process, he documents photography's inability to capture time or different perspectives with single frames. But he also shows how fragmentation and the reorganization of fragments open up new perceptual possibilities and spatial experiences.

Lipchik, who assembles his works from various motifs, strives for a similar effect in his painting: "When painting I find I can have a lot of control over the perspective I allow the viewer to see, as does a filmmaker but limited to what the camera and physics can achieve. Oftentimes I am using an overhead perspective or even over the shoulder view to imply (just as filmmakers do) a minimizing or watching viewpoint on my figures. You might even say an out of body or spiritual viewpoint on simulated figures."[3] What's interesting is that in so doing, he is at least as grounded in the canon of modernism and post-war painting as he is in 21st century digital image production.

Lipchik's garishly lit, multi-perspectival summer images, like *Biker* [▸ **P. 104**] or *Garden Hose* [▸ **P. 60**] which were made in 2019 at the same time as the images of *Windows Into Exile*, draw on typical shots from 80s gay porn films, citing the clean American Apparel look. They seem like ironic, brightly colored responses to Willem de Kooning's lewdly uptight hetero statement about his expressive female nudes, which were provocative for postwar society: "Flesh is the reason oil paint was invented." Lipchik's queer acrylic bodies are fragmented, but not fleshy; they are smooth, artificial, to be licked and eaten. They are not psychologized, charged with guilt or shame, but available in an entirely pragmatic way. Paintings are feminized by default, writes U.S. art historian and theorist W.J.T. Mitchell. They are treated as something that has to arouse desire in the viewer, while they themselves don't reveal signs of desire in any way, or even an awareness that they are being looked at—as if the viewer were voyeuristically peering through a keyhole. Lipchik creates a gay counterpart to this effect with almost surgical means. His anonymous avatars have no faces, no eyes, are only bodies. As one-dimensional objects of desire, they are unable to return the viewer's gaze. Yet there is something hard and abysmal in these pop images, a latent violence that seems almost threatening. In 2020, a dystopian shadow fell over everything, the digital summer turned to mystical end time.

3. MELANCHOLIA

Lipchik's cycle *Visions of Song* is a tribute to the great American poets, to Robert Frost, to the Beat poets Allen Ginsberg and Jack Kerouac, to James Baldwin. But most of all, it alludes to the gay poet and transcendentalist Walt Whitman (1819–1892), who sang of the dawn of industrialization, democracy, indigenous culture, and a spiritual experience of nature. Whitman fits with Lipchik's repertoire so well because he eroticizes the American dream of democracy like a male body. In *I Sing the Body Electric* in his famous poetry collection *Leaves of Grass* (1855) for example, he sings of America as if it were a collective organism connected by railroad lines, utility poles, working, fraternal, loving bodies. Lipchik's paintings from *Visions of Song* were created toward the end of Trump era, when climate catastrophe was also becoming increasingly obvious. It was the time of devastating wildfires in California and Australia, where not only small towns and suburbs went up in flames, but millions of animals died, entire populations burned. With democracy collapsing and nature burning, the images seem as if Whitman's electric communal body has shattered into its limbs. In some images, the bodies are sallow and ashen like dried wood, the arms and legs marked with spray paint like trees destined to be cut down. There is planting, building, repotting, trying to save what can still be saved. Somewhere there is already another fire. It seems as if every frivolity, every touch of café society has disappeared. But there are still the same motifs, the fences, the hammers, the sword-like leaves—Lipchik shows almost the same scenes under construction, albeit in a more precarious light. Observation, which was once something more voyeuristic, is now more reminiscent of surveillance by cameras and drones, aerial images from disaster areas.

Yet here in this dying world, another theme that has determined Lipchik's work from the beginning starts to emerge more clearly: culture and nature are now almost completely interpenetrated in his bodily architectures. This recalls the sci-fi horror film *Annihilation* (2018) where a mysterious alien life form infiltrates an area on the American West Coast. The "shimmer" mutates humans, animals, and plants into the most bizarre forms, breeding new creatures: human flowers, shark crocodiles. Natalie Portman plays a molecular biologist who ventures with her team into "Area X," an area cordoned off by the military. In the film's key scene, the psychologist, Jennifer Jason Leigh, tells Portman, "It's destroying everything." And she replies, "It's not destroying. It's making something new." This departure from binary thinking and purely human categories is also what Marxist-feminist theorists and historians of science like Donna Haraway and Anna Tsing have been calling for. For the earth to survive, Tsing and Haraway argue, we must give up our dominance and redefine our role in the cosmos, as well as the relationship between culture, science, and nature. For we are already living in the ruins of capitalism, in an age of annihilation, exploitation, and extinction, in a situation that is increasingly precarious for most living beings. To understand this situation, we need not only facts but also multi-perspectival narratives, experiences that help us to emotionally and creatively connect with other species, to learn other ways of thinking and perceiving. In the process, Haraway and other thinkers and activists are developing all sorts of SF terms: *science fact, science fiction, speculative feminism, speculative fabulation.* The stories that emerge, however, do not tell of space adventures, of distant worlds to be colonized, of a last-minute rescue. They tell of a new ecological and social diversity created by contamination and extinction. Tsing and Haraway speak of "worlding" or "world-making". But in their thought, it is not only humans and patriarchal capitalism that make worlds, but all species and non-living things as well: bacteria, plants, mammals, insects, birds, crabs, nematodes, fungi, machines, cyborgs, algorithms. Everything is intertwined, entangled, needs and conditions each other.

These discourses shape the current art world, and they also play a role for Lipchik, but he doesn't illustrate them. Ruthless as the shimmer in *Extinction,* he takes this current thinking and clones it together with the romantic, decadent, super-gay motifs he already dealt with in *Windows Into Exile.* His next series, *Above the Surface*, combines Haraway's figure of the cyborg with Hollywood, ancient mythologies, Pre-Raphaelite art into a kind of Wagnerian *Götterdämmerung*. If things were austere in between, decadence and narcissism make their return here. *Above the Surface* acts as a sort of meta-commentary on Lipchik's earlier works—like a reflection of a reflection, a mirror looking into a mirror.

His avatars become even harder, more crystalline. Much like in the TV series *American Gods*, the deities have returned to earth, this time to the abandoned suburbs of the white lower middle class. The garden and pool become mythologically charged sites of homoeroticism and death. Whereas in the series, the "old" gods of indigenous peoples, former slaves, and immigrants compete against the "new" globalized techno gods, Lipchik has simply morphed them together. The collaged cubist aesthetic of the figures staring into mirrors, smartphones, and watery surfaces recall early computer animations from the 1980s, like the paintbox characters in the Dire Straits video *Money For Nothing* (1985). They aren't actually deities either, but memes of goddesses, avatar containers to be filled with new speculative narratives. In *Elizabeth Taylor's Reflection* (2021) [► P. 106], Lipchik has one avatar gaze at mirror-smooth water while wearing the famous ruby necklace Taylor got as a gift from her husband, Hollywood producer Mike Todd. But the chunky figure wrought together in paint bears no resemblance to Liz Taylor, or to a woman at all. It is genderless. Lipchik has reduced recognizability to the minimum, leaving only the jewelry and a sunken stare into the reflection. This Liz could also be the avatar of a gay teenager—as Lipchik once was, growing up in the conservative working-class town of Erie, Pennsylvania—who recognizes his sexual identity in the water, his desires, his future, very likely narcissistic manifestations. There's something romantic and yearning about that, but also something incredibly melancholic.

Night falls in Lipchik's paintings. Moons or planets appear, his figures bathing in their light. A fissure runs through reality, and something yet unknown comes shining out. Perhaps it's the start of a new age, but more likely it's the possibility of annihilation looming. The moon bathers, the longings, the immersion in premonitions, mythological and archetypal images, the end-time vibe are all strikingly reminiscent of Lars von Trier's *Melancholia* (2011). The film tells of the last days on Earth as a giant blue planet called Melancholia hurtles towards it. The apocalypse is narrated from the perspective of the severely depressed Justine (Kirsten Dunst). Accompanied by the sounds of the prelude to Wagner's opera *Tristan und Isolde*, we see her stone-like face, she opens her eyes. Birds fall dead from the sky, a horse sinks into the ground softening like hot tar. Lightning strikes from Justine's electrostatically charged hands, while the sky darkens with sulfurous clouds. With this vision, von Trier makes it clear right from the start that things are coming to an end. And he does it through choreographed dreamlike slow-motion shots that resemble tableaux vivants, old master paintings, the Surrealism of Dora Carrington, or Dali's dreamscapes, or Hitchcock's 1945 psychological thriller *Spellbound*. This artificiality creates a strange, almost cold distance from death. The closer the planet comes to impact, the less real and more stylized the operatic the world becomes.

This corresponds with Justine's nature, as she plays the role of the decadent yet realistic heroine—a seer who is the first to realize that humanity along with everything living will be wiped out. The first part of the film shows how this realization renders her incapable of living. Her depression costs the protagonist her job and her marriage, which was to be sealed at the chateau estate of her conservative bourgeois sister Claire (Charlotte Gainsbourg) with an extravagant wedding party. Justine can no longer stand up, eat, or wash herself. But when it becomes clearer that her visions are actually coming true, that the world can't be saved, she wakes up, filled with a great clarity. While her sister, who had previously been so capable, becomes increasingly hysterical, refusing to face the truth, Justine says hard-boiled things like: "The earth is evil. We don't need to grieve for it."[4] At the same time, she develops a paradoxical zest for life. She lies naked in the woods at night and takes moon baths in the strangely diffuse green light of the alien planet. Marxist philosopher Slavoj Žižek calls her attitude optimistic: "If you really want to do something good for society, if you want to avoid all totalitarian traps you really should go [see the film]. We all should go to make this—let me call it, although I am a total materialist—'fundamental spiritual experience' of accepting that someday everything will finish."[5] This factual certainty helps Kirsten Dunst's character care for her family in an almost Buddhist, spiritual way. Just before Melancholia hits and atomizes the earth, the nihilistic and depressed Justine builds her sister and nephew a magical shelter out of sparse branches to calm them and die with them.

"Highly romantic" is how von Trier described his film, also in reference to Wagner.[6] But beneath the film's "romantic" operatic quality lies a hard, materialist truth that Melancholia confronts us with: the end of humanity won't be preserved by any human memories. There are no more bodies, no more sites of memory. There is literally nothing. At the end of the film, viewers unexpectedly find themselves gazing at a black screen for a minute with no sound. There are no "posthuman" narratives in this sense either, they are merely a construction, a hopeless attempt to maintain control and somehow imagine a life after the end. Yet it is precisely from this hopelessness, this profoundly pessimistic attitude, that one can draw strength, just like Justine does in the film. The rituals Lipchik shows in his latest paintings in the exhibition at Kunstpalais radiate a material-spiritual energy similar to Justine's shelter. They are magical constructions that help us hold on to the grand narratives a little longer before the hard facts speak. As Justine says to her family as they start looking for an escape, a new story, a new beginning, "Life is only on Earth. And not for long."[7]

1 Personal correspondence with the artist, 23.11.2021.
2 Ibid.
3 Ibid.
4 Internet Movie Database (IMDb), https://www.imdb.com/title/tt1527186/characters/nm0000379 [last accessed May 24, 2022].
5 Slavoj Žižek, The Optimism of Melancholia (Big Think), June 26, 2012, https://www.youtube.com/watch?v=eUIjoYDKETM [last accessed May 22, 2022].
6 Lars von Trier and others tell about *Melancholia*'s visual style, YouTube, 21.02.2012, 0:50: https://www.youtube.com/watch?v=HAMOR898yyc [last accessed May 22, 2022].
7 Internet Movie Database (IMDb), https://www.imdb.com/title/tt1527186/characters/nm0000379 [last accessed May 24, 2022].

OLIVER KOERNER VON GUSTORF

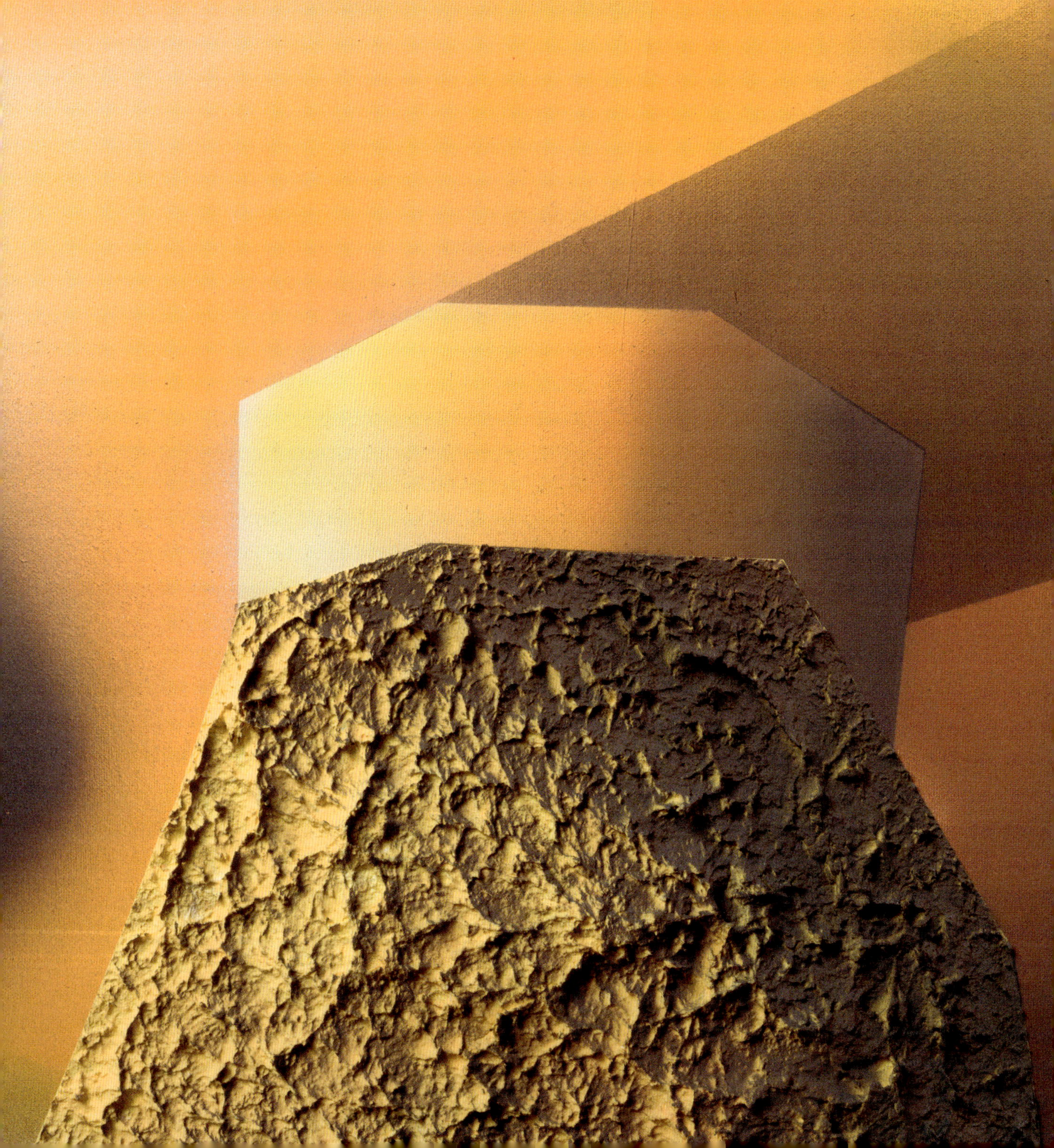

MONDBADEN IN ENDZEITEN

Brandon Lipchiks romantischer Materialismus

1. WHITE LOTUS

All diese geilen, zersplitterten Körper, die auf Brandon Lipchiks jüngeren Gemälden im Mondlicht baden. Wie Ophelia auf dem berühmten Gemälde von John Everett Millais treiben sie bleich in Swimming-Pools, verschlungen in Plastikschläuchen, wie in Schlingpflanzen, Schlangen oder endlos langen Schwänzen, aus denen sie sich mit Chlorwasser besprenkeln. Sie blicken hoch, in den nächtlichen Himmel, lümmeln sich mit ihrer künstlichen, schimmernden Haut in Jacuzzis, auf dem Rasen, tanzen auf Podesten, nehmen Selfies auf, ficken, betrachten ihre Spiegelbilder. Die ganze Welt ist eine Spiegelung, ein Traum. Vielleicht ist dieses Licht, das sie grün, violett, blau anstrahlt, auch kein Mondlicht, sondern das Licht von Scheinwerfern, fremden Gestirnen, die schwer am Firmament hängen. Vielleicht sind es auch keine Körper, sondern zusammengemorphte Avatare, Architekturen, Oberflächen und Materialien, die lediglich an Körper erinnern, die sich, kaum dass man den Blick abwendet, zu etwas Anderem zusammensetzen, zu klobigen, rasiermesserscharfen Blättern, Scherben, Schatten.

Trotz des „Mystischen" oder „Erotischen", das diese Körperarchitekturen ausstrahlen, vermitteln sie ein Gefühl von Normierung, Funktionalität, etwas Abwaschbares. Das mag an der Rendering-Software liegen, mit der Lipchik seine Bilder komponiert, um sie dann auf die Leinwand zu projizieren und dann das digitale Image mit Airbrush, Klebeband und Pinseln als Malerei zu materialisieren. Lipchiks Welt wird mit denselben Mitteln erzeugt wie die 3D-Visualisierungen von Games, Messeständen, Shops, Garagen. Die Verbindung von industriellen, plakativen Methoden mit „künstlerischer" oder „authentischer" Handschrift, von Funktionalem mit Heiligem, reflektiert eine globale Kulturlandschaft, die ähnlich funktioniert. Da ist dieses Versprechen eines „einmaligen Erlebnisses", von absoluter Einzigartigkeit und Originalität, von Liebe, Schönheit, inneren und äußeren Abenteuern, das aber vor einer Matrix der völligen Homogenisierung und Kommerzialisierung abgelegt wird.

Alle Träume werden ganz individuell auf dich zugeschnitten, Baby: Millionen fahren nach Disneyland, aber für jeden ist es ein unvergleichliches Erlebnis. Millionen tummeln sich auf Grindr, TikTok, Instagram und Tinder, posen dieselben Posen, fotografieren dieselben Bärte, Nippel, Tattoos, Negligés, kochen dasselbe Essen, machen dieselben Memes, unterlegen ihre Clips mit Harry Styles *As it Was*, pumpen ihre Bizepse und Ärsche auf, backen Muffins oder bauen Tiny Houses. Alle nutzen dieselben Filter, aber sicher war es einmalig und bestimmt wartet da draußen schon jemand, der ganz anders ist. Nicht ohne Hintersinn erinnern Lipchiks Pool- und Gartenlandschaften an amerikanische Vororte, an Ferienressorts wie in der US-Fernsehserie *The White Lotus* (2021), in denen von der Architektur bis zum Interior Design und zum Unterhaltungsprogramm verschiedene exotische oder romantische „Themen" durchgespielt werden. Die Art-Deco-Tapete ist geplottet, die Palmen eingeflogen, die marokkanischen Fliesen aus Plastik gestanzt, die Mitarbeiter*innen unter Mindestlohn. Alles in dieser modularen Erlebniswelt kann nach Bedarf abgezogen, zusammengeklappt, saisonal erneuert, gefeuert werden. Die

Körper der Konsument*innen werden auf dieselbe Weise zu Event-Baustellen, mit Diäten, Wellness und Training aufgepimpt, unterspritzt, abgesaugt, geschliffen, geschnitten, gefärbt.

Der Körper ist ein kapitalistischer Körper. Und so dekliniert Lipchik in seiner Malerei kommerzialisierte und industrielle Farbpaletten, Formensprachen und Symbole durch. Die Braun- und Espresso-Töne, die matten Grüns und Graus, die er auf seinen mystischen Bildern wie *Howling Snake* (2020) [▶ S. 114] in seiner Ausstellung *Visions of Song* in der Berliner Galerie Robert Grunenberg einsetzt, könnte man auch in Mid-Century-Boutique-Hotels mit faken Eames-Möbeln finden, die stilisierten Aststrukturen der Bäume auf einer nordischen Designertasse entdecken. Lipchik macht schon hier unmissverständlich klar, was in seinen jüngsten Gemälden noch weiter ausgeführt wird. Er zeigt, wie vorgefertigt auch unsere extremsten Selbstentwürfe sind, wie limitiert die antrainierten, performativen Gesten unseres Instagram-tauglichen Lebens – in dem wir immer süchtiger danach werden, alles zu teilen, uns selbst wie ein Produkt zu branden, unsere Alleinstellungsmerkmale hervorzuheben. In einer schnellen, jungen Kunstszene, die sich natürlich auch zunehmend auf Instagram vermarktet, erscheint ein Jahr wie ein Äon. So gehört Lipchiks Malerei, die er mit Mitte Zwanzig nach dem Abschluss seines Studiums an der Rhode Island School of Design und der Brown University produzierte, bereits zum „Frühwerk". Zugleich gibt es auf dem Markt auch einen bestimmten Aufmerksamkeitszwang, über den nicht offen gesprochen wird. So wie junge Kunst inzwischen sofortige, fast erotische Attraktion wecken soll, smart, attraktiv und heiß sein muss, wie High-End-Design, müssen es auch die Künstler*innen sein. Das Werk, die Biografie, der eigene Look, die ästhetischen und konzeptionellen Strategien müssen gleichermaßen begehrlich sein, „gut aussehen".

2. A BIGGER SPLASH

Lipchik, der schon zu Studienzeiten als Model arbeitete und von einer der weltweit größten und wichtigsten Agenturen vertreten wurde, wuchs quasi mit dem visuellen Vokabular von Looks, Posen, der Verbindung von Mode, Kunstgeschichte, Popkultur und Erotik auf. Die Bilder, die zwischen 2018 und 2019 entstehen, haben eine paradoxe sexualisierte Aufladung. Lipchik dekonstruiert digital Männerkörper, Räume, Landschaften, dekorative Objekte, Fauna, zerlegt sie in rudimentäre abstrakte Formen. Doch seine Praxis unterscheidet sich ganz erheblich von Avery Singer, die als Godmother der Post-Internet-Malerei bereits in den frühen 2010er-Jahren mit Rendering-Programmen und Airbrush arbeitete und nachfolgende Generationen prägte. In ihren Bildern, wie ihrem wohl berühmtesten Gemälde *The Studio Visit* (2012), thematisierte sie ihre Rolle und ihr Leben als Künstlerin, die Vermittlung und Vermarktung von Kunst, die Diskrepanz zwischen den Ritualen zeitgenössischer Malerei und der digitalen Bildproduktion. Das Faszinierende an Singer war, dass ihre Bilder die banale, demokratische Ästhetik von Games und Rendering-Programmen dem modernen und sehr männlichen Pathos von Konstruktivismus, Futurismus und Kubismus entgegenstellte. Singer knüpfte damit unter neuen Vorzeichen an die formalen Debatten, ästhetischen und konzeptionellen Strategien von US-Malerinnen wie Laura Owens, Amy Sillman oder Charlene van Heyl an, die den Malerei-Diskurs in den USA der letzten beiden Dekaden entscheidend geprägt haben.

Doch auch wenn er die visuelle Sprache der sogenannten Post-Digital-Malerei nutzt, agiert der sechs Jahre jüngere Lipchik aus einer ganz anderen Position. In *Windows Into Exile* bezieht er sich nicht dezidiert auf die Diskurse der aktuellen Malerei oder das Betriebssystem Kunst, auch wenn er davon geprägt ist: „Während des Studiums interessierte ich mich sehr für die Arbeit von Julie Mehretu. Mich begeisterte ihre Praxis, Informationen aus Architekturplänen und realen Strukturen zu extrahieren und diese in ein Rendering einzubauen, um daraus Abstraktionen zu schaffen. Ich war fasziniert, wie sie digitale Werkzeuge für ihre Arbeit einsetzte. Offensichtlich hatten alle, die einen Computer hatten, Zugang zu dieser Technologie. Ich bekam das Gefühl, dass es nur ein weiteres Handwerkszeug für Künstler*innen ist, um etwas zu erschaffen."[1] Lipchik greift in seiner digital-analogen Malerei eine ganz andere Agenda auf: die hypersensible schwule Ästhetik, die queeren Codes der Café Society und des späteren Jetsets der Sixties und Seventies. Er arbeitet mit Themen wie Interior Design, Dekor, angewandter Kunst, Illustration. Der Titel der Ausstellung spielt auf den Roman *Exil in Capri* (1959) des französischen Schriftstellers Roger Peyrefitte an, der auf dem Leben von Baron Jacques d'Adelswärd-Fersen (1880–1923) basiert. Der Pariser Aristokrat wird 1903 wegen päderastischer Beziehungen zu Pariser Schuljungen verurteilt und zu einer *persona non grata* in den Salons der Stadt erklärt. Daraufhin geht er ins Exil nach Capri, wo er mit seinem langjährigen, jüngeren Freund Nino Cesarini in einer erlesen eingerichteten Jugendstilvilla, der Villa Lysis, lebt, die nach dem Dialog Platons über Freundschaft und homosexuelle Liebe benannt wurde. Über dem Eingang ließ Fersen die lateinische Inschrift AMORI ET DOLORI SACRUM (*Der Liebe und dem Leid geweiht*) anbringen. 1923 nimmt er sich mit einer Überdosis Kokain das Leben.

Der Schwule oder der Dandy, der sich in der selbstgewählten Isolation oder im Exil eine dekadente Fantasiewelt schafft, in der er vollendet dahinsiecht und meistens auch stirbt, gehört seit dem Ende des 19. Jahrhunderts zu den Topoi der anbrechenden Moderne. Einer der Pioniere war Joris-Karl Huysman mit seinem 1884 erschienenen Kultbuch *À rebours* (*Gegen den Strich*), in dem Jean Floressas Des Esseintes, ein exzentrischer junger Adeliger sich in seine erlesen gestaltete Villa zurückzieht, um zu sterben. In einer Schlüsselszene des Romans beklebt er den Panzer einer lebenden Riesenschildkröte mit Diamanten, damit sie zum Teppich passt. Das Tier verendet an seinem Stilwillen. Mit Oscar Wildes Roman *Das Bildnis des Dorian Gray* (1890) und Thomas Manns *Der Tod in Venedig* (1911) wurde dieses Motiv weiter in der Massenkultur verewigt. Dabei geht es immer auch um einen weiter gefassten Themenkomplex: Um Künstlichkeit, absolute ästhetische Sensibilität, das Handeln *gegen die Natur*. Das heißt, gegen das biologische Geschlecht, gegen die Fortpflanzung, gegen das Alter, gegen den Zwang, sich dem Leben und der sich selbst als „natürlich" betrachtenden Gesellschaft unterzuordnen. Und in diesem Themenkomplex bewegen sich auch die Avatare, die Lipchiks Malerei bevölkern. Dabei haben die Lebensunfähigkeit und die Faszination des Todes als Programm etwas radikal Emanzipatorisches und Befreiendes.

Lipchik, der auch Fersens Villa in Capri besucht, dekonstruiert in *Windows Into Exile* nicht nur die bourgeoise, an Antike und Klassik angelehnte Ästhetik des Barons und seiner Zeitgenossen, wie etwa des Fotografen Wilhelm Plüschow. Er reagiert auch auf die Tatsache, dass das Begehren Jungs und jungen Männern aus der Arbeiterklasse oder Bauernfamilien galt. Lipchik konstruiert semi-abstrakte, völlig zeit- und klassenlose Interieurs, eine ungeheuer physische, verführerische, plastische Trompe-l'œil-Malerei. Er lässt die Leinwand aussehen, wie eine digitale Baustelle, als sei sie aus Photoshop-Ebenen zusammengezimmert, aus deren Tiefen dreidimensionale Formen emportauchen: die Muskeln eines Oberarms, grüne, wie aus Raufasertapete geschnittene Blätter, Haarwirbel, Werkzeuge wie Hammer und Säge, Amphoren, Polaroids, Eisenzäune, Nippel, hart und plastisch wie die Süßigkeiten in einem Candy Store. Zugleich sind seine Avatare dekadent oder romantisch, wie Figuren in der symbolistischen Malerei, der Literatur und Musik des 19. Jahrhunderts. Natürlich spielt Lipchik mit der Wave-Preppy-Ästhetik von Luca Guadagninos *Call Me By Your Name* (2017), lässt sogar den berühmt berüchtigten Pfirsich auftauchen. Aber auch das ist eine Anspielung auf eine dekadente, hedonistische Ära. Hemmungslos sexualisiert er die Oberfläche – mit Airbrush-Tulpen, die auf den Bildern sitzen wie Lippenstift-Abdrücke auf Kleenex-Tüchern, mit plastischen, minzigen, gelben, pinken Farblachen, die wie Sperma oder flüssiger Lack auf der Leinwand treiben. Wie die pastösen Farbschlieren, die er aus Gips modelliert, erinnern sie an die Art und Weise, wie Laura Owens ihren Bildern einen skulpturalen Touch gibt und expressive, affektgeladene Gesten persifliert.

Doch Lipchik braucht diesen konzeptionellen Abstand nicht, er setzt die künstlichen Spritzer, Schlieren und Blüten ohne Scham wie verführerische dekorative Elemente ein. Seine Capri-Serie buchstabiert ein nostalgisches Alphabet des homosexuellen Geschmacks durch. Dazu gehören Cocteaus und Cecil Beaton ebenso wie David Hockneys Poolgemälde und der melancholische Jetset-Glamour aus dem Hockney-Film *A Bigger Splash* (1973). Und anders als etwa Avery Singer, die Mal-Roboter und Digitaldruck einsetzt, um auf ihren perfekt fotorealistisch gemalten Bildern konzeptionelle Distanz zur genialischen Berührung der Leinwand mit dem Pinsel zu erzeugen, geht Lipchik hier einen umgekehrten, eher outsiderischen Weg. Immer wieder hat er auf die Frage, warum er seine digitalen Bilder überhaupt auf Leinwand malen muss, geantwortet, dass ihm dieser physische Kontakt enorm wichtig ist, dass Malerei für ihn eine beinahe sexuelle Komponente hat. Er nimmt den Weg über die digitale Bildproduktion, um so zu einer queeren Malerei zu gelangen, die extrem physisch ist, ohne machohaft zu werden. So wie David Hockney in seinem Spätwerk zur digitalen Malerei auf dem iPad kommt, findet Lipchik über das Digitale zu einer analogen, extrem sinnlichen, malerischen Form, die skulpturale Züge hat.

„Ich glaube, ich fühlte mich mit Hockney verbunden, nachdem ich seine Gemälde und diese visuellen Erzählungen über Pools gesehen hatte", sagt Lipchik. „Der Pool war ein Symbol, das ich im Zusammenhang mit Americana sehe. Ich denke, er steht für Wohlstand, Freizeit, amerikanische Träume und Hollywood-Phantasien, die man immer wieder in Filmen sieht. Ich habe ähnliche Erfahrungen gemacht, als ich in den Suburbs aufwuchs – anders als in Hollywood, aber in ähnlicher Weise. Der Pool war auch der Ort, an dem ich begann, die Tiefen meiner eigenen Sexualität zu entdecken. Und das Thema ist geblieben."[2] Eines von Lipchiks absoluten Lieblingsgemälden ist Hockneys 1972 entstandenes *Portrait of an Artist* (*Pool with Two Figures*), das auch im Hockney-Biopic *A Bigger Splash* (1973) eine zentrale Rolle spielt. Es zeigt Hockneys Freund Peter Schlesinger, der in einer Berglandschaft am Pool steht und auf eine im Wasser schwimmende Figur blickt. Die eckigen Formen des Pools, der Kacheln und Steinplatten ergeben ein Netz aus horizontalen und vertikalen Linien, in das beide Figuren eingebettet sind. Interessanterweise tut Lipchik in seiner Malerei etwas Ähnliches wie das, was Hockney hier so meisterlich vormacht: Er verbindet die beiden Genre Porträt- und Landschaftsmalerei. Hockneys Bild entsteht in der für ihn traumatischen Trennungsphase von Schlesinger. Das Gemälde ist eine Montage aus verschiedenen zeitlichen und räumlichen Ebenen, zusammengesetzt aus Fotos, nachgestellten Szenen und einem Shooting mit Schlesinger, die Hockney malerisch zusammenfügt. *Portrait of an Artist* (*Pool with Two Figures*) thematisiert das Verschwimmen von äußerem und innerem Erleben, physischem und emotionalem Abstand, Performativität und Authentizität, die verzerrte, zersplitterte, medialisierte Wahrnehmung von Körpern, Orten, Gefühlen – Themen, die auch Lipchiks Malerei beherrschen.

Diese multiperspektivische visuelle Erzählung hat Hockney dann in den frühen 1980er-Jahren mit seinen Polaroid-Arbeiten weitergetrieben. Diese Porträts oder Landschaften setzen sich aus bis zu 120, im Raster angeordneten Polaroids zusammen, von denen jedes einzelne eine andere Perspektive zeigt. Das heißt, wenn Hockney einen Menschen neben einem Tisch fotografiert auf dem ein Blumenstrauß steht, bewegt er sich um den Menschen, den Tisch, den Blumenstrauß, macht Nahaufnahmen von Details wie Blüten oder Schuhen, entfernt sich bei anderen Aufnahmen wieder. Man kann sagen, er umkreist Subjekte und Objekte und bewegt sich durch den Raum wie eine Drohne, die kontinuierlich Aufnahmen macht. Er dokumentiert dabei die Unfähigkeit der Fotografie, mit Einzelbildern Zeit oder verschiedene Perspektiven festzuhalten. Aber er zeigt auch, wie mit Fragmentierung und Reorganisation der Fragmente neue Wahrnehmungsmöglichkeiten und Raumerfahrungen eröffnet werden.

Lipchik, der seine Werke aus verschiedenen Motiven zusammenmontiert, strebt in seiner Malerei einen ähnlichen Effekt an: „Beim Malen merke ich, welche Kontrolle ich über die Perspektive habe, dass ich genau wie ein Filmemacher bestimme, was der Betrachter sehen soll, wobei der Filmemacher auf das beschränkt ist, was die Kamera oder die Physik hergeben. Oft nehme ich eine über dem Kopf schwebende Perspektive ein oder zeige den Blickwinkel über die Schulter, um genau wie im Film buchstäblich ‚von oben herab' auf die Figur zu blicken oder zu verdeutlichen, dass sie beobachtet wird. Man könnte sogar sagen, ich vermittle eine außerkörperliche oder spirituelle Sichtweise auf meine simulierten Figuren".[3] Das Interessante daran ist, dass er dabei mindestens so im Kanon der Moderne und der Nachkriegsmalerei verankert ist wie in der digitalen Bildproduktion des 21. Jahrhunderts.

Lipchiks grell ausgeleuchtete, multiperspektivische Sommer-Bilder, die wie *Biker* **[▸ S. 104]** oder *Garden Hose* **[▸ S. 60]** 2019 zeitgleich mit den Bildern von *Windows Into Exile* entstehen, greifen typische Einstellungen aus schwulen 80er-Jahre-Pornofilmen auf, zitieren den cleanen American-Apparel-Look. Sie wirken wie ironische, knallbunte Reaktionen auf das lüstern verklemmte Hetero-Statement von Willem de Kooning zu dessen expressiven, für die Nachkriegsgesellschaft provokanten Frauenakten: „Fleisch ist der Grund, warum die Ölfarbe erfunden worden ist." Lipchiks queere Acryl-Körper sind fragmentiert, aber nicht fleischig, sondern glatt, artifiziell, zum Anlecken und Aufessen. Sie sind nicht psychologisiert, mit Schuld oder Scham beladen, sondern auf eine ganz pragmatische Weise verfügbar. Standardmäßig werden Bilder feminisiert, schreibt der US-Kunsthistoriker und Theoretiker W.J.T. Mitchell. Sie werden als etwas behandelt, das im Betrachter oder der Betrachterin Begehren zu wecken hat, während sie selbst in keiner Weise irgendwelche Anzeichen eines Begehrens preisgeben, oder auch nur eines Bewusstseins davon, dass sie von jemandem angeblickt werden – ganz so, als würden die Betrachter*innen voyeuristisch durch ein Schlüsselloch gucken. Lipchik erzeugt diesen Effekt in der schwulen Version mit geradezu chirurgischen Mitteln. Seine anonymen Avatare haben kein Gesicht, keine Augen, sind nur Körper. Sie können also nicht zu den Betrachter*innen zurückblicken, sondern sind einseitige Objekte der Begierde. Doch da ist etwas Hartes, Abgründiges in diesen poppigen Bildern, eine latente Gewalt, die fast bedrohlich wirkt. 2020 fällt dann ein dystopischer Schatten über alles, der digitale Sommer verwandelt sich in eine mystische Endzeit.

3. MELANCHOLIA

Lipchiks Zyklus *Visions of Song* ist eine Hommage an die großen amerikanischen Dichter, an Robert Frost, die Beat-Poeten Allen Ginsberg und Jack Kerouac, an James Baldwin. Vor allem aber spielt er auf den schwulen Poeten und Transzendentalisten Walt Whitman (1819–1892) an, der die beginnende Industrialisierung, die Demokratie, die indigene Kultur und eine spirituelle Erfahrung der Natur besang. Whitman passt so gut in das Repertoire von Lipchik, weil er den amerikanischen Traum der Demokratie wie einen männlichen Körper erotisiert. Etwa in *I Sing the Body Electric* in seinem berühmten Gedichtband *Leaves of Grass* (1855), in dem er Amerika wie einen kollektiven Organismus besingt, der verbunden ist durch Eisenbahnlinien, Strommasten, arbeitende, brüderliche, liebende Körper. Lipchiks Gemälde aus *Visions of Song* entstehen in der auslaufenden Trump-Ära, in der auch die Klima-Katastrophe immer unübersehbarer wird. Es ist die Zeit der verheerenden Waldbrände in Kalifornien und Australien, in der nicht nur Kleinstädte und Vororte in Flammen aufgehen, sondern Millionen von Tieren sterben, ganze Populationen verbrennen. Die Bilder wirken, als sei Whitmans elektrischer, kommunaler Körper mit der kollabierenden Demokratie und der verbrennenden Natur in seine Gliedmaßen zersplittert. Auf einigen Bildern sind die Körper fahl und äschern, wie vertrocknetes Holz, die Arme und Beine sind mit Sprühfarbe markiert wie Bäume, die zum Fällen bestimmt sind. Es wird gepflanzt, gebaut, umgetopft, zu retten versucht, was noch zu retten ist. Irgendwo brennt es schon wieder. Es scheint, als sei jede Frivolität, jeder Anflug von Café Society verschwunden. Doch da sind noch immer dieselben Motive, die Zäune, die Hammer, die schwertartigen Blätter – Lipchik zeigt fast die gleichen im Bau befindlichen Szenerien, nur in einer prekäreren Version. Das Beobachten, das vorher eher ein voyeuristischer Akt war, erinnert jetzt vielmehr an die Überwachung durch Kameras und Drohnen, Luftbilder aus Katastrophengebieten.

Zugleich beginnt sich hier, in dieser absterbenden Welt, ein anderes Thema deutlicher herauszukristallisieren, das Lipchiks Arbeit von Anfang an bestimmt hat: Kultur und Natur sind in seinen Körperarchitekturen inzwischen fast vollständig voneinander durchdrungen. Das erinnert an den Sci-Fi-Horrorfilm *Auslöschung* (2018), in dem eine geheimnisvolle außerirdische Lebensform ein Gebiet an der amerikanischen Westküste infiltriert. Der „Schimmer" lässt Menschen, Tiere, Pflanzen in die bizarrsten Formen mutieren und züchtet neue Geschöpfe: Menschenblumen, Haifischkrokodile. Natalie Portman spielt eine Molekularbiologin, die mit einem Team in das vom Militär abgesperrte Gebiet „Area X" vordringt. In der Schlüsselszene des Films sagt die Psychologin, Jennifer Jason Leigh, zu Portman: „Es zerstört alles." Und die entgegnet: „Es zerstört nicht. Es schafft etwas Neues." Dieser Abschied von binärem Denken und rein menschlichen Kategorien ist auch das, was feministisch-marxistische Theoretikerinnen und Naturwissenschaftshistorikerinnen wie Donna Haraway oder Anna Tsing fordern. Damit die Erde überleben kann, sagen Tsing und Haraway, müssen wir unsere Vorherrschaft aufgeben und unsere Rolle im Kosmos, das Verhältnis zwischen Kultur, Wissenschaft und Natur neu bestimmen. Denn wir leben bereits heute in den Ruinen des Kapitalismus, in einem Zeitalter der Vernichtung, Ausbeutung und Auslöschung, in einer für die meisten Lebewesen immer prekärer werdenden Situation. Um diese Situation zu begreifen, brauchen wir nicht nur Fakten, sondern auch multiperspektivische Erzählungen, Erfahrungen, die helfen, uns emotional und kreativ mit anderen Spezies zu verbinden und andere Formen des Denkens und des Wahrnehmens zu erlernen. Dabei entwickeln Haraway und andere Denker*innen und Aktivist*innen lauter SF-Begriffe: *science fact, science fiction, speculative feminism, speculative fabulation.* Die Stories, die dabei herauskommen, erzählen allerdings nicht von Weltraumabenteuern, von fernen, zu kolonialisierenden Welten, von einer Rettung in letzter Minute. Sie erzählen von einer neuen ökologischen und sozialen Diversität, die durch Kontamination und Ausrottung entsteht. Tsing und Haraway sprechen von „world-making". Doch in diesem Denken machen nicht nur der Mensch und der patriarchale Kapitalismus Welten, sondern alle Spezies und auch Nicht-Lebendes: Bakterien, Pflanzen, Säugetiere, Insekten, Vögel, Krebse, Fadenwürmer, Pilze, Maschinen, Cyborgs, Algorithmen. Alles ist ineinander verwickelt, verheddert, braucht und bedingt einander.

Diese Diskurse prägen den aktuellen Kunstbetrieb. Auch für Lipchik spielen sie eine Rolle, doch er illustriert sie nicht. Skrupellos wie der Schimmer in *Auslöschung* nimmt er dieses aktuelle Denken und klont es mit den romantischen, dekadenten, super-schwulen Motiven zusammen, mit denen er sich bereits in *Windows Into Exile* beschäftigte. Seine nächste Serie, *Above the Surface*, verbindet Haraways Denkfigur des Cyborgs mit Hollywood, antiken Mythologien, präraffaelitischer Kunst zu einer Art Wagnerianischen Götterdämmerung. Wurde es zwischendurch karg, kehren hier wieder Dekadenz und Narzissmus zurück. *Above the Surface* agiert quasi als Meta-Kommentar zu Lipchiks früheren Arbeiten – wie die Reflexion einer Reflexion, ein Spiegel, der in den Spiegel blickt.

Seine Avatare erhalten eine noch kristallinere und härtere Qualität. Ähnlich wie in der TV-Serie *American Gods* sind Gottheiten auf die Erde zurückgekehrt, in diesem Fall in die verlassenen Vororte der weißen Lower Middle Class. Der Garten und der Pool werden zu mythologisch aufgeladenen Orten der Homoerotik und des Todes. Treten in der TV-Serie die „alten" Gött*innen der indigenen Völker, von ehemaligen Sklav*innen und Immigrant*innen, gegen die „neuen" globalisierten Techno-Gött*innen an, hat Lipchik sie einfach zusammengemorpht. Die Figuren, die in Spiegel, auf Smartphones und Wasseroberflächen starren, erinnern in ihrer kubistisch-collagierten Ästhetik an frühe Computeranimationen aus den 1980er-Jahren, etwa die Paintbox-Charaktere in dem Dire-Straits-Video *Money For Nothing* (1985). Es sind eigentlich auch keine Gottheiten, sondern Memes von Gött*innen, Avatar-Behälter, die mit neuen spekulativen Narrativen gefüllt werden. Lipchik lässt auf *Elizabeth Taylor's Reflection* (2021) **[▶ S. 106]** einen Avatar mit dem berühmten Rubin-Halsband, das Taylor von ihrem Mann, dem Hollywood-Produzenten Mike Todd, geschenkt bekam, auf eine spiegelglatte Wasseroberfläche blicken. Doch die malerisch zusammenmontierte, klobige Gestalt hat weder Ähnlichkeit mit Liz Taylor noch überhaupt mit einer Frau, sondern ist geschlechtslos. Lipchik hat die Wiedererkennbarkeit auf ein Minimum reduziert, nur den Schmuck und den versunkenen Blick aufs Spiegelbild gelassen. Diese Liz könnte auch der Avatar eines schwulen Teenagers sein – wie einst Lipchik, der in der konservativen Arbeiterstadt Erie in Pennsylvania aufwuchs –, der im Wasser seine sexuelle Identität, seine Sehnsüchte, seine zukünftigen, wahrscheinlich narzisstischen Manifestationen erkennt. Das hat etwas Romantisches, Sehnsüchtiges, aber auch etwas unglaublich Melancholisches.

Es wird Nacht in Lipchiks Bildern. Es tauchen Monde oder Planeten auf, in deren Licht sich seine Gestalten baden. Ein Riss geht durch die Wirklichkeit, aus dem etwas noch völlig Unbekanntes strahlt. Vielleicht ist es der Beginn einer neuen Zeit, aber vielmehr lauert da die Möglichkeit der Auslöschung. Die Mondbäder, die Sehnsüchte, das Eintauchen in Vorahnungen, mythologische und archetypische Bilder, die Endzeitstimmung erinnern frappant an Lars von Triers *Melancholia* (2011). Der Film erzählt von den letzten Tagen der Erde, auf die ein riesiger, blauer Planet zurast, der Melancholia heißt. Erzählt wird die Apokalypse aus der Sicht der schwer depressiven Justine (Kirsten Dunst). Unterlegt mit den Klängen der Prélude zu Wagners Oper *Tristan und Isolde* sehen wir ihr versteinertes Gesicht, sie öffnet die Augen. Vögel fallen tot vom Himmel, ein Pferd versinkt wie heißer Teer im aufweichenden Boden. Blitze schlagen aus Justines elektrostatisch aufgeladenen Händen, während der Himmel sich mit schwefeligen Wolken verdunkelt. Von Trier macht mit dieser Vision gleich zu Beginn klar, dass es zu Ende geht. Und er tut das mit traumartig choreografierten Zeitlupenaufnahmen, die Tableaux vivants ähneln, die altmeisterliche Malerei, den Surrealismus von Dora Carrington, Dalis Traumlandschaften oder Hitchcocks 1945 entstandenen Psychothriller *Spellbound* (*Ich kämpfe um dich*) zitieren. Diese Künstlichkeit schafft eine merkwürdige, fast kalte Distanz zum Tod. Je näher wir dem Aufprall des Planeten kommen, desto weniger real und desto stilisierter, opernhafter wird die Welt.

Das entspricht der Verfassung von Justine, die hier die Rolle der dekadenten, aber zugleich realistischen Heldin spielt – eine Seherin, die als Erste erkennt, dass die Menschheit, alles Lebende ausgelöscht wird. Der erste Teil des Films zeigt, wie lebensunfähig sie dadurch wird. Ihre Depressionen kosten sie ihren Job, ihre Ehe, die auf dem Schlossgut ihrer bourgeoisen, konservativen Schwester Claire (Charlotte Gainsbourg) mit einer fulminanten Hochzeitsfeier besiegelt werden soll. Justine kann nicht mehr aufstehen, nicht mehr essen, sich nicht waschen. Doch als deutlicher wird, dass ihre Visionen tatsächlich eintreffen, dass es keine Rettung für die Welt gibt, wacht sie wieder auf, ist erfüllt von großer Klarheit. Während ihre vorher so patente Schwester immer hysterischer wird, der Wahrheit nicht ins Auge blicken will, sagt Justine abgebrühte Sachen wie: „Die Erde ist böse. Wir müssen nicht um sie trauern.“[4] Zugleich entwickelt sie eine paradoxe Lebensfreude. Sie liegt nachts nackt im Wald und nimmt Mondbäder im seltsam diffusen grünen Licht des fremden Planeten. Der marxistische Philosoph Slavoj Žižek nennt ihre Haltung optimistisch: „Wenn Sie wirklich etwas Gutes für die Gesellschaft tun wollen, wenn Sie alle totalitären Fallen vermeiden wollen, sollten Sie wirklich gehen [und diesen Film ansehen]. Wir alle sollten gehen, um diese – ich nenne es mal, obwohl ich ein totaler Materialist bin – ‚fundamentale spirituelle Erfahrung‘ zu machen, zu akzeptieren, dass eines Tages alles enden wird.“[5] Diese faktische Gewissheit hilft Kirsten Dunsts Figur im Film, sich auf eine fast buddhistische, spirituelle Weise um ihre Familie zu kümmern. Kurz bevor Melancholia einschlägt und die Erde atomisiert, baut die nihilistische und depressive Justine ihrer Schwester und ihrem Neffen aus spärlichen Ästen eine magische Schutzhütte, um sie zu beruhigen und mit ihnen zu sterben.

„Hochgradig romantisch“ hat von Trier, auch in Anspielung auf Wagner, seinen Film genannt.[6] Doch unter der „romantischen“ Opernhaftigkeit des Films verbirgt sich eine harte, materialistische Wahrheit, mit der uns Melancholia konfrontiert: Das Ende der Menschheit wird durch keine menschlichen Erinnerungen bewahrt. Es gibt keine Körper, keinen Ort für die Erinnerung mehr. Da ist buchstäblich nichts. Am Ende des Films blicken die Zuschauer*innen völlig unerwartet für eine Minute auf eine schwarze Leinwand, ohne Ton. Es gibt in diesem Sinne auch keine „posthumanen“ Erzählungen, sie sind lediglich eine Konstruktion, der aussichtslose Versuch, die Kontrolle zu bewahren und sich irgendwie ein Leben nach dem Ende vorzustellen. Doch genau aus dieser Hoffnungslosigkeit, aus einer zutiefst pessimistischen Haltung kann man, wie Justine im Film, Kraft beziehen. Die Rituale, die Lipchik auf seinen jüngsten Gemälden in der Ausstellung im Kunstpalais zeigt, strahlen eine ähnlich materiell-spirituelle Energie wie Justines Schutzhütte aus. Es sind magische Konstruktionen, die helfen, noch ein bisschen an den Großen Erzählungen festzuhalten, bevor die harten Fakten sprechen. Wie sagt Justine zu ihrer Familie, als sie damit beginnen, einen Ausweg, eine neue Story, einen Neuanfang zu suchen: „Leben gibt es nur auf der Erde. Und nicht mehr lange.“[7]

1 Persönliche Korrespondenz mit dem Künstler, 23.11.2021.
2 Ebd.
3 Ebd.
4 Internet Movie Database (IMDb), https://www.imdb.com/title/tt1527186/characters/nm0000379 [letzter Zugriff: 24.05.2022].
5 Slavoj Žižek, The Optimism of Melancholia (Big Think), 26.06.2012, https://www.youtube.com/watch?v=eUIjoYDKETM [letzter Zugriff: 22.05.2022].
6 Lars von Trier and others tell about *Melancholia*’s visual style, YouTube, 21.02.2012, 0:50, https://www.youtube.com/watch?v=HAMOR898yyc [letzter Zugriff: 22.05.2022].
7 Internet Movie Database (IMDb), https://www.imdb.com/title/tt1527186/characters/nm0000379 [letzter Zugriff: 24.05.2022].

WORKS
ARBEITEN

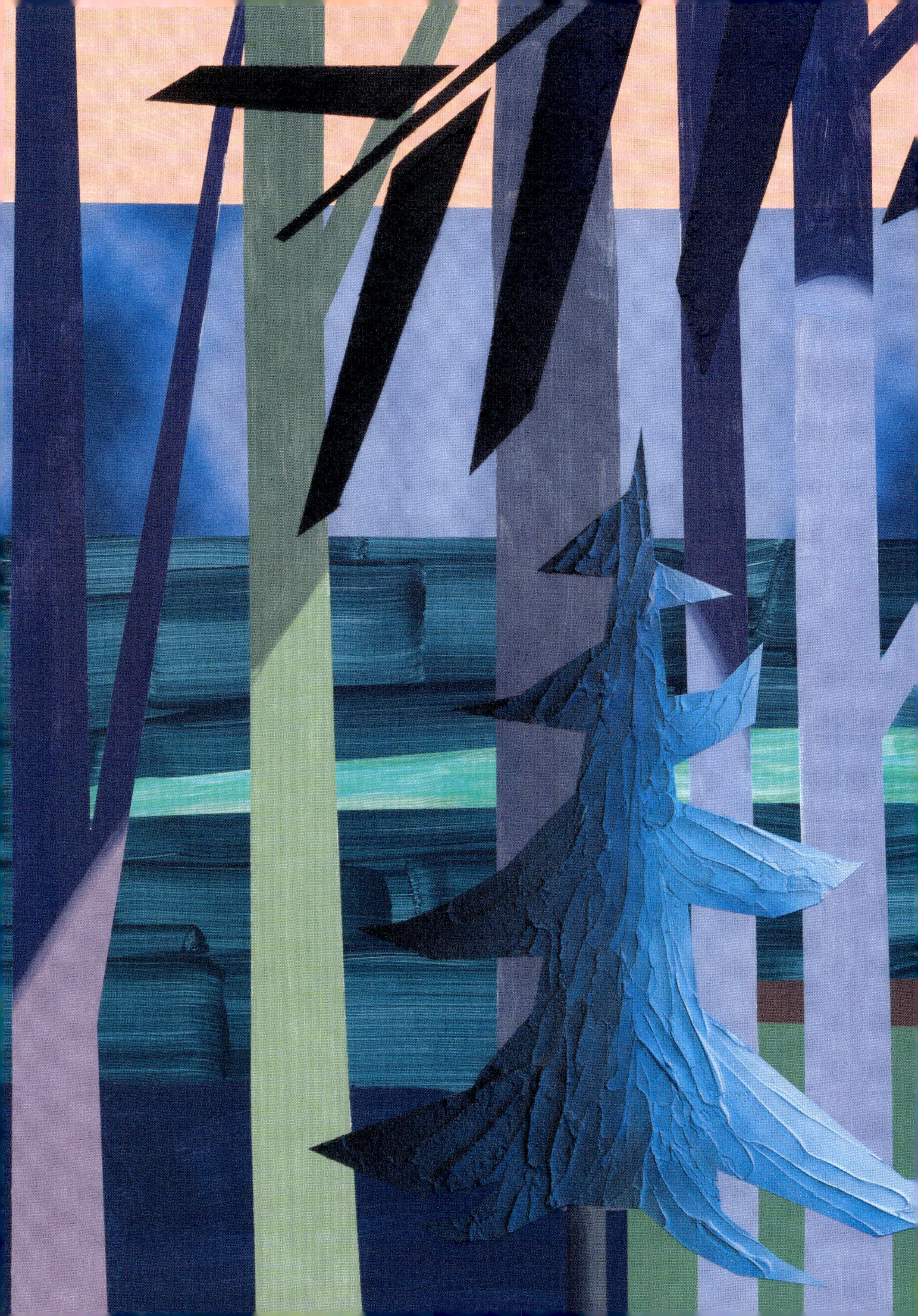

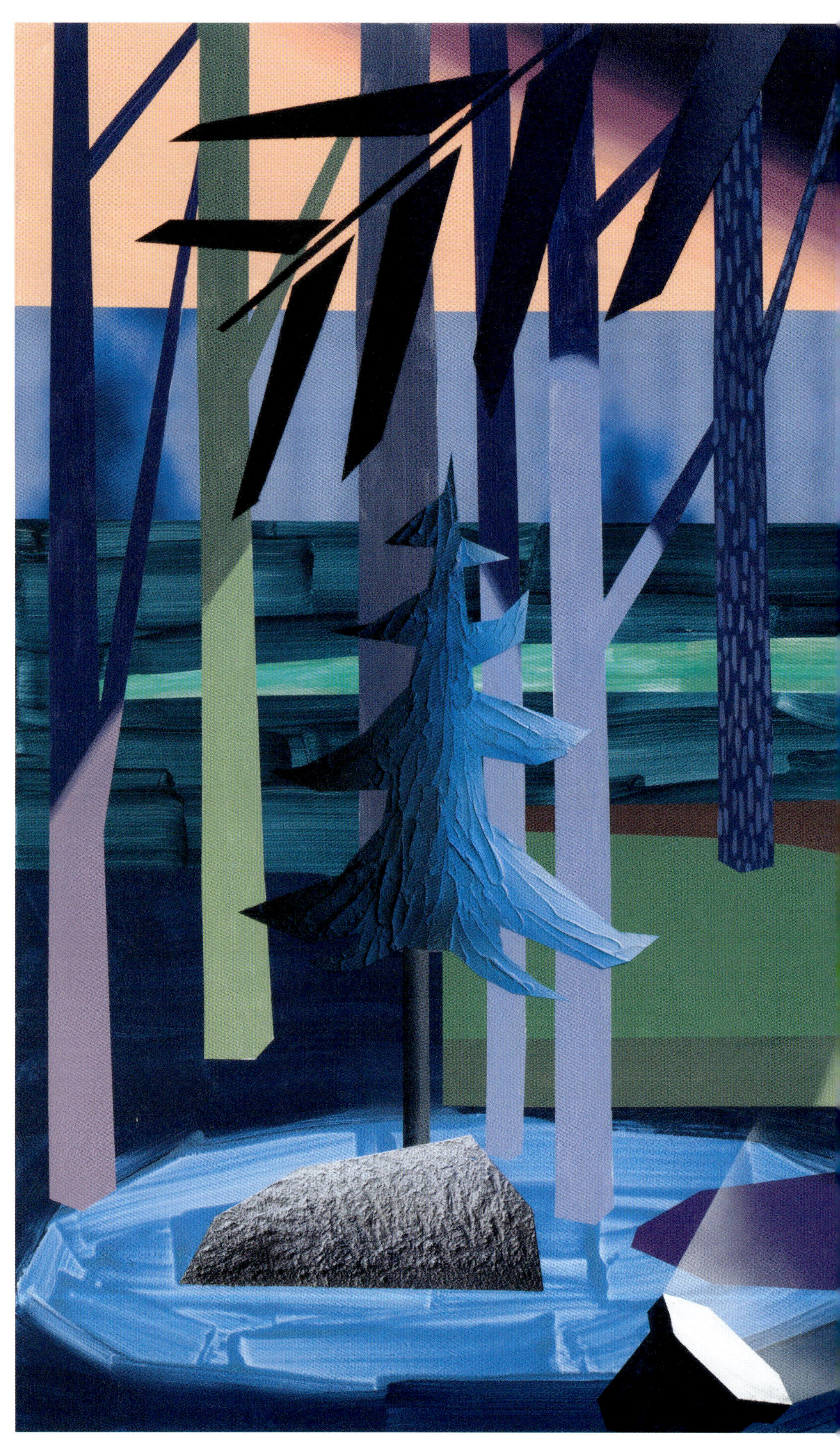

FOREST STAGE
2022 · 175 × 250 cm

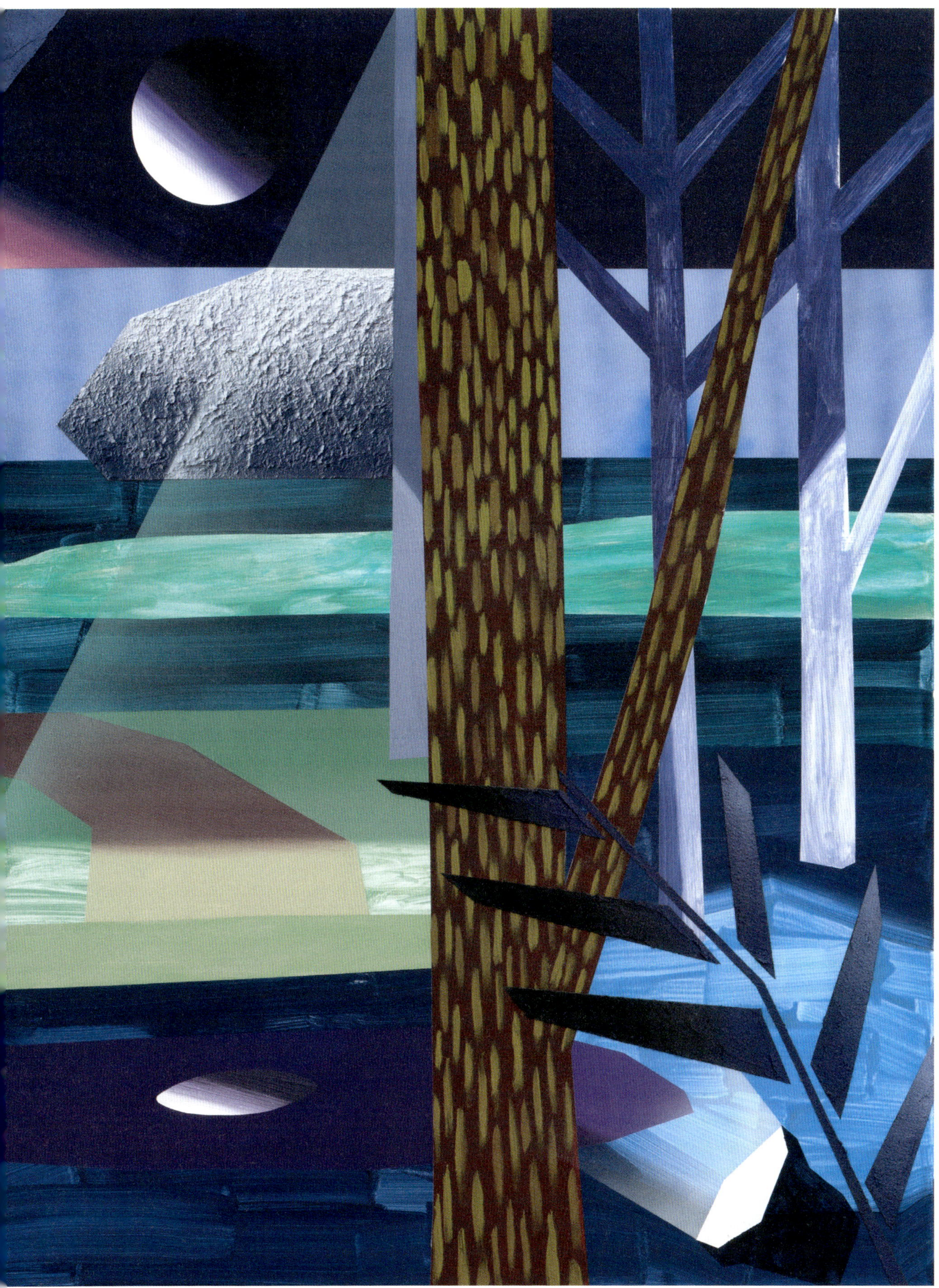

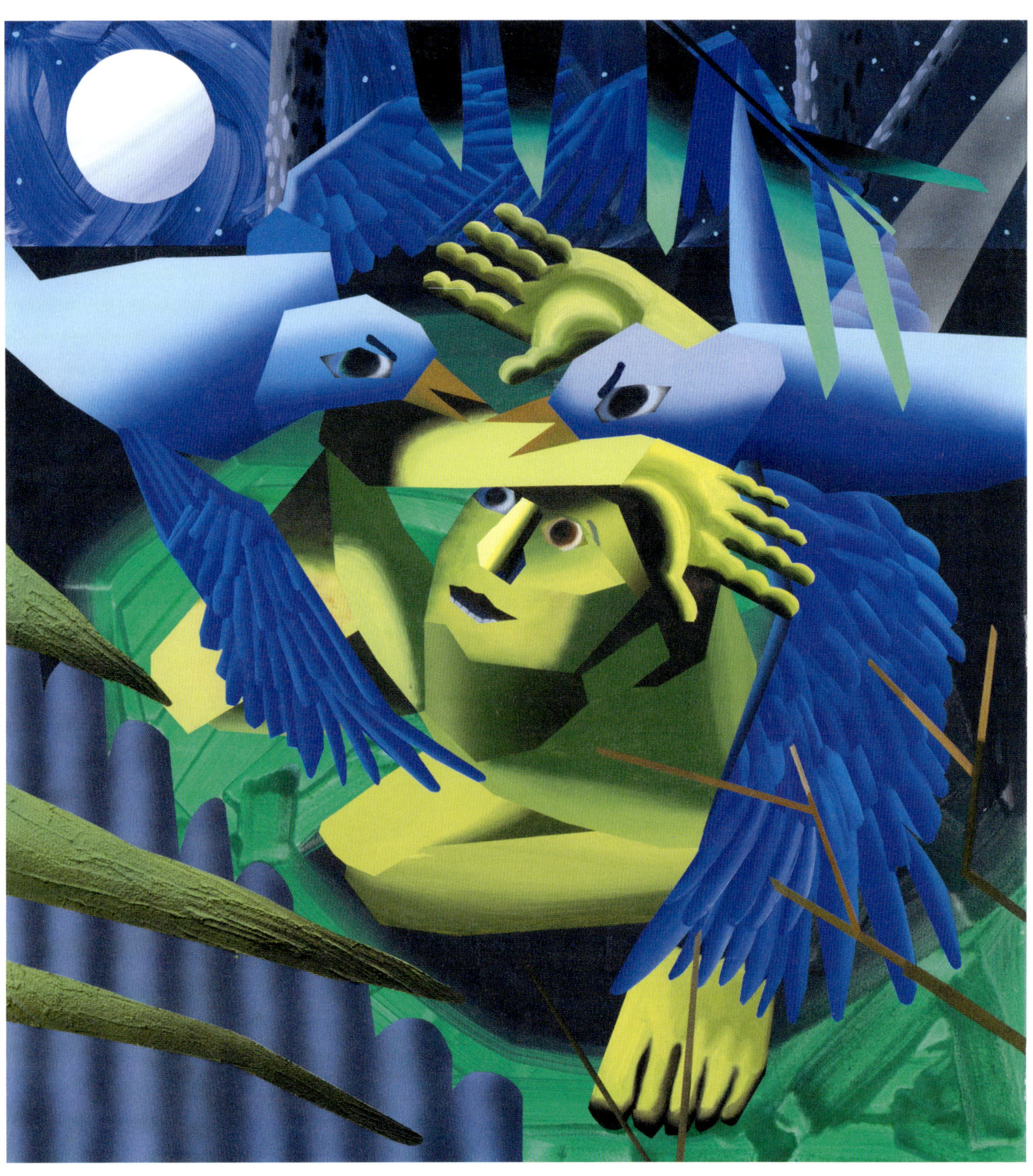

BIRD ATTACK 2022 · 170 × 158 cm

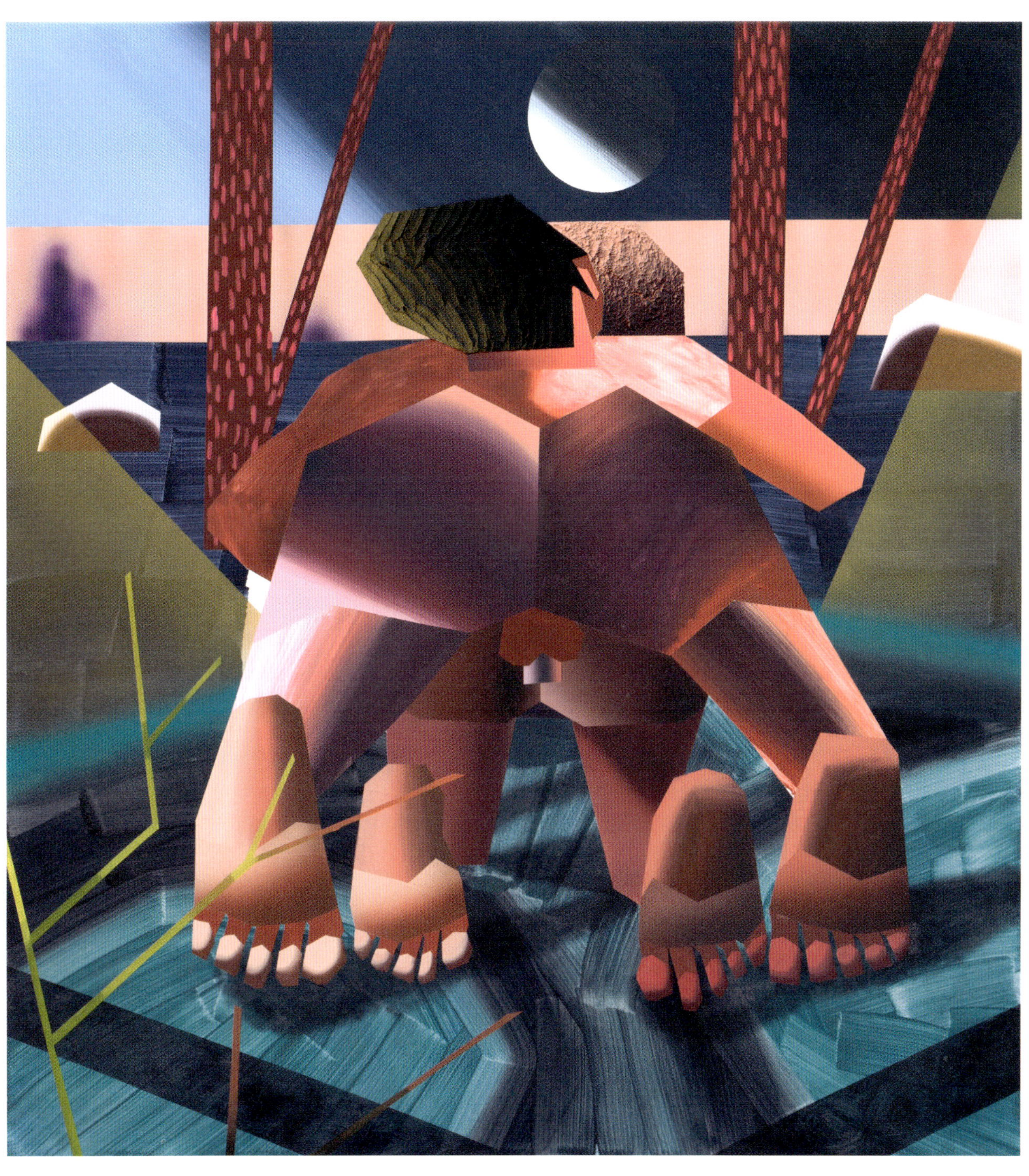

WALK IN THE WOODS 2022 · 170 × 158 cm

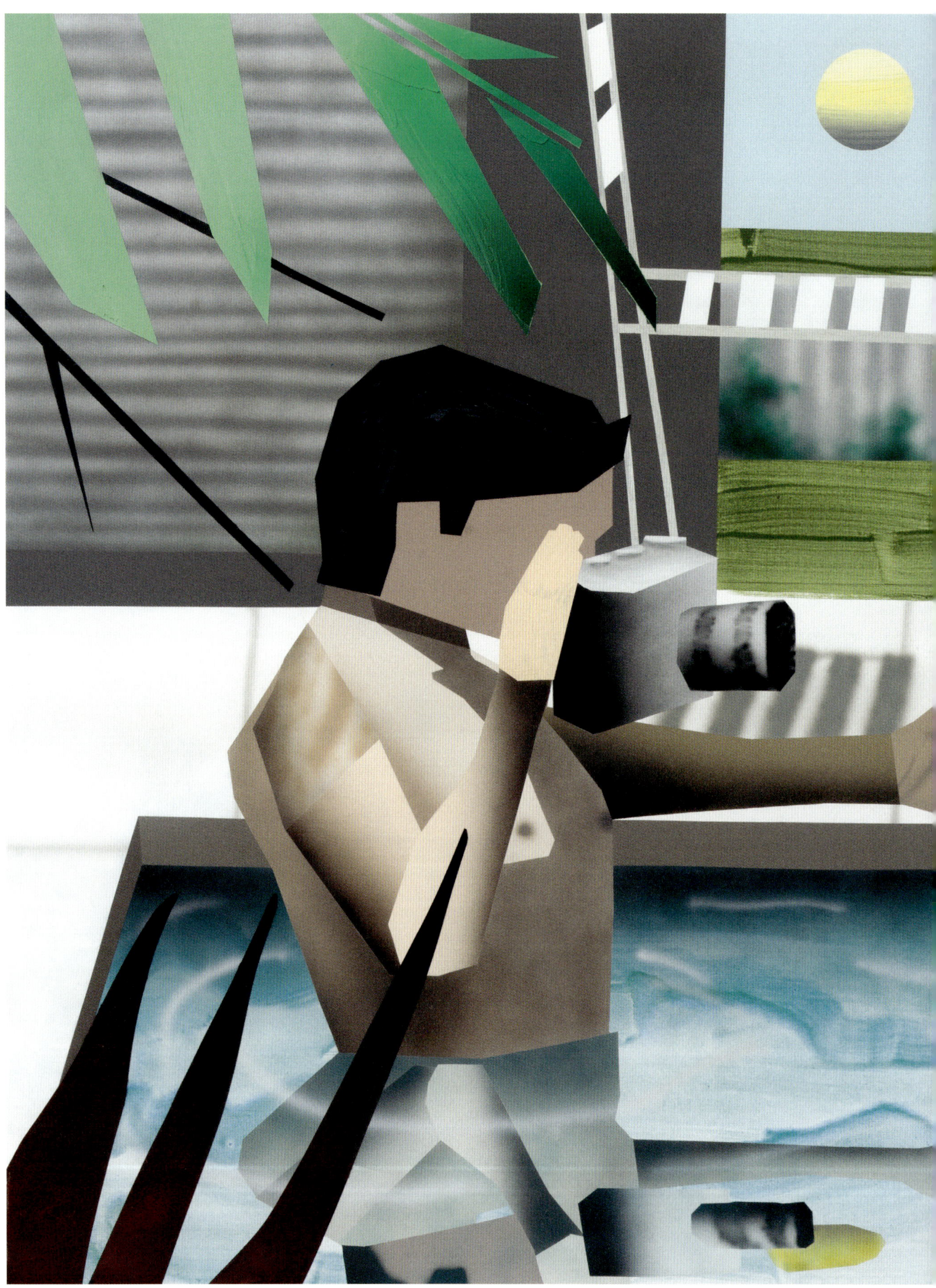

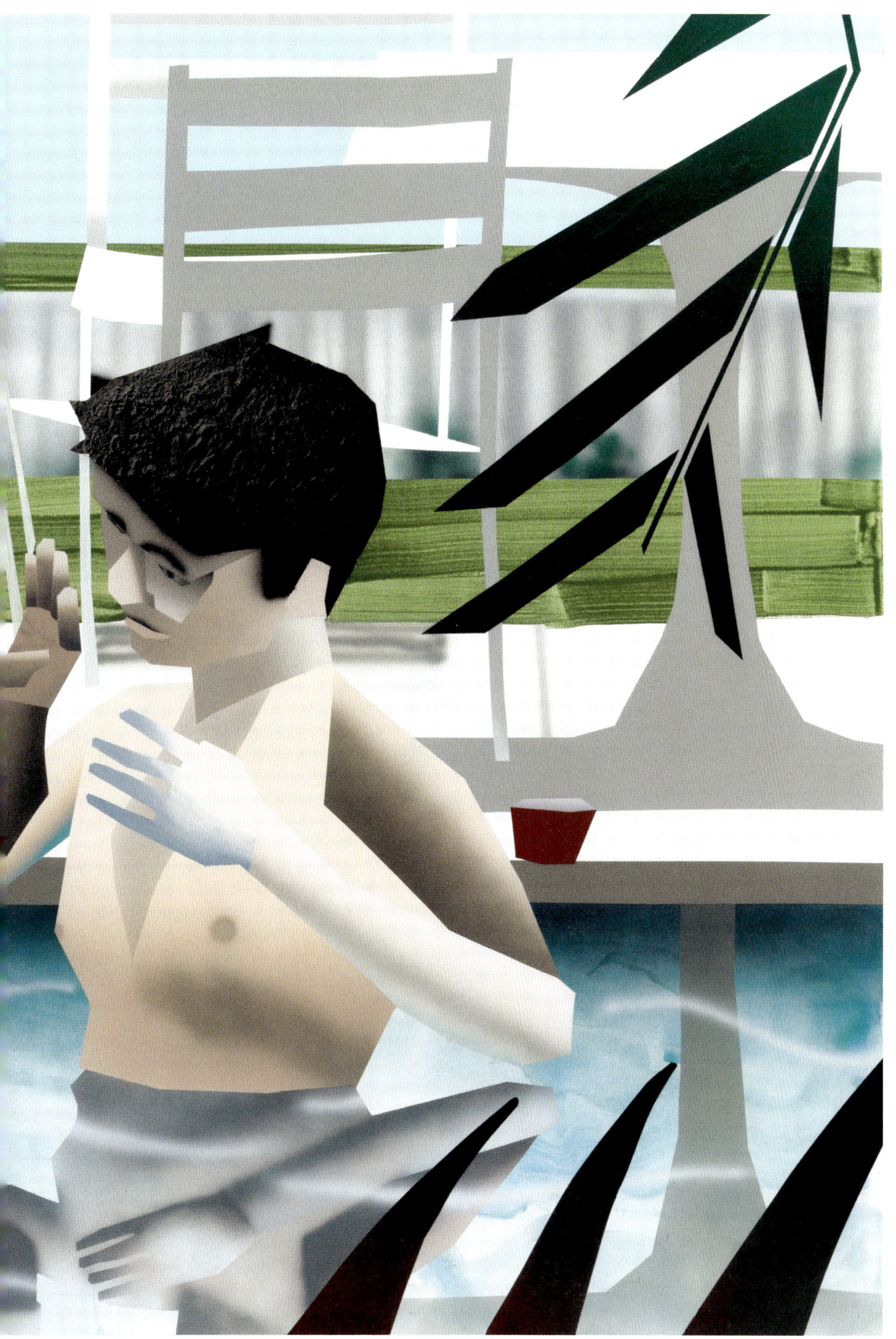

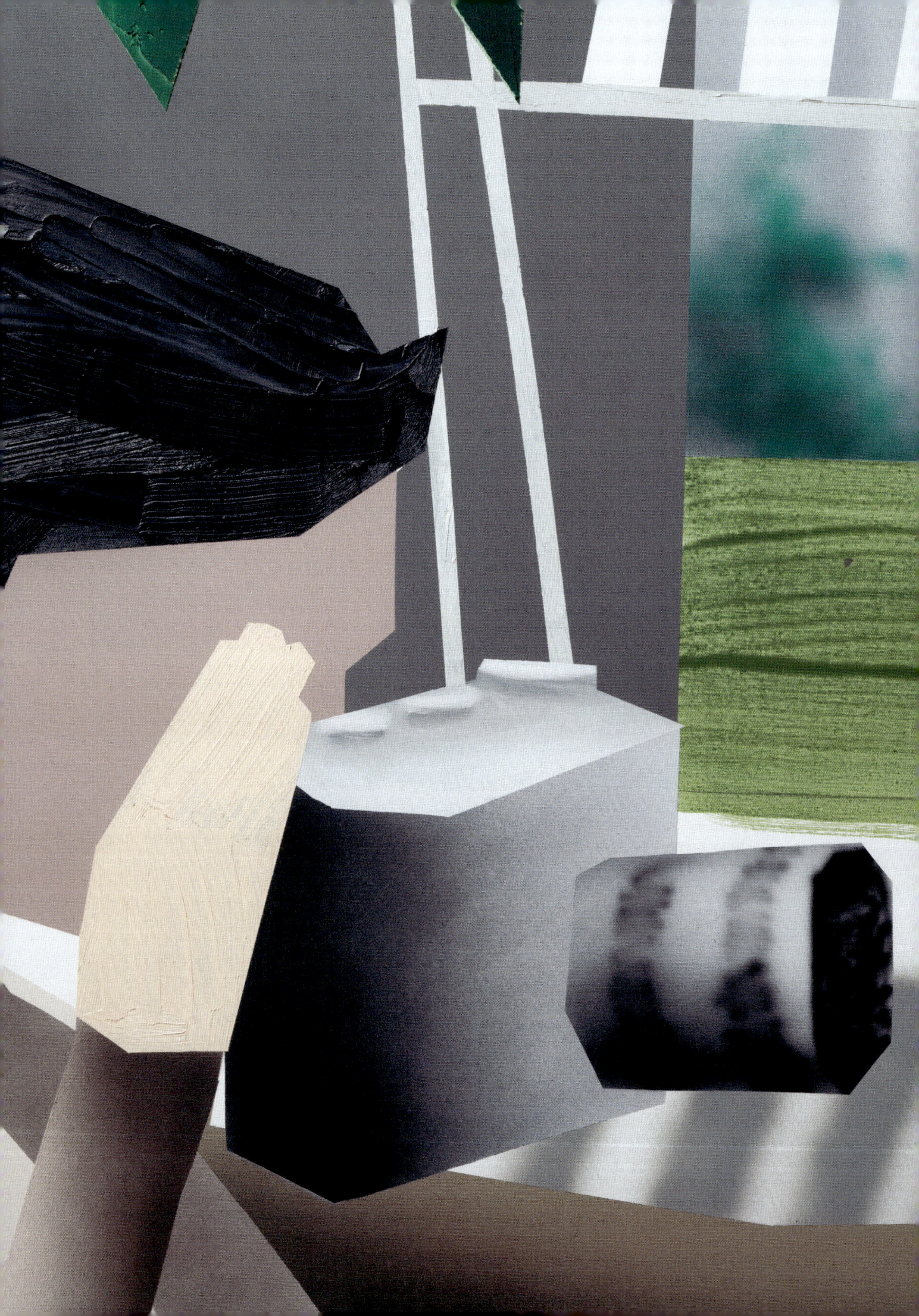

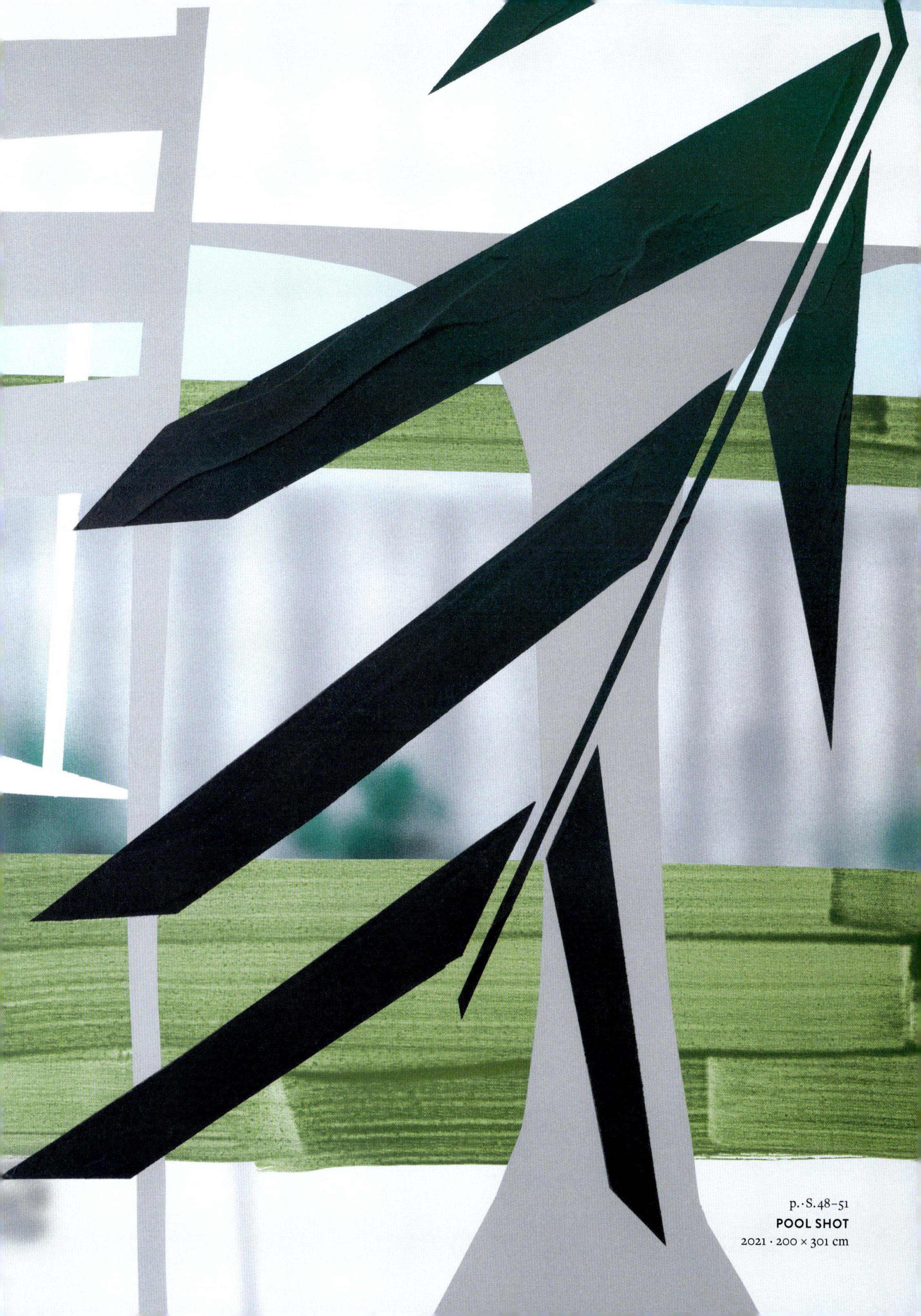

p. · S. 48–51
POOL SHOT
2021 · 200 × 301 cm

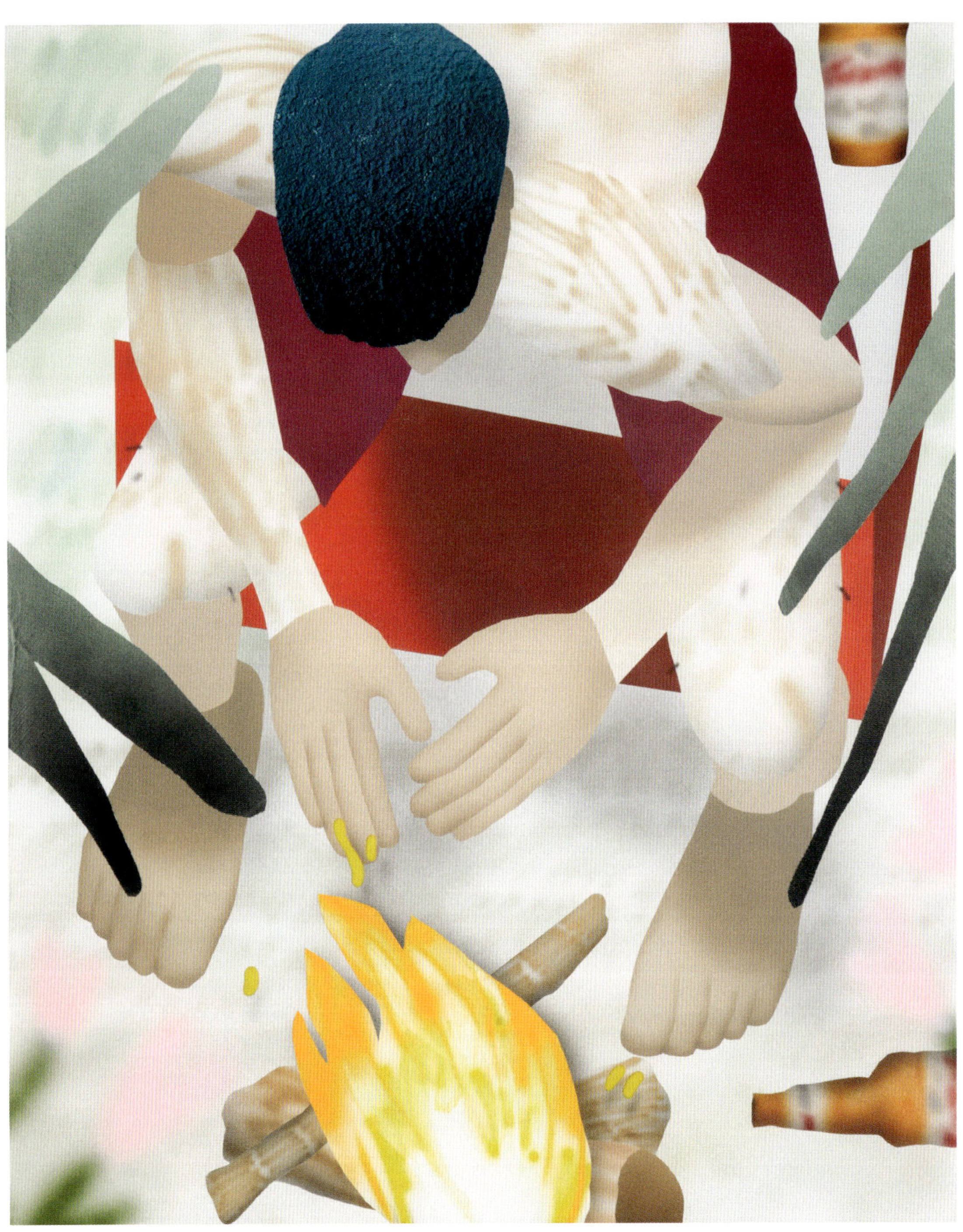

CAMPFIRE 2020 · 120 × 100 cm

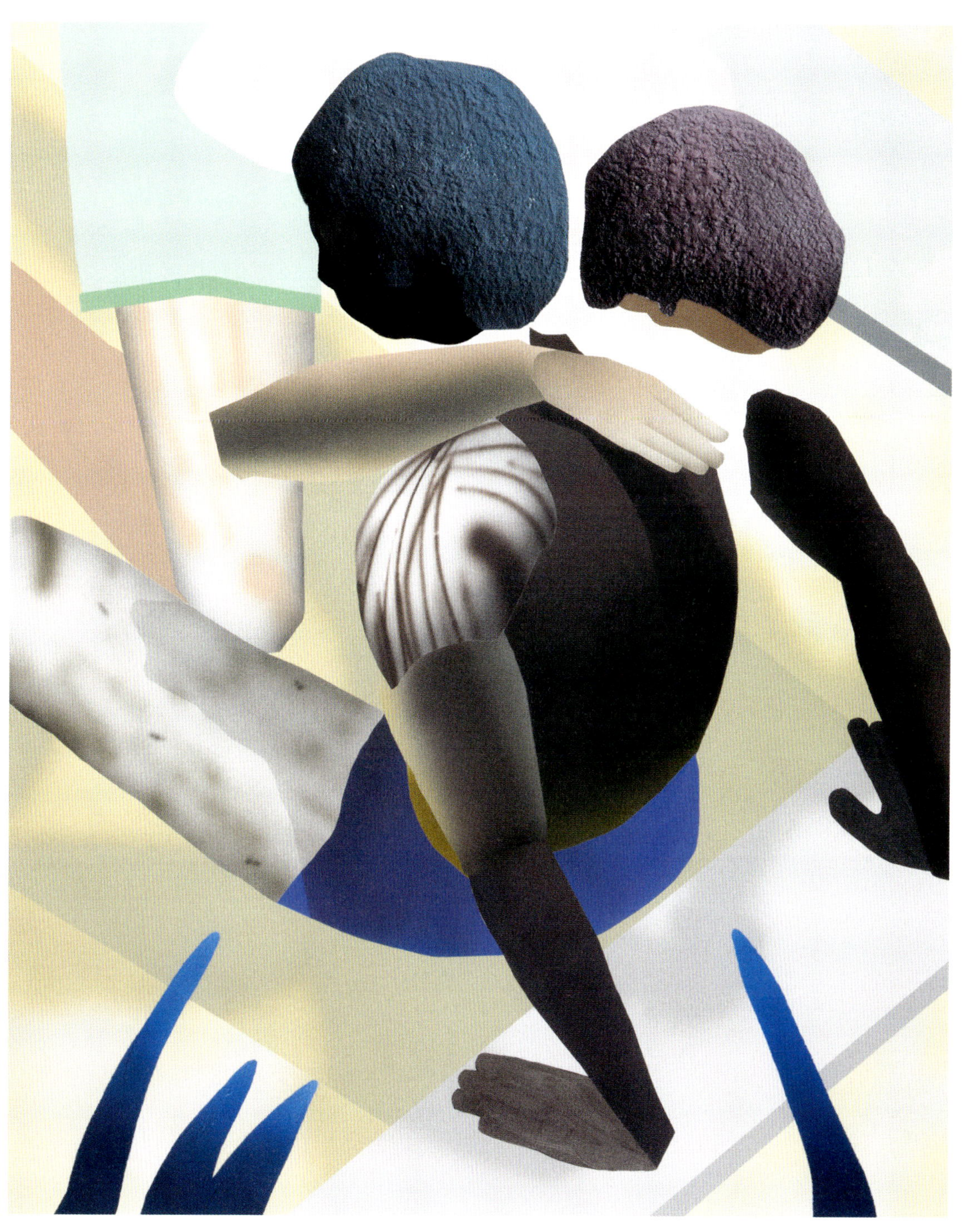

CUDDLE 2020 · 120 × 100 cm

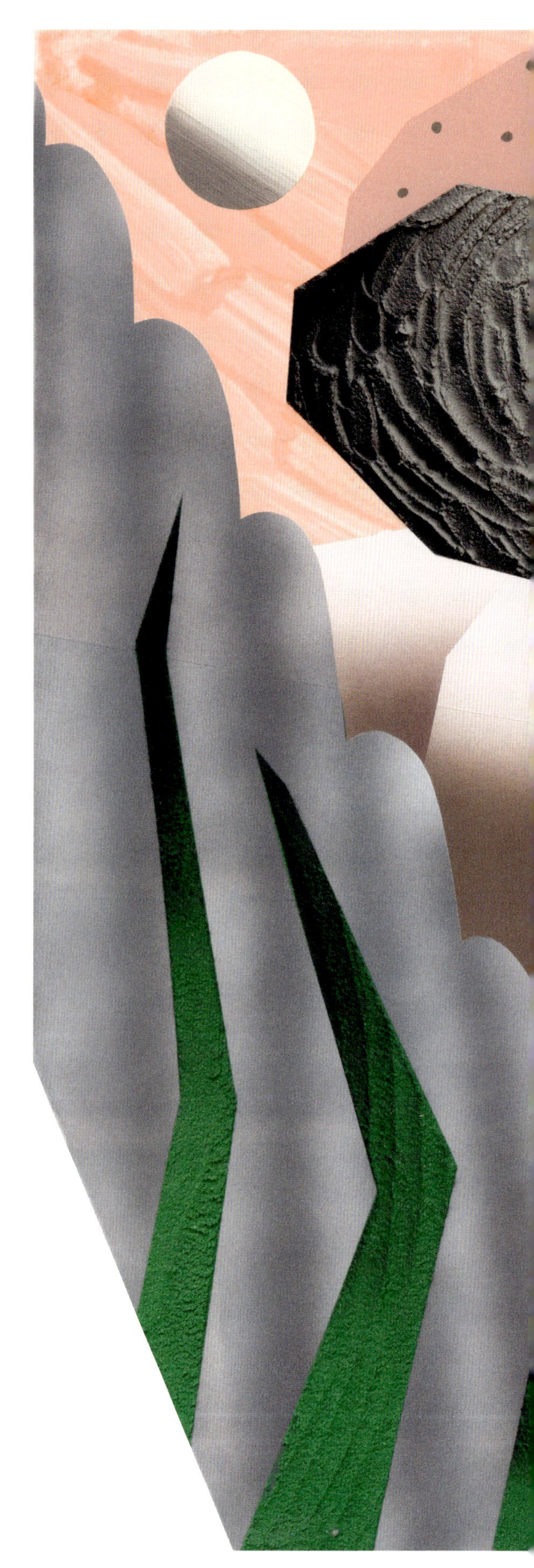

RAINSHOWER TREE
2022 · 117,5 × 100,5 cm

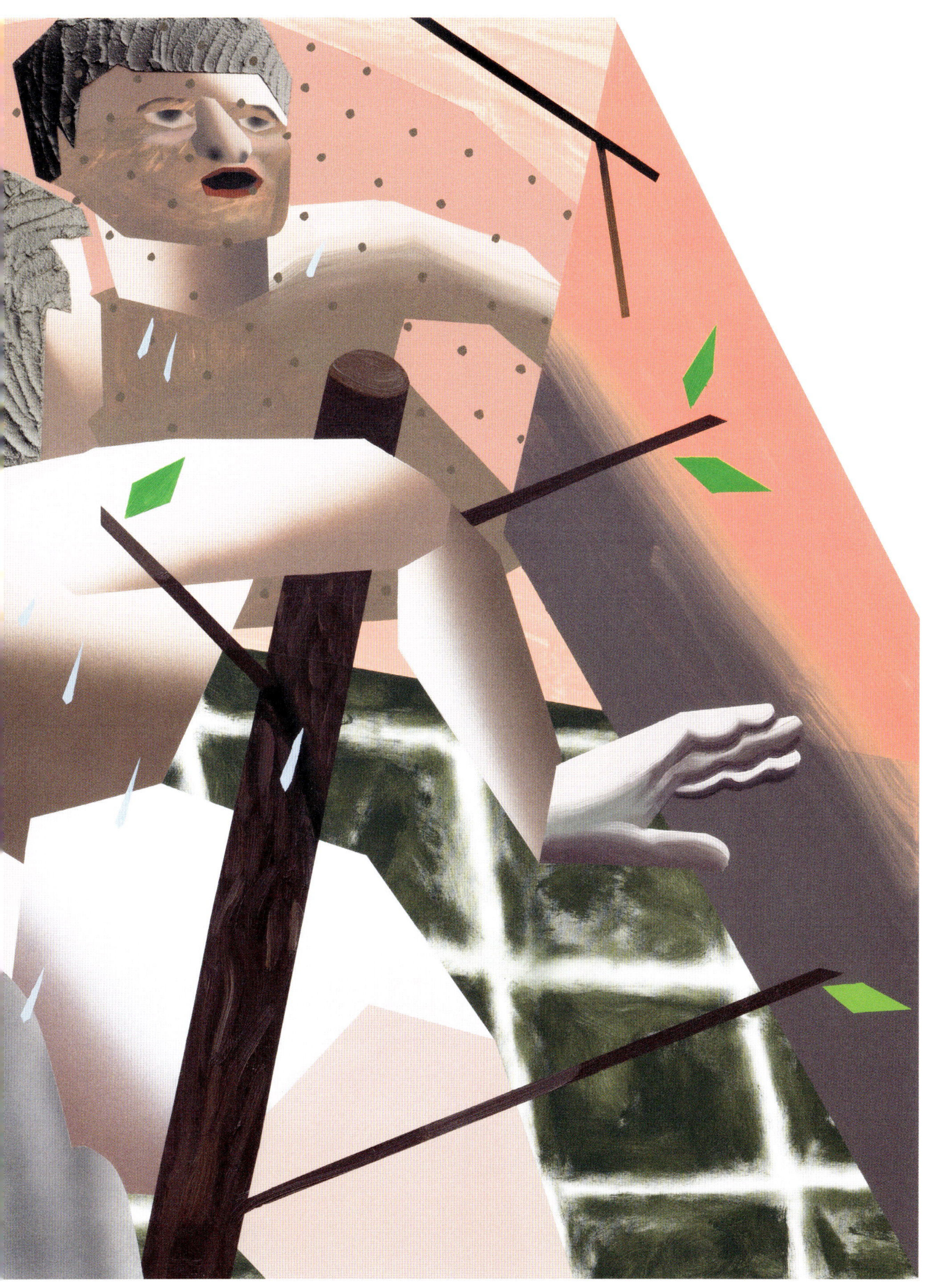

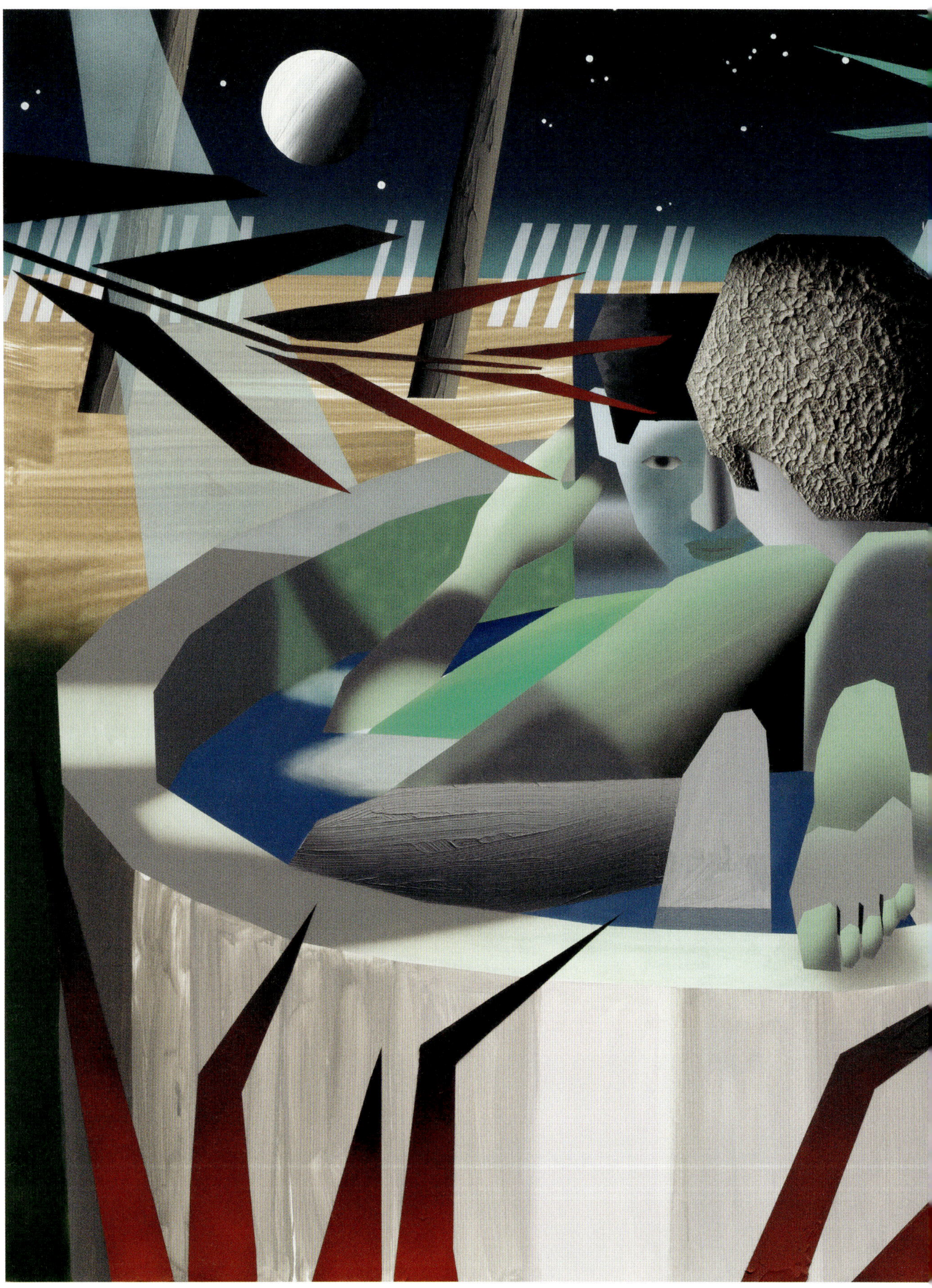

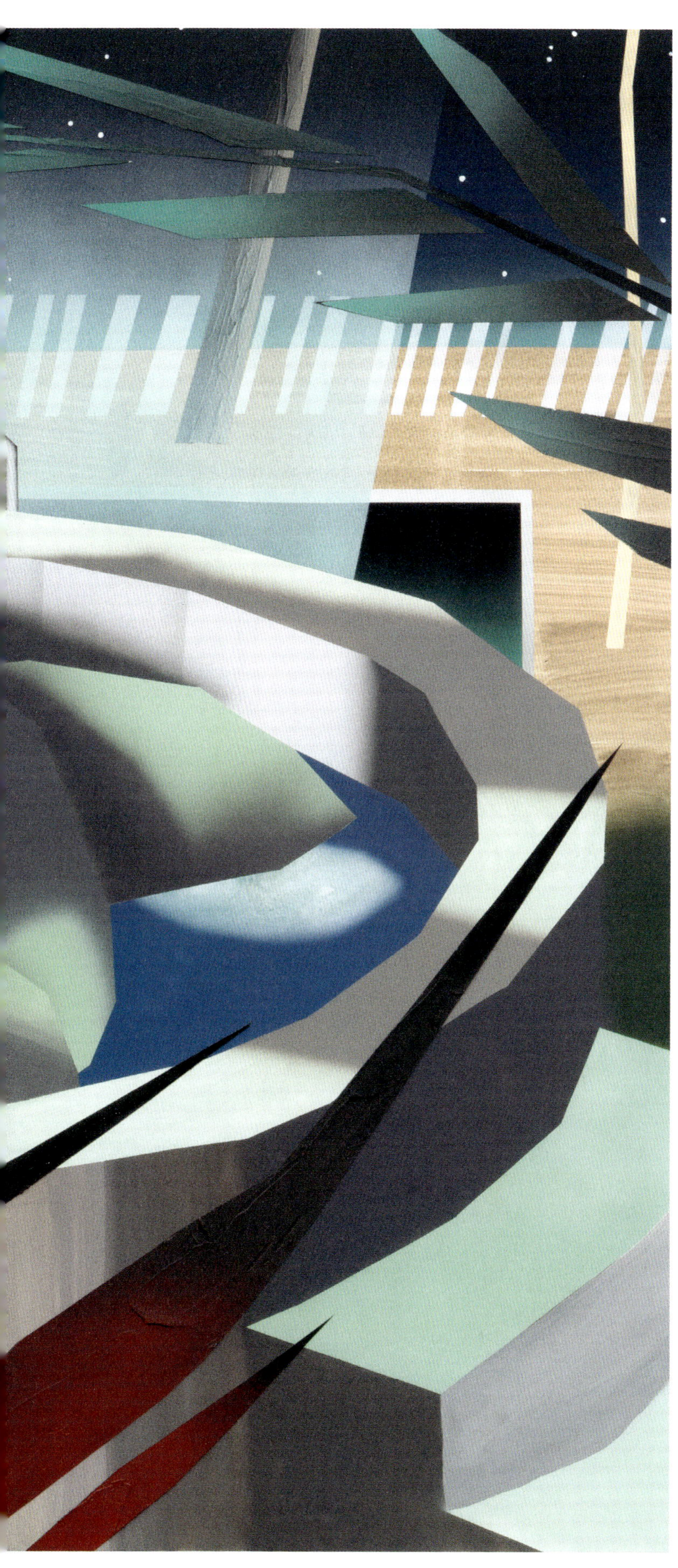

HOT TUB WATCH
2021 · 175 × 223,5 cm

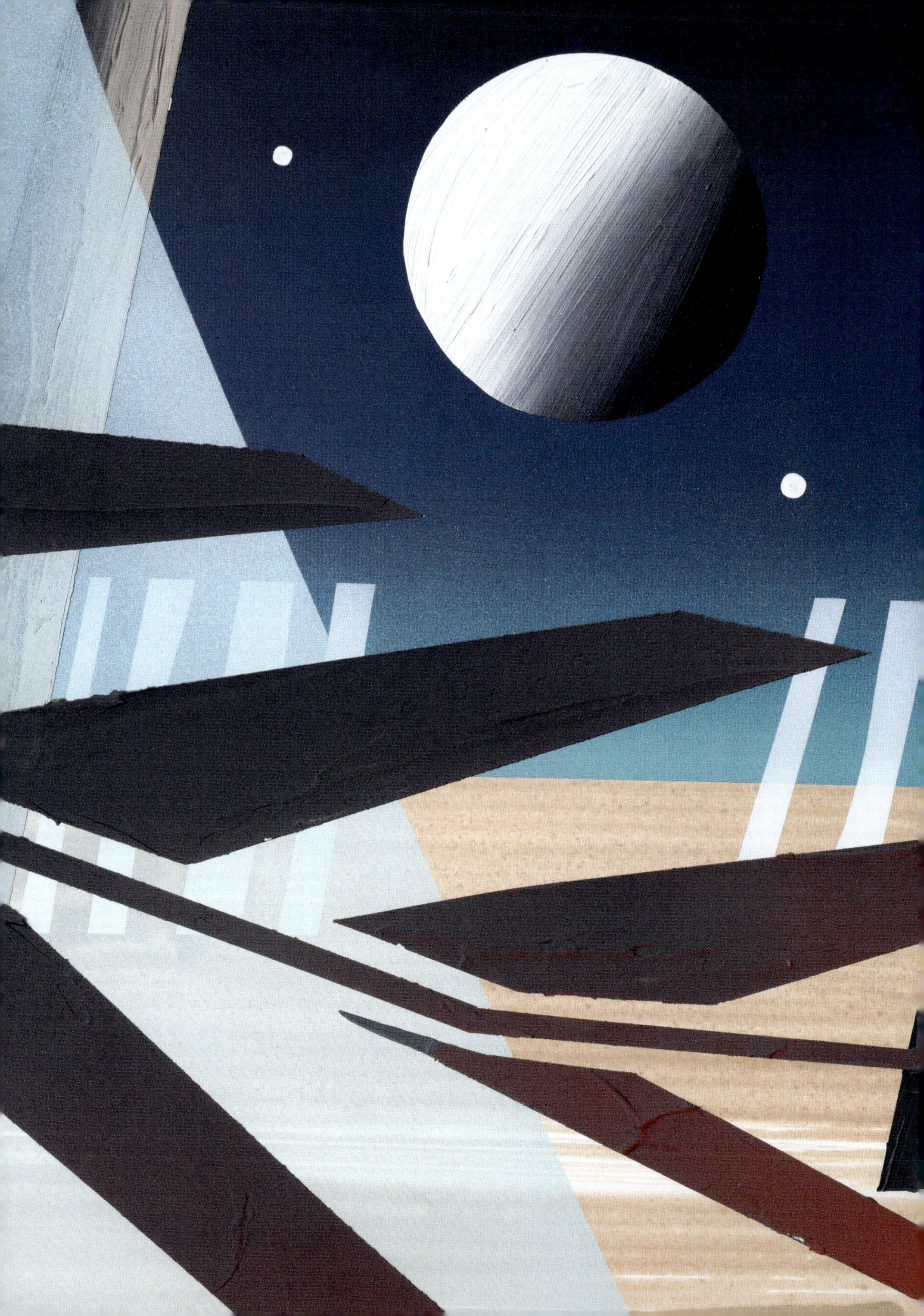

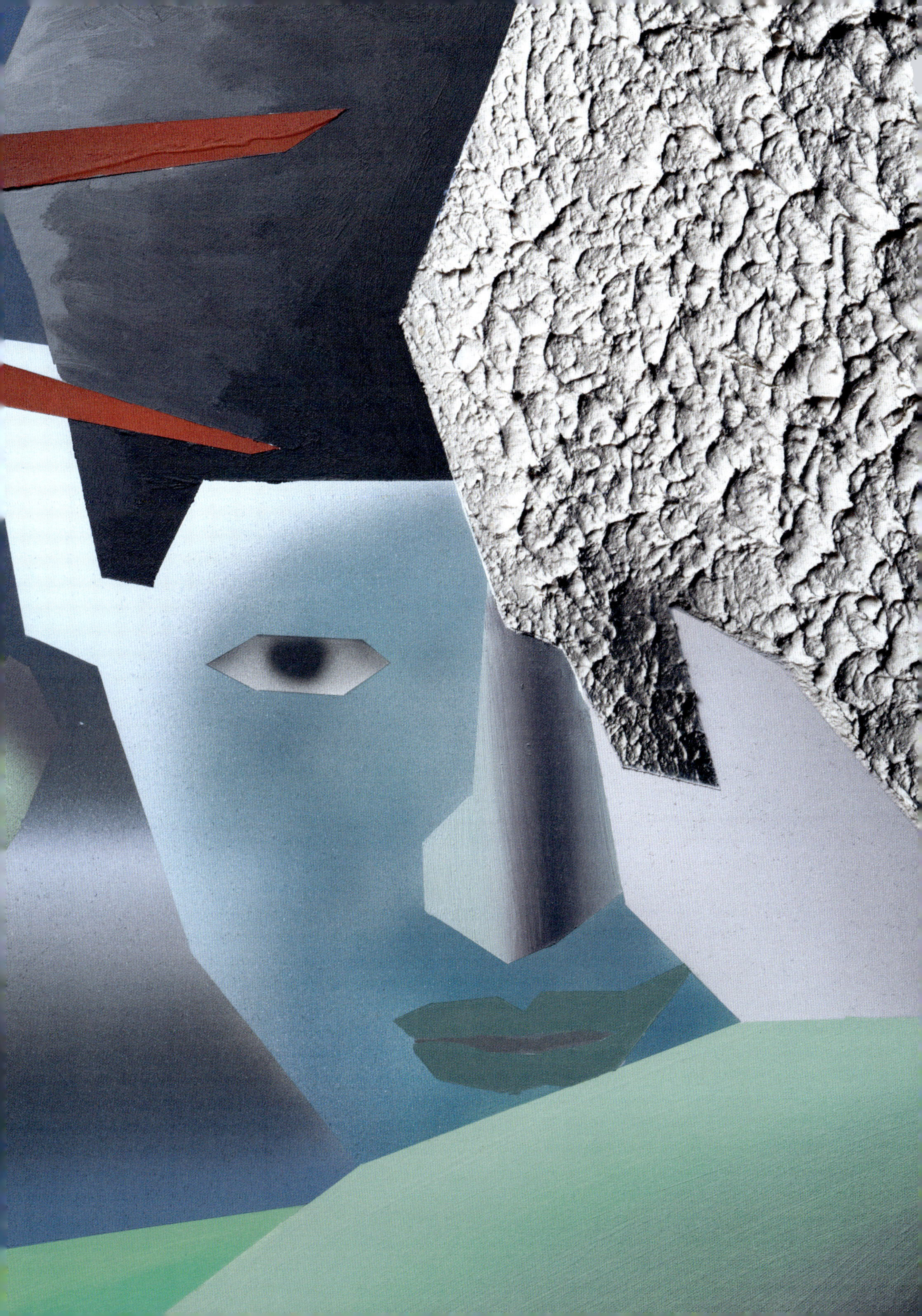

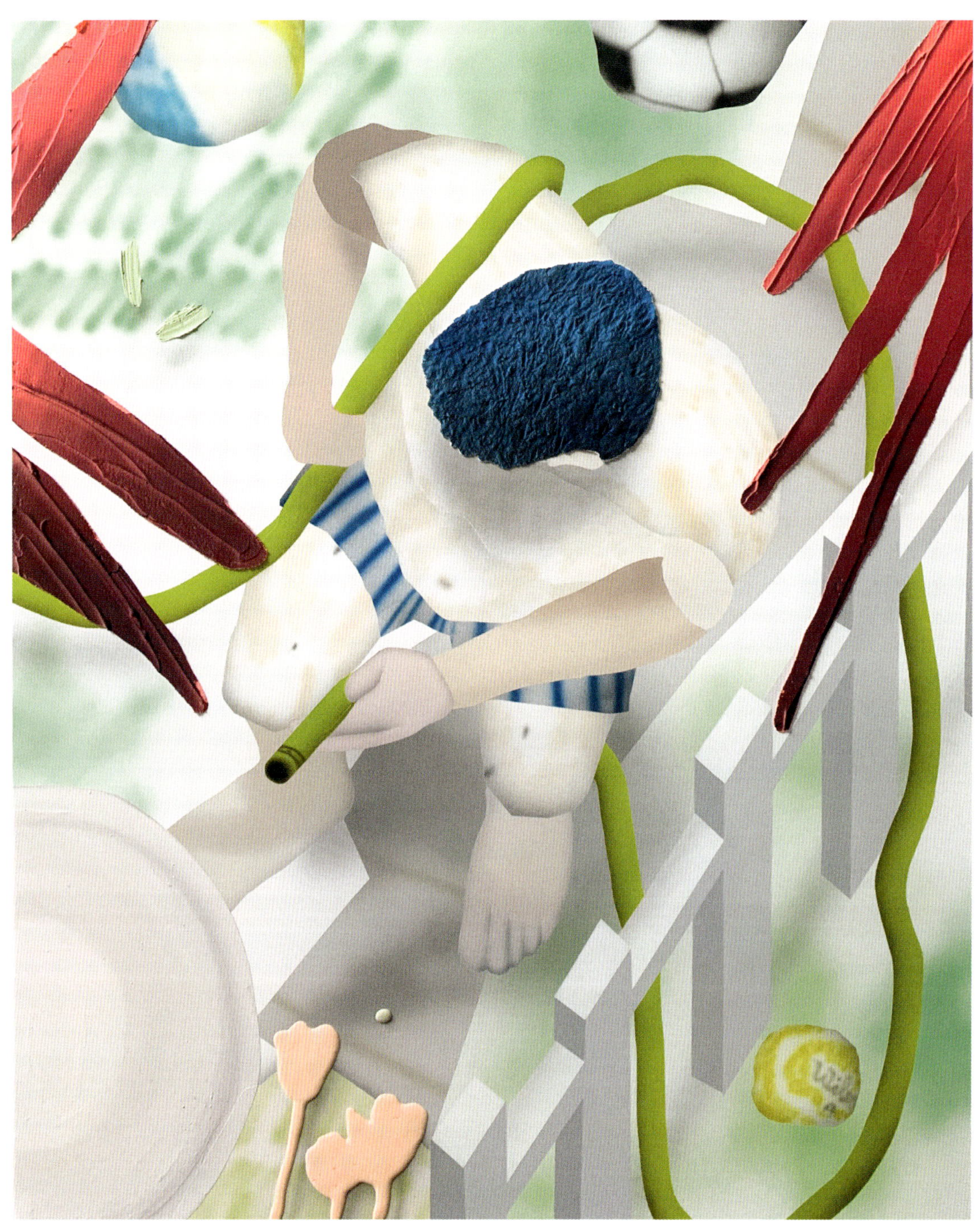

GARDEN HOSE 2019 · 120 × 100 cm

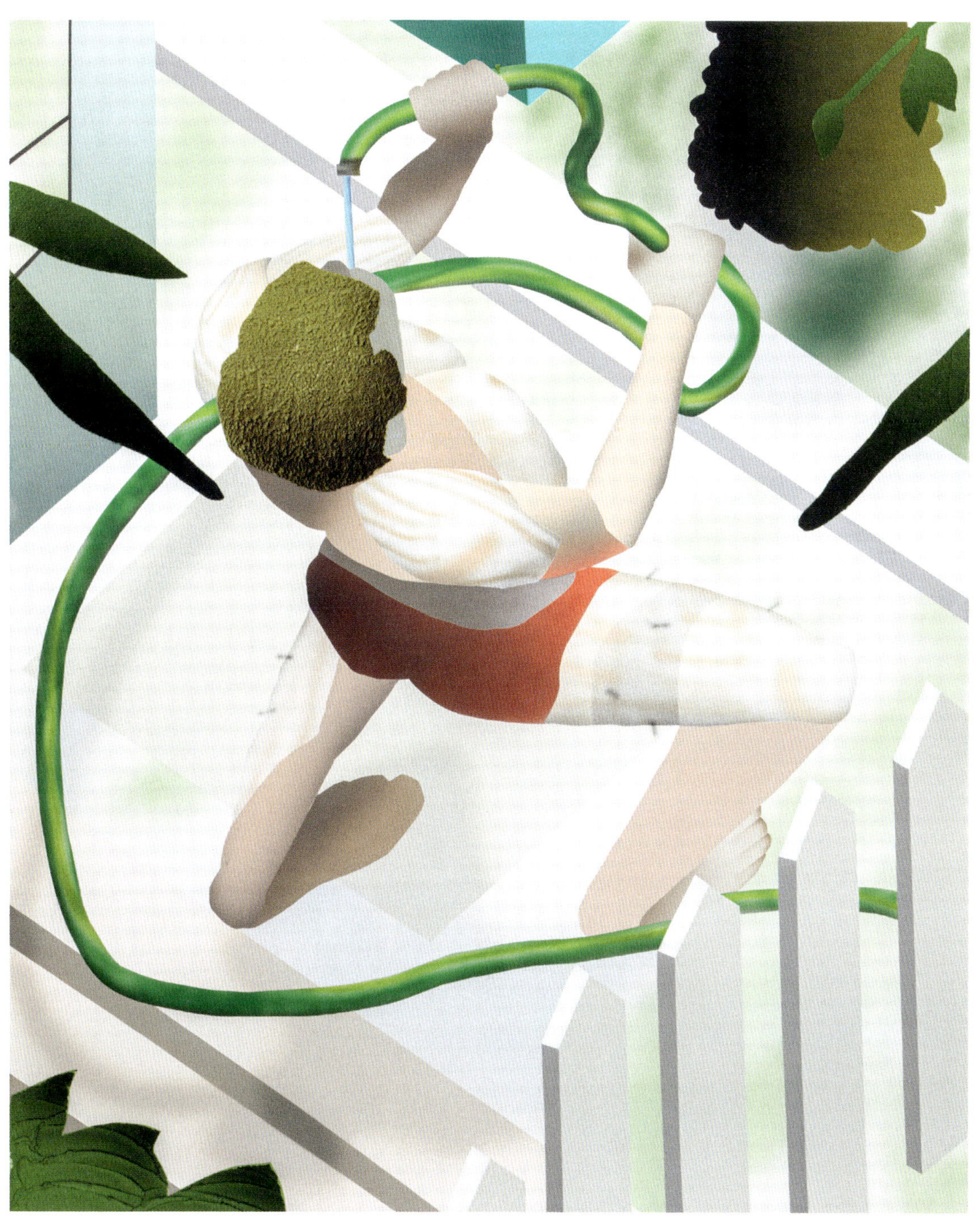

WATER HOSE 2020 · 120 × 100 cm

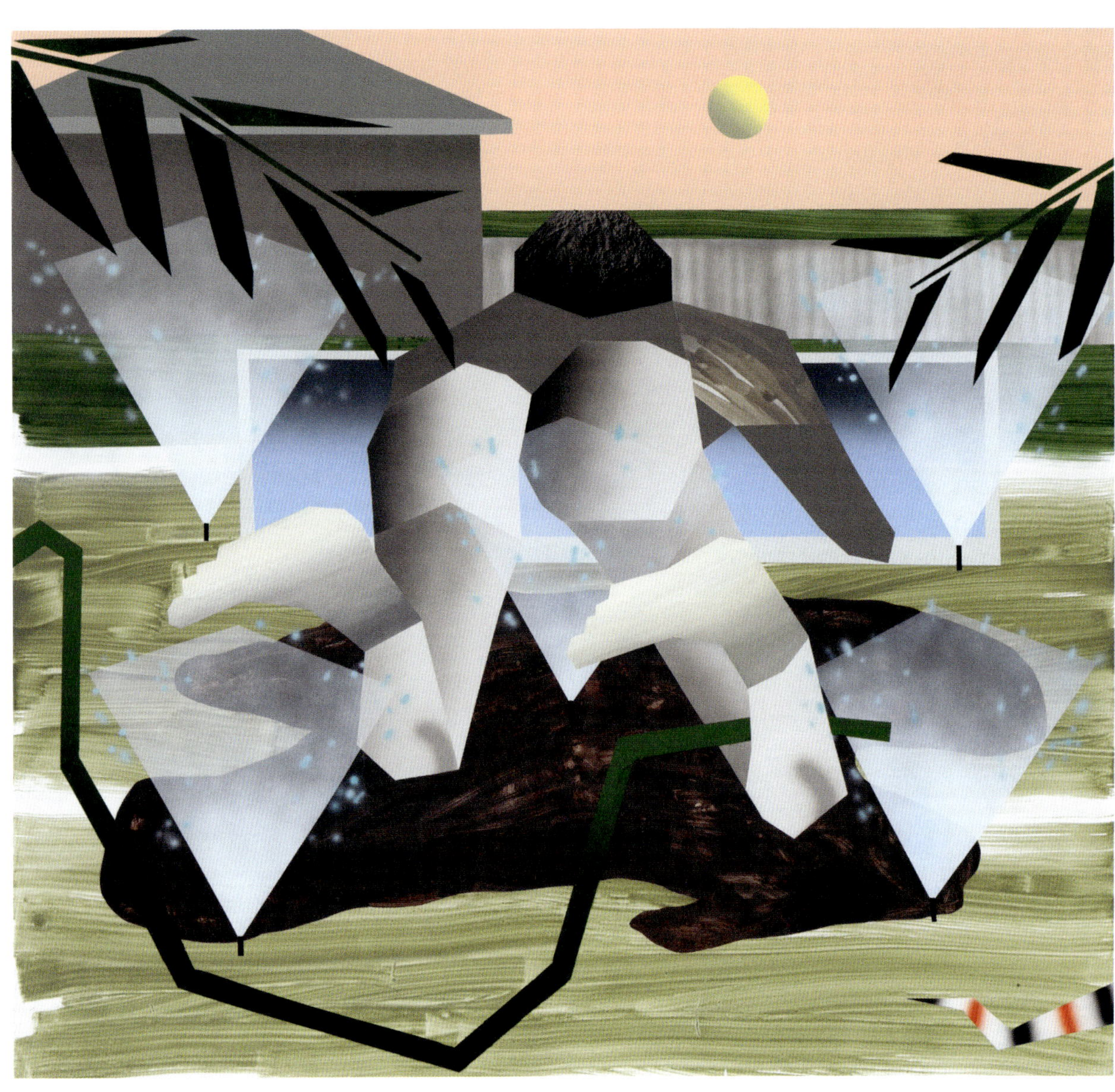

SPRINKLERS 2021 · 185 × 200 cm

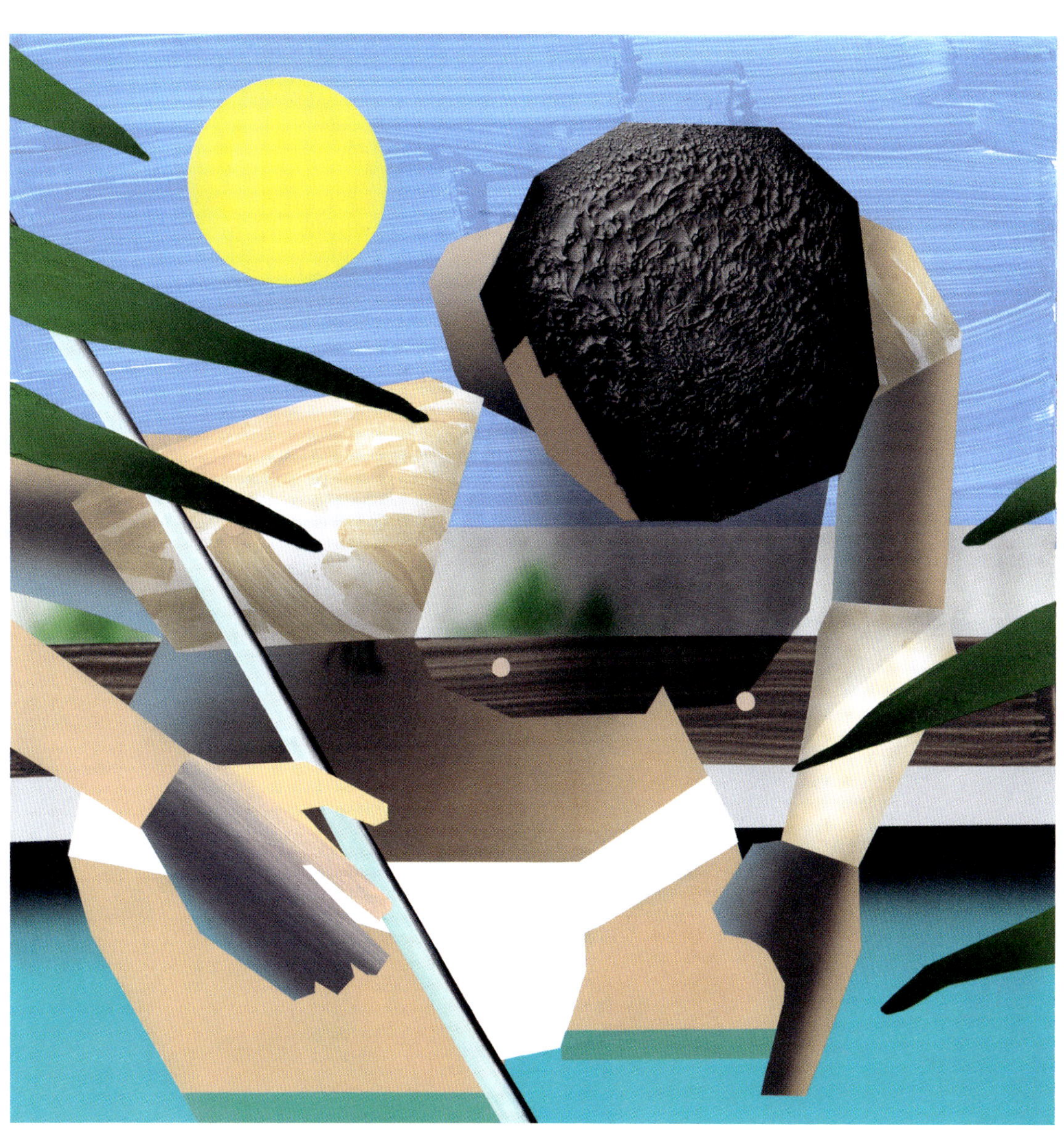

POOL BOY 2021 · 120 × 120 cm

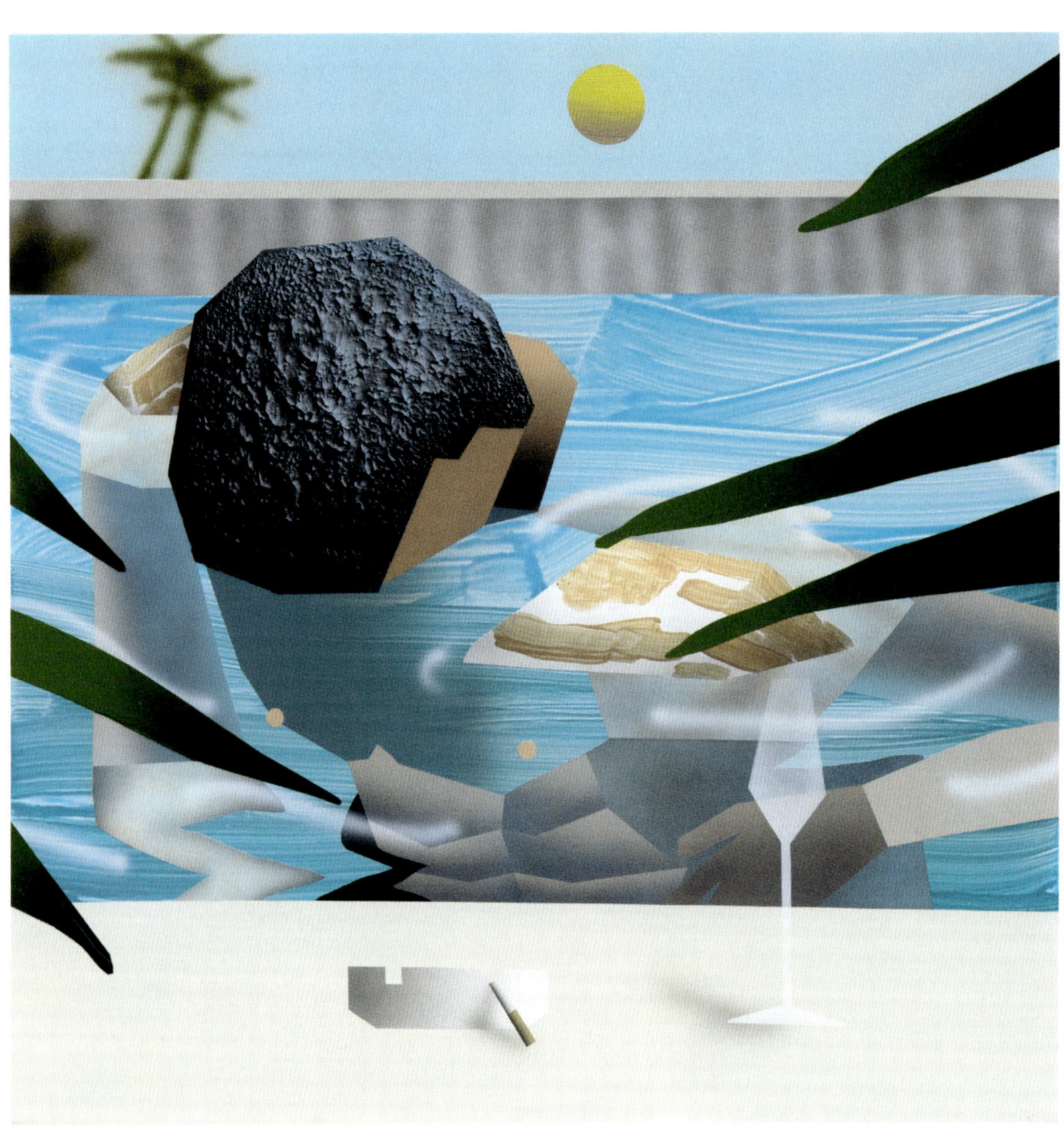

SUBMERGE 2021 · 120 × 120 cm

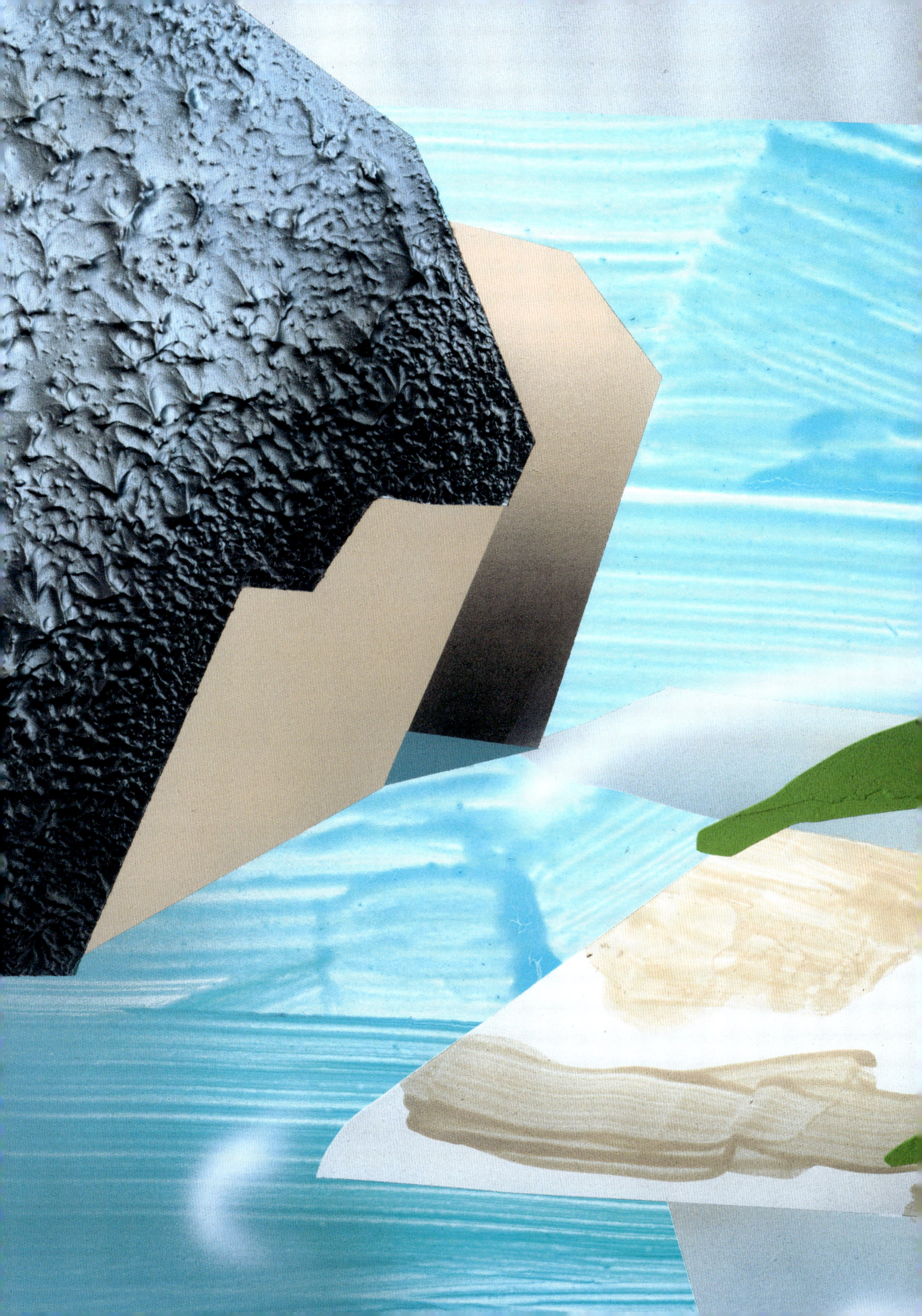

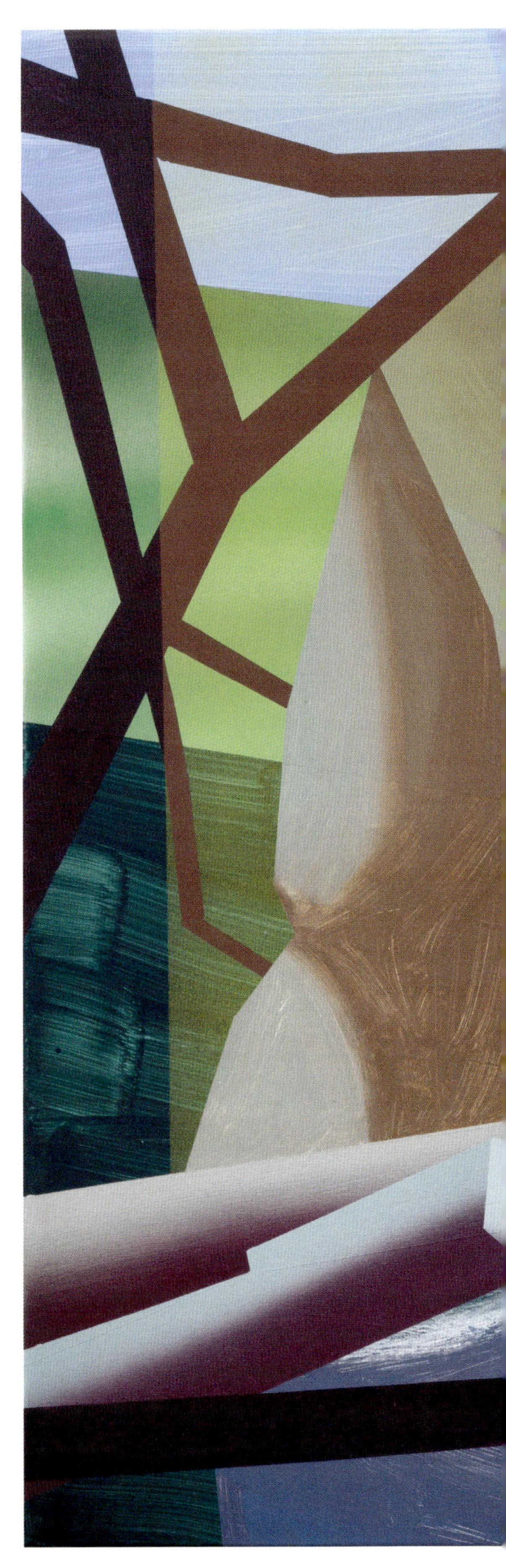

LOOKING THROUGH YELLOW LIGHT
2022 · 101 × 117 cm

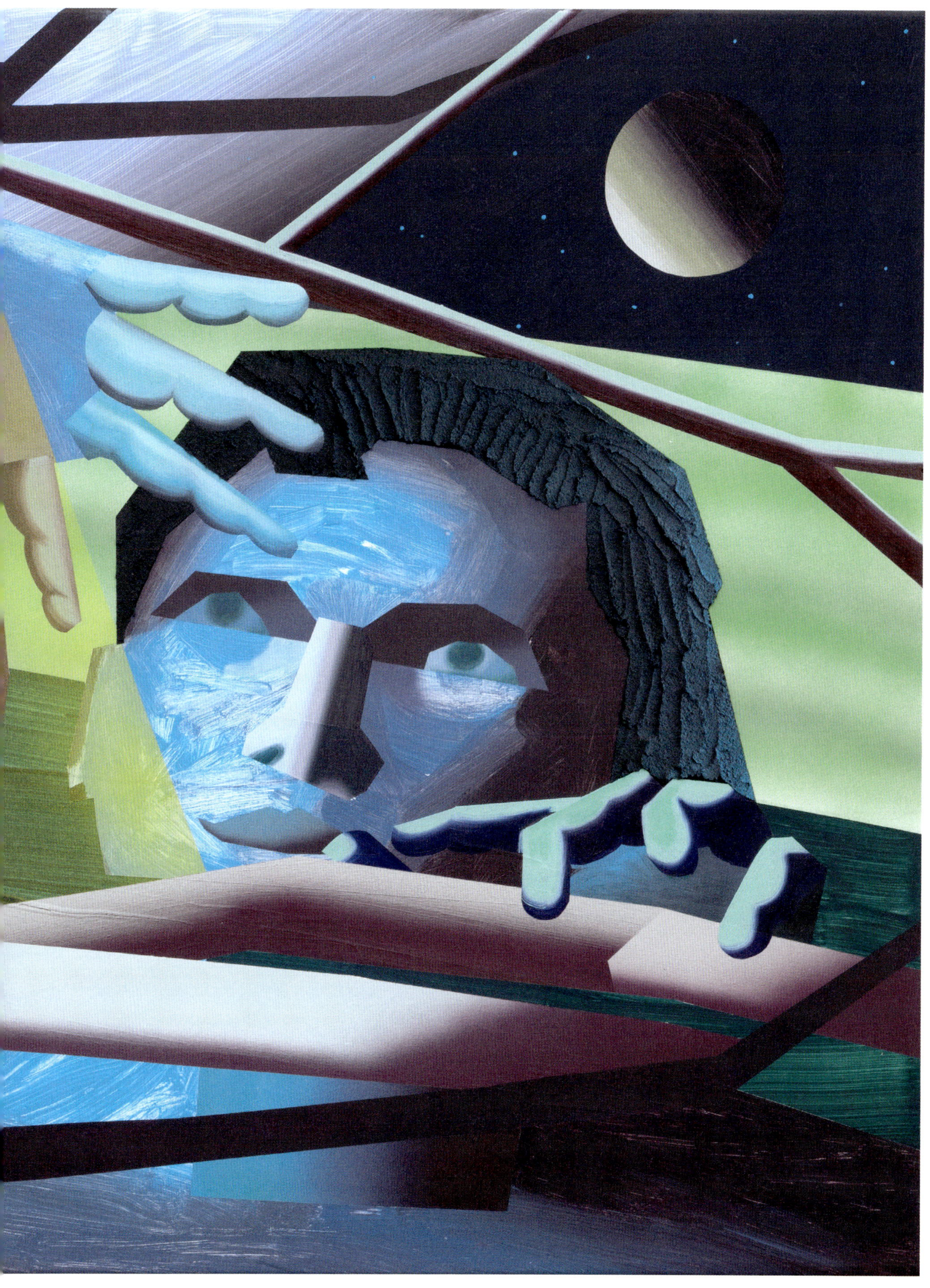

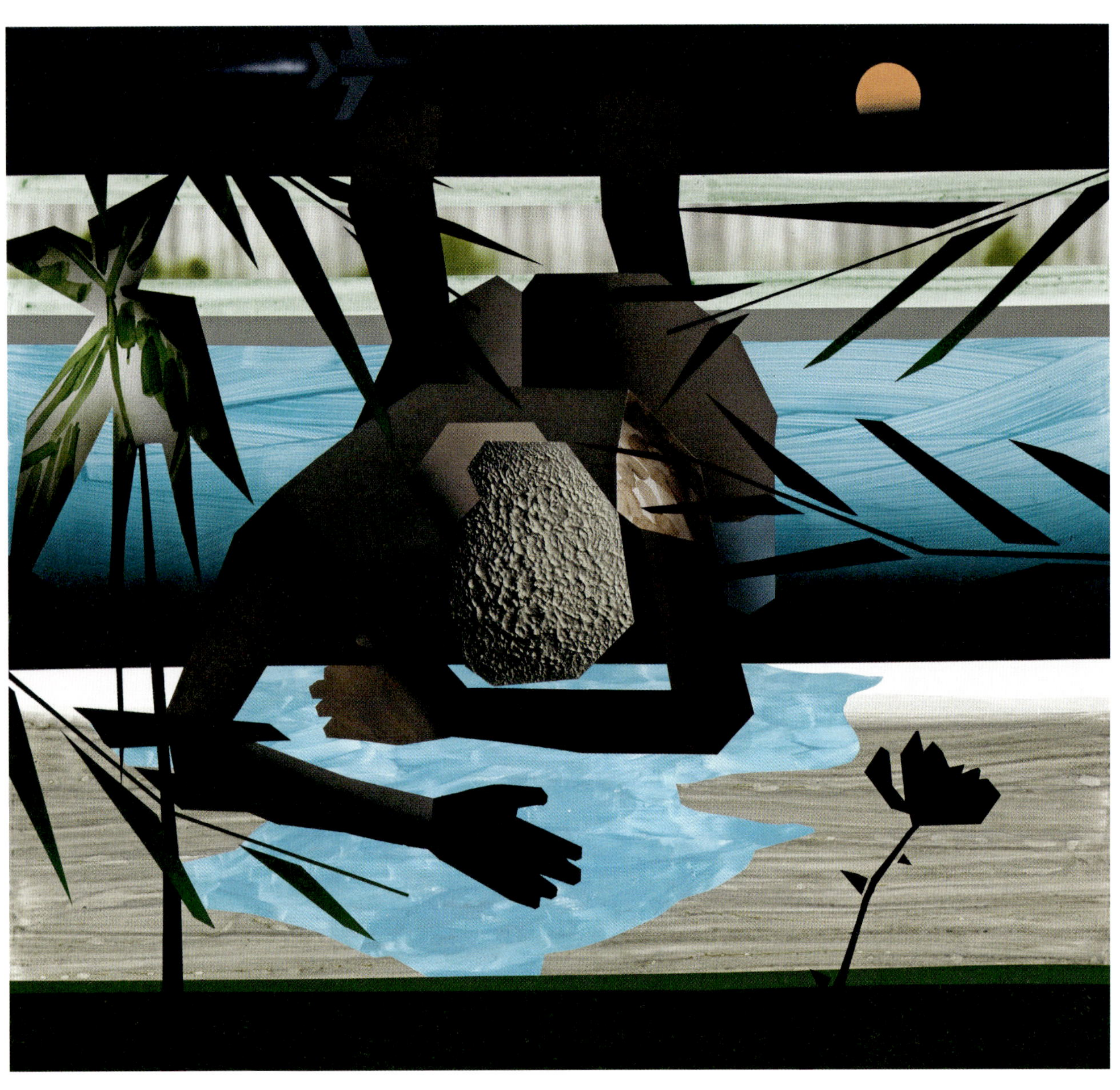

CHEMTRAIL SKY 2021 · 140 × 150 cm

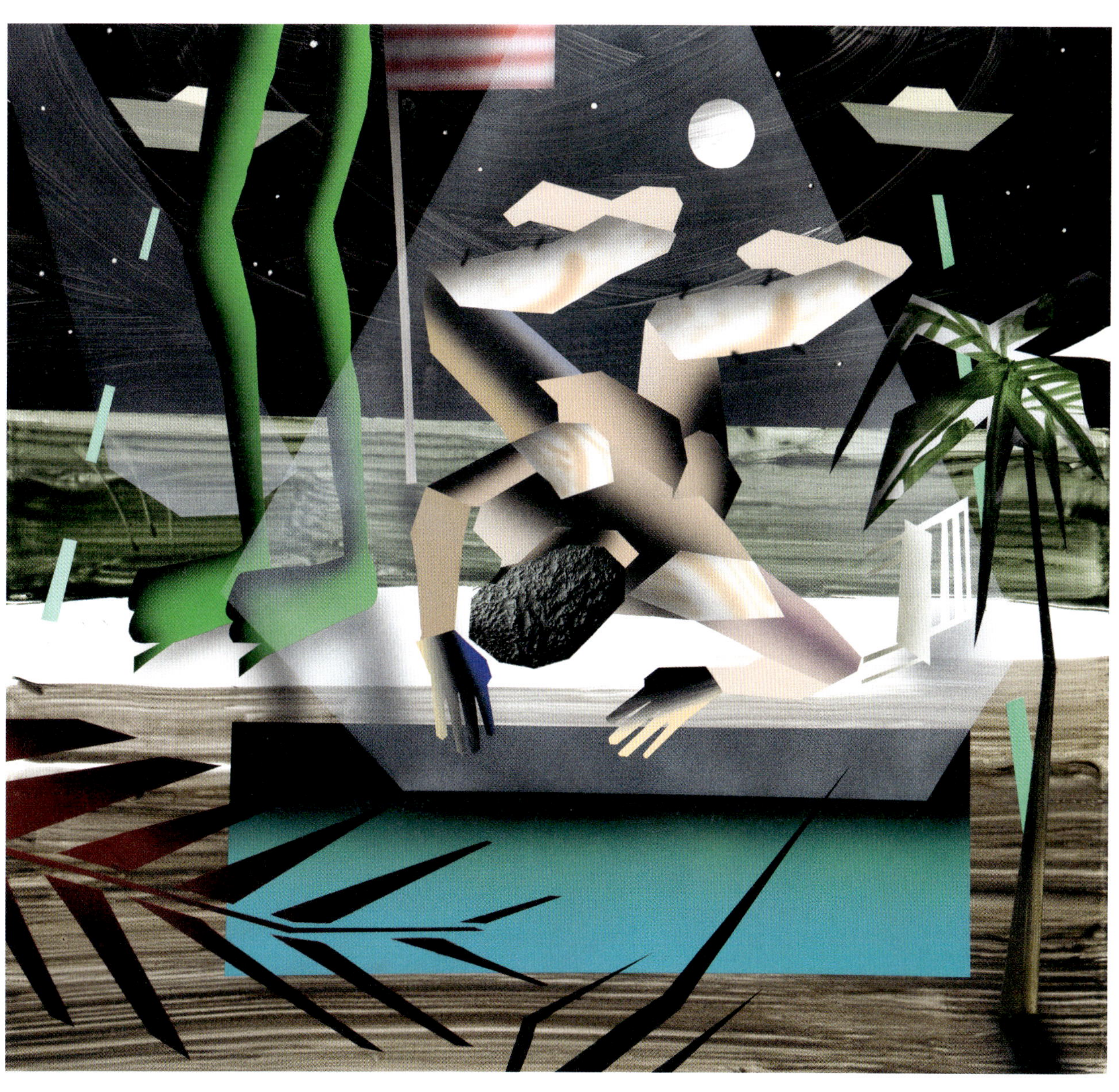

ABDUCTION 2021 · 138 × 150 cm

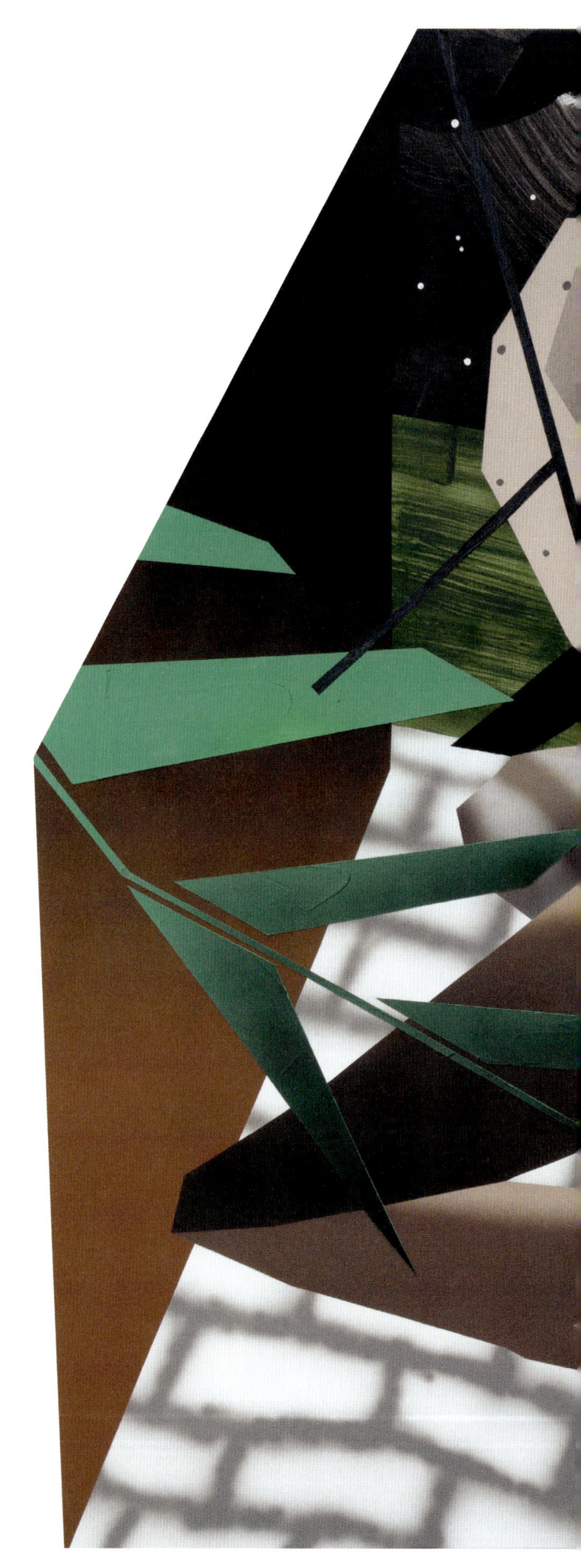

RAINSHOWER
2021 · 198,5 × 236 cm

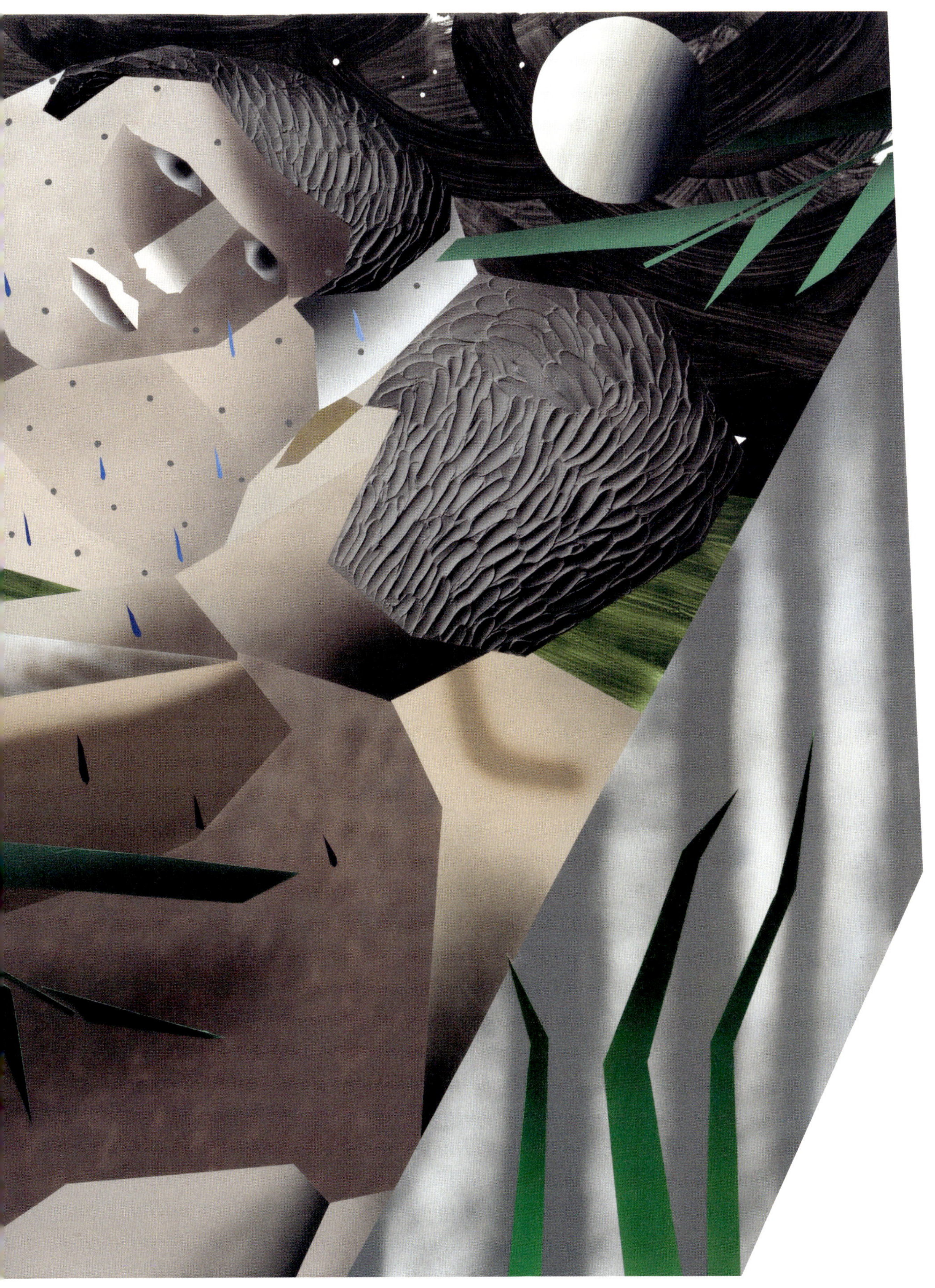

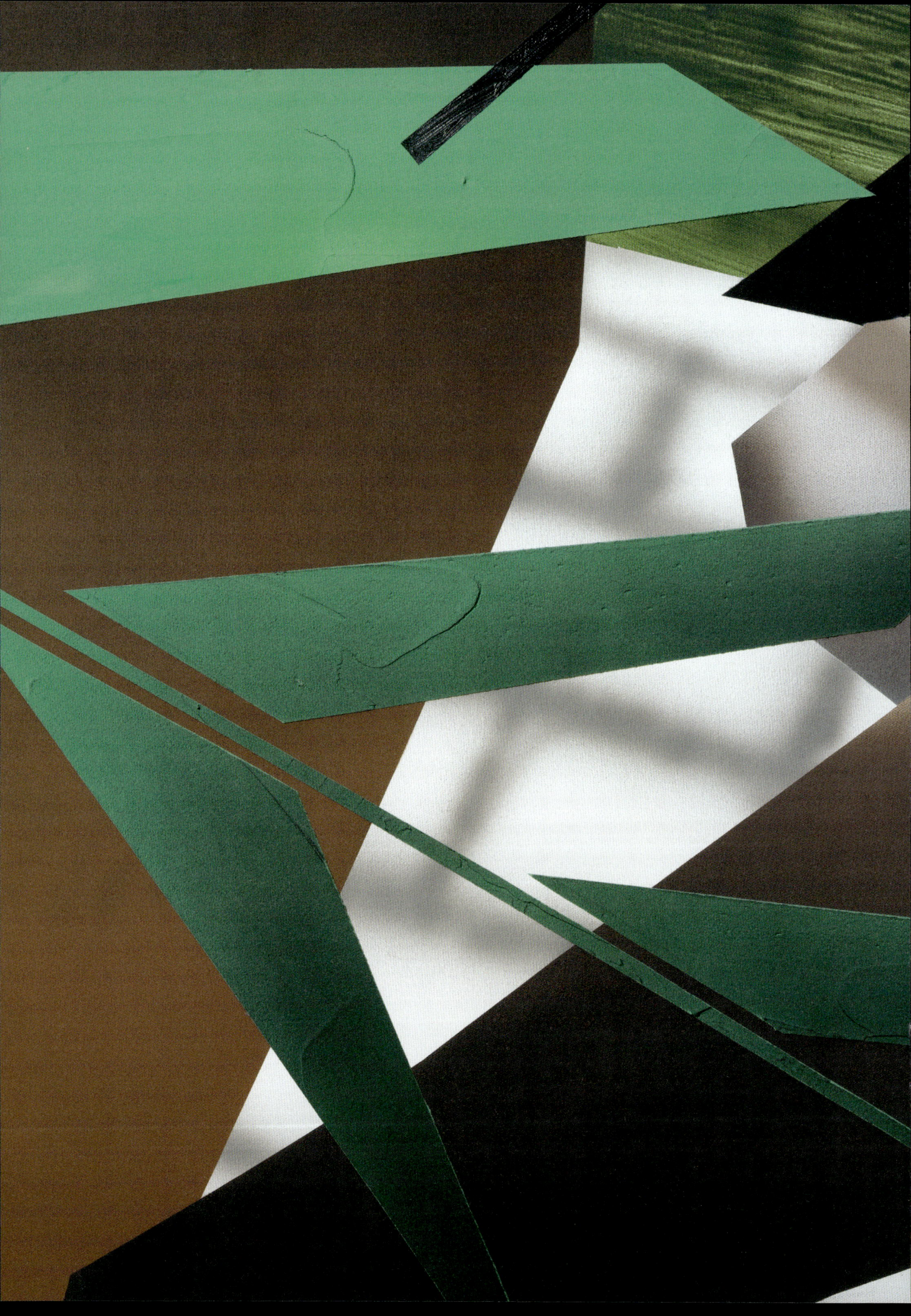

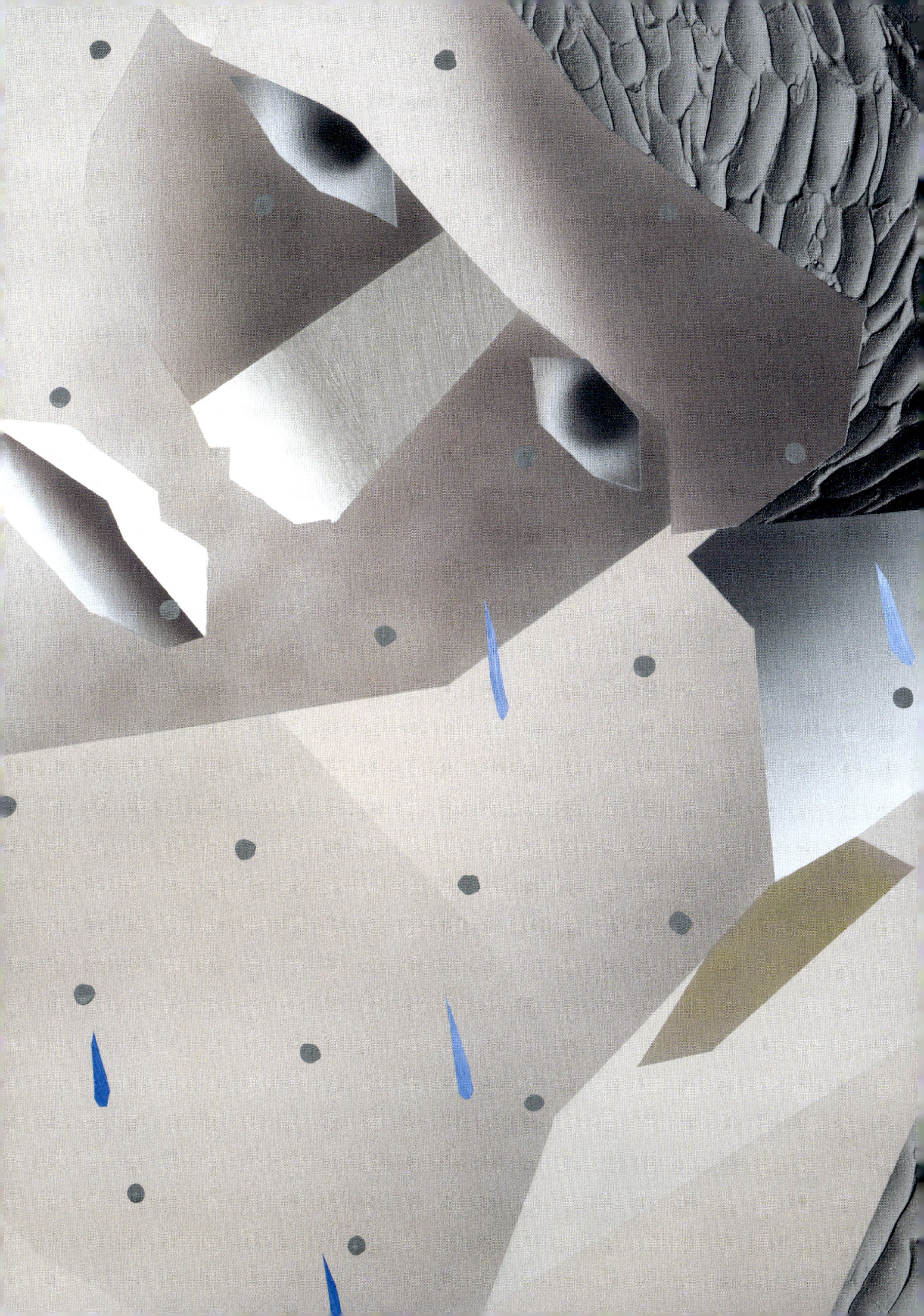

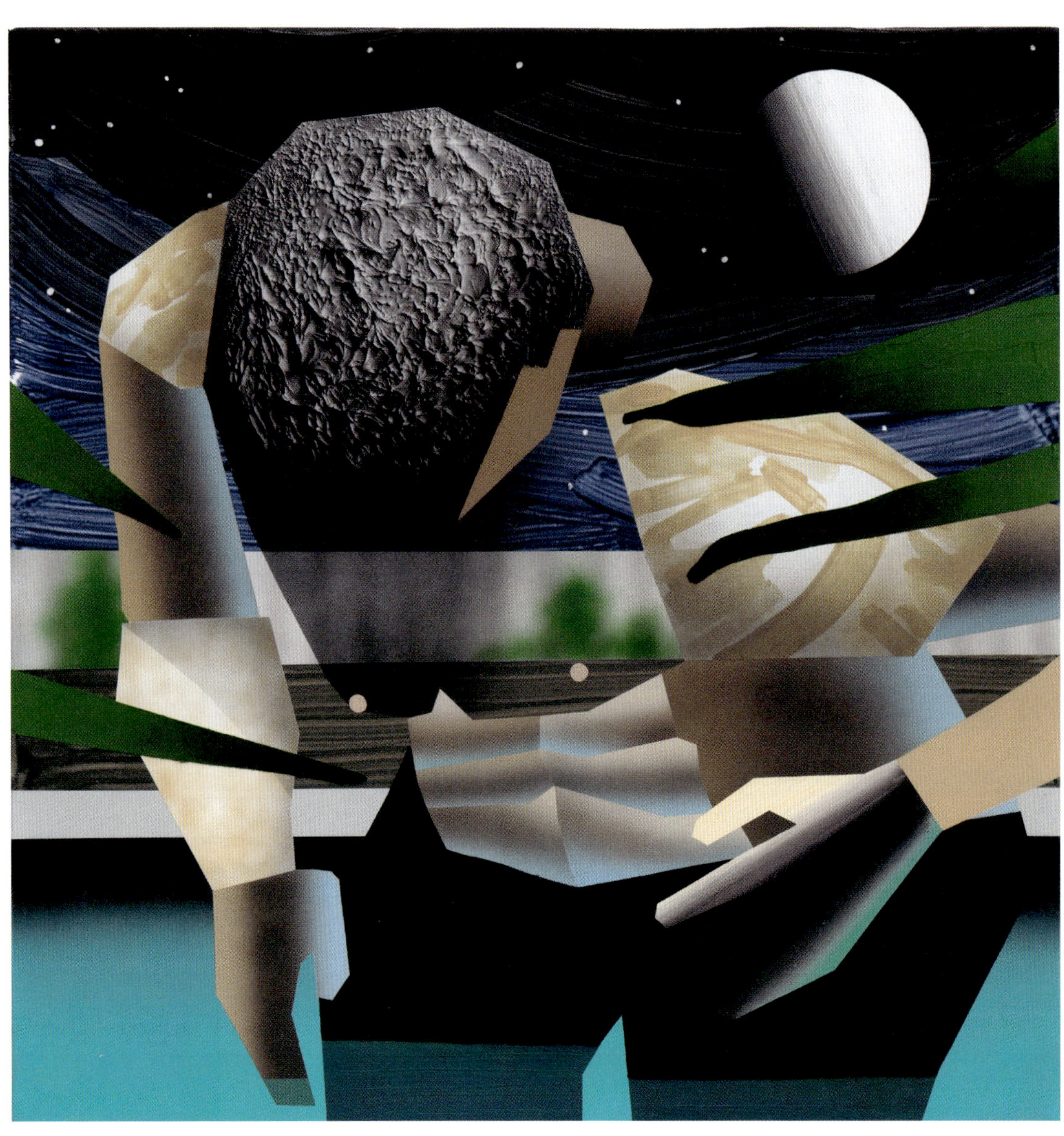

MOON SWIM 2021 · 120 × 120 cm

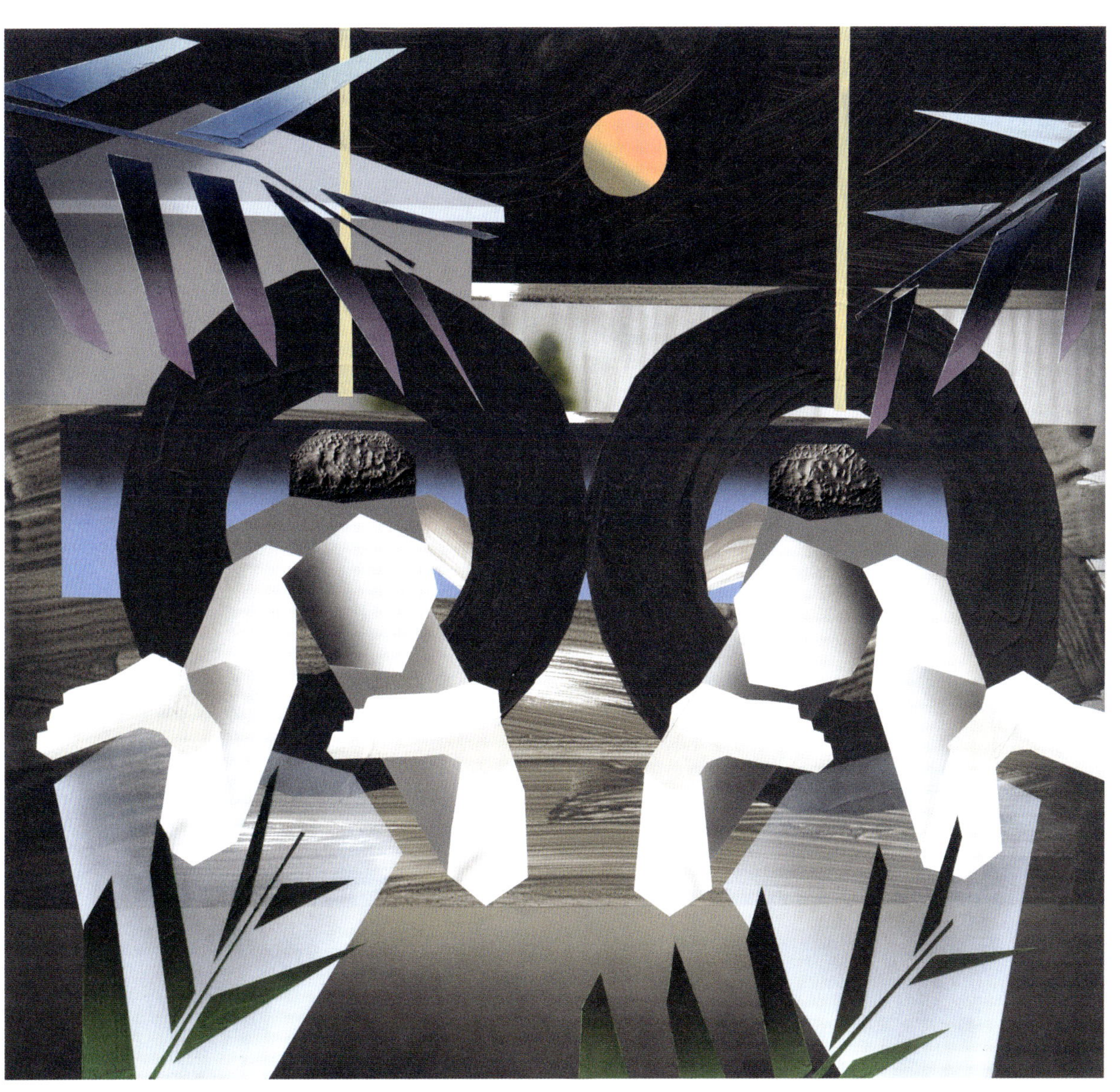

TIRE SWINGS 2021 · 138 × 150 cm

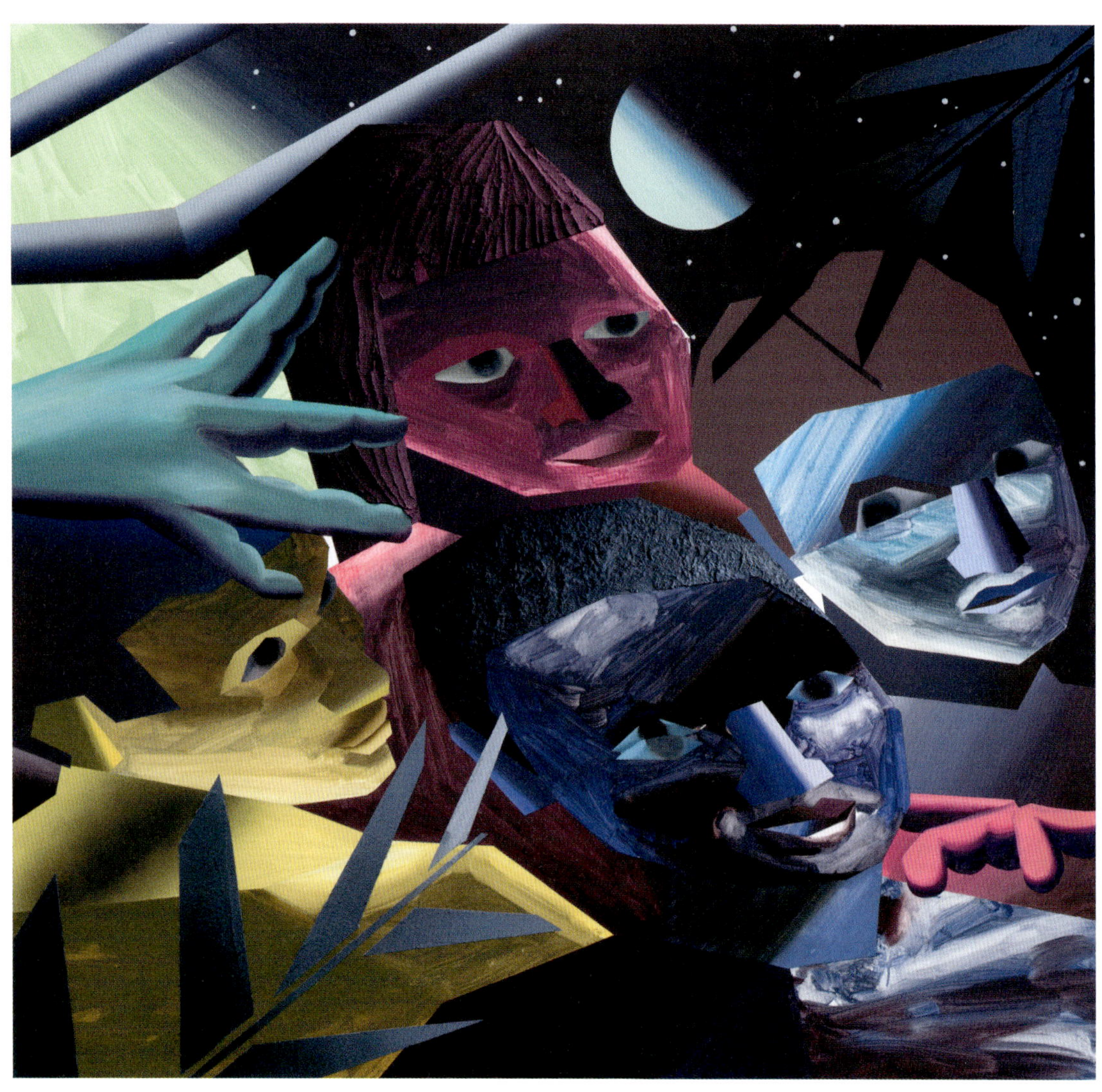

THE AUDIENCE 2022 · 140 × 150 cm

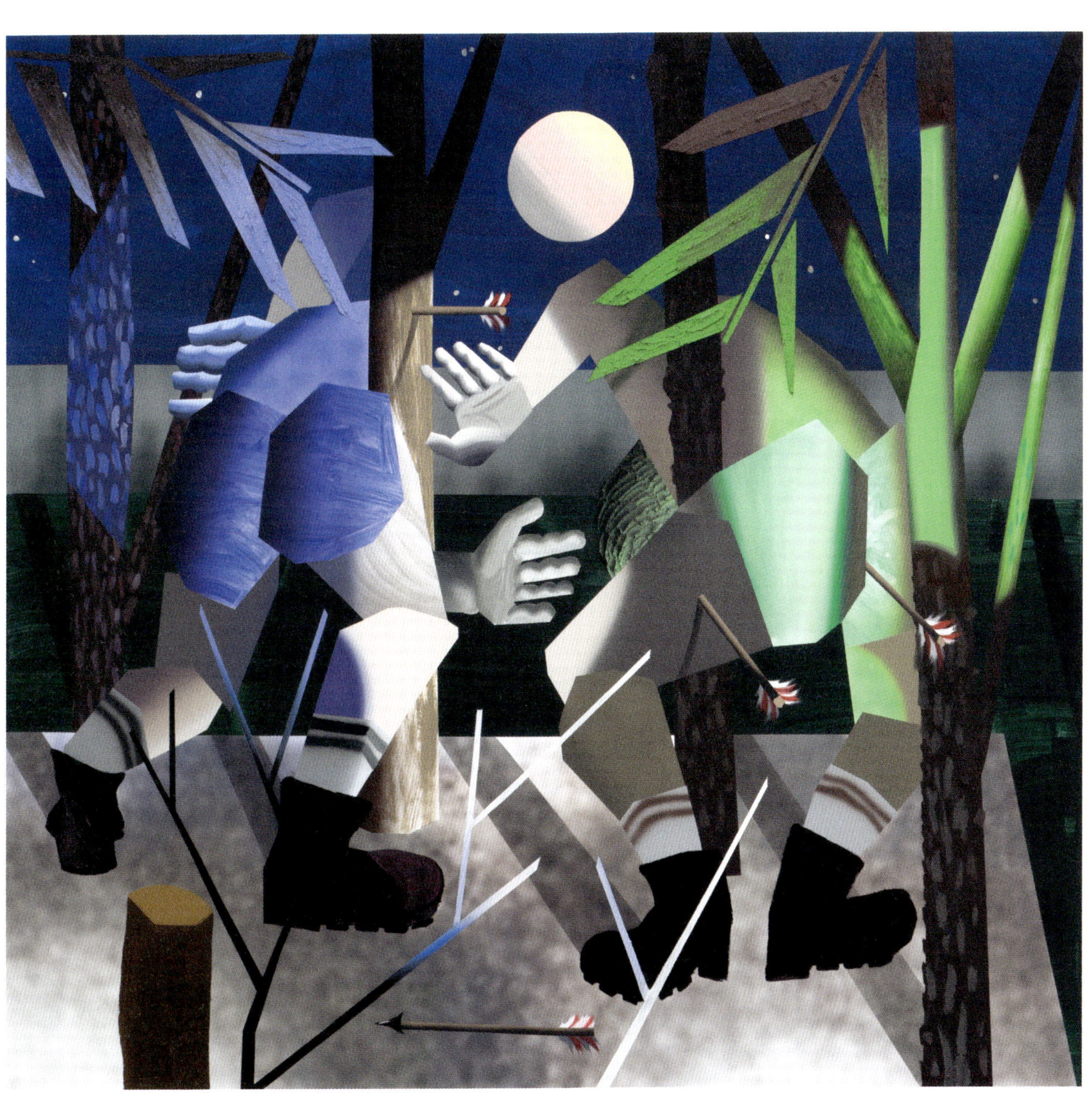

SEBASTIAN'S REVENGE 2022 · 200 × 186 cm

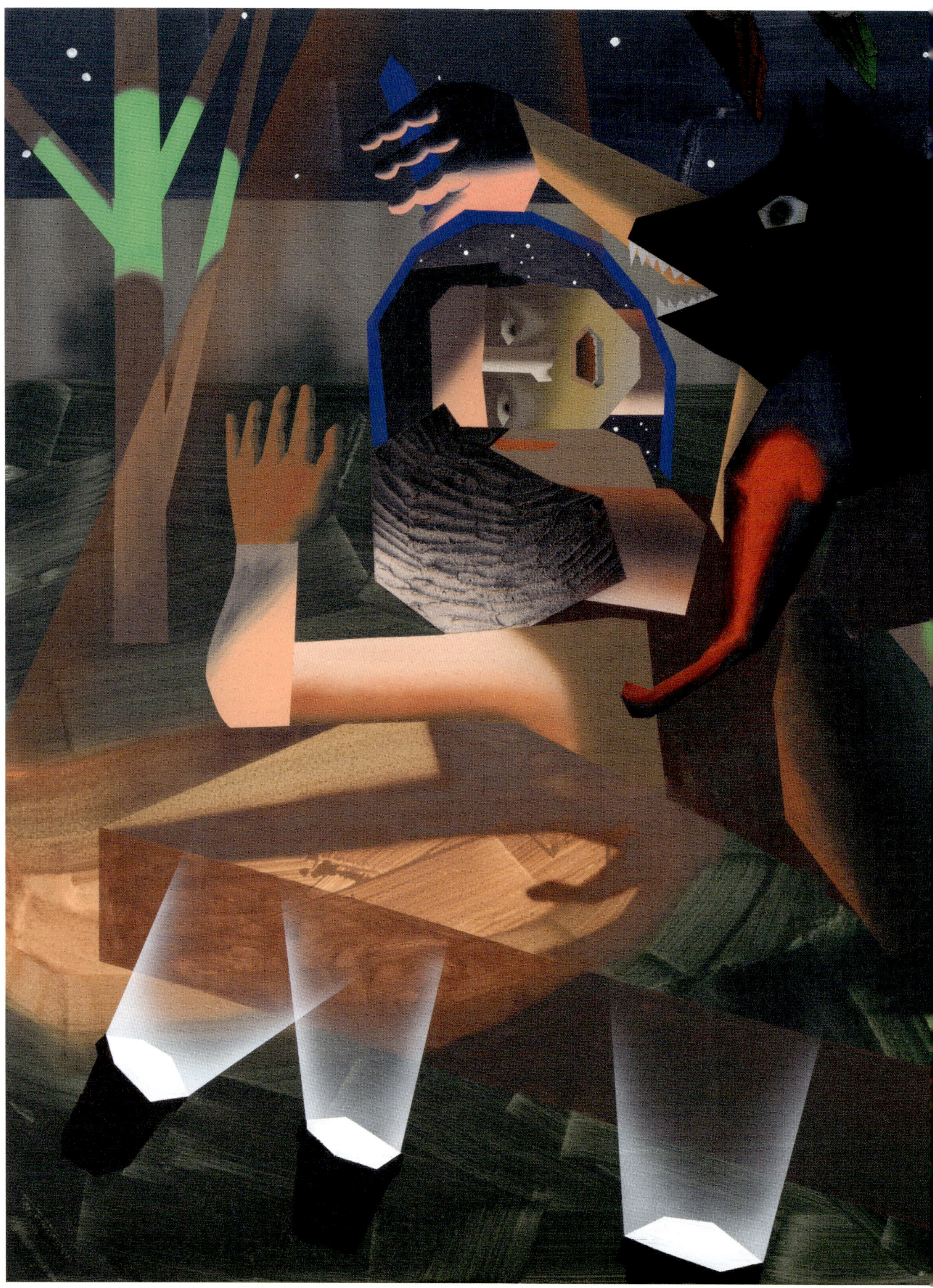

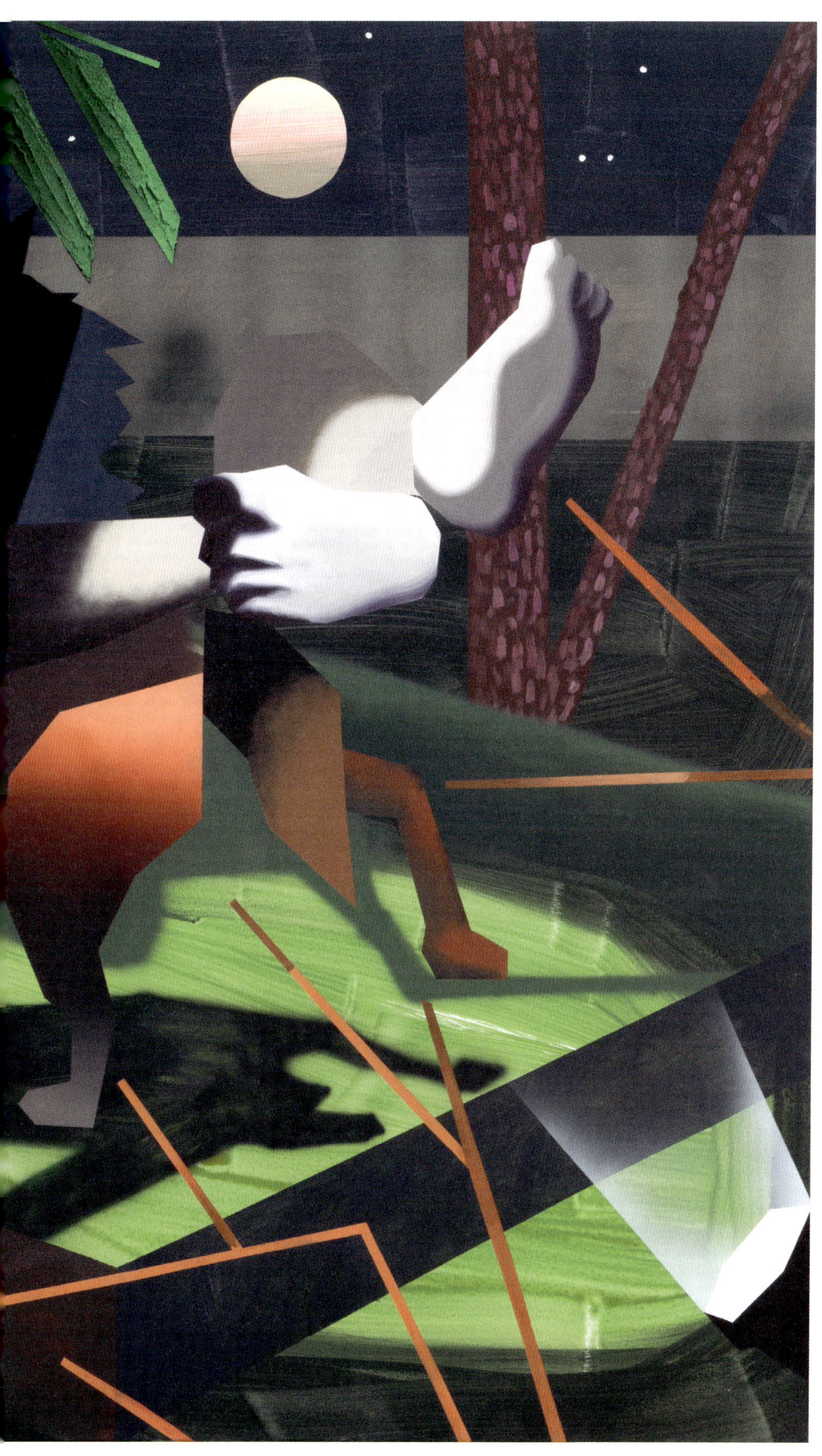

A BEAUTY AND THE BEAST
2022 · 175 × 250 cm

VIRTUAL REALITY

p. · S. 81–89

FEAR AND FANTASY

Render Stills of Virtual Reality · 2022

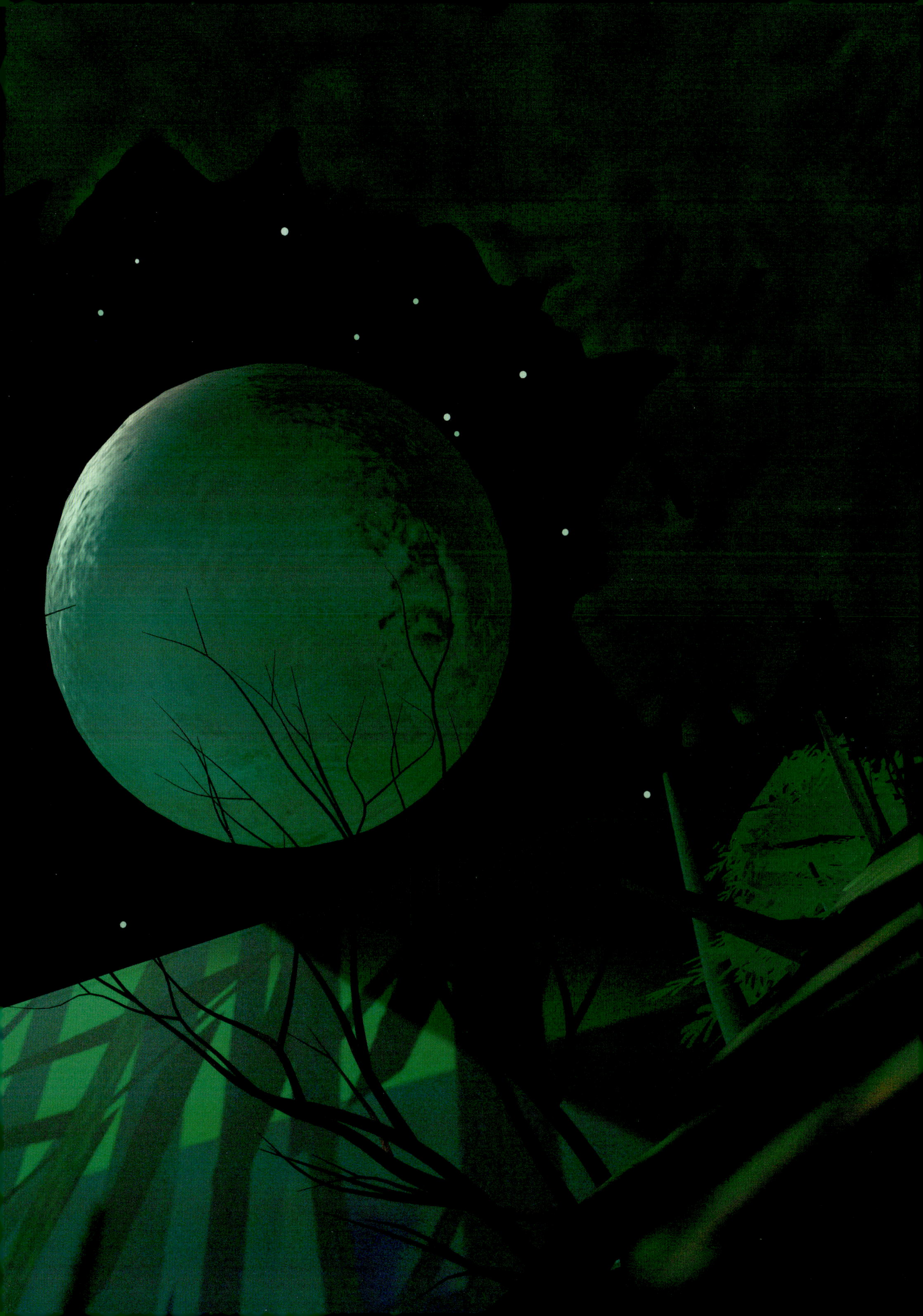

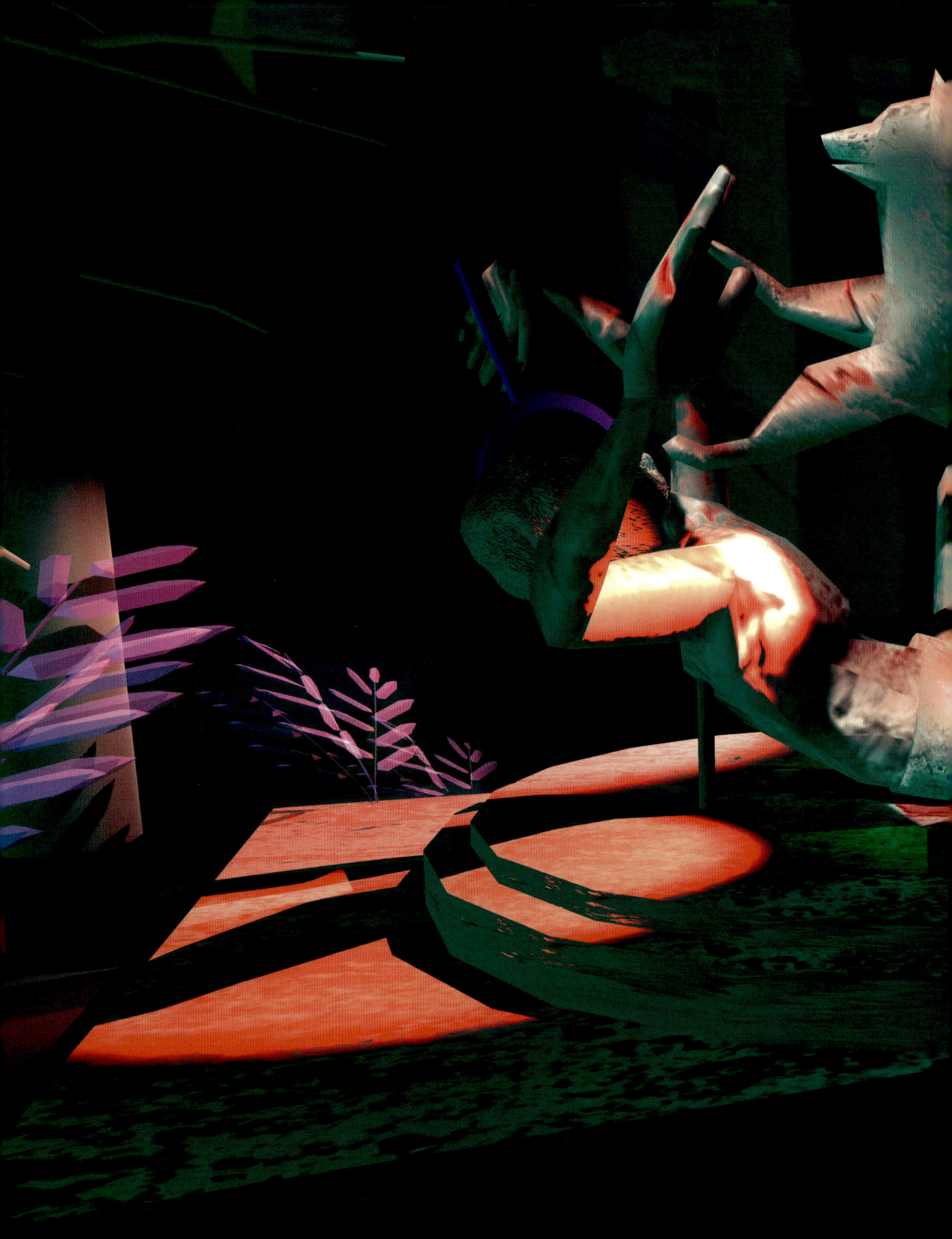

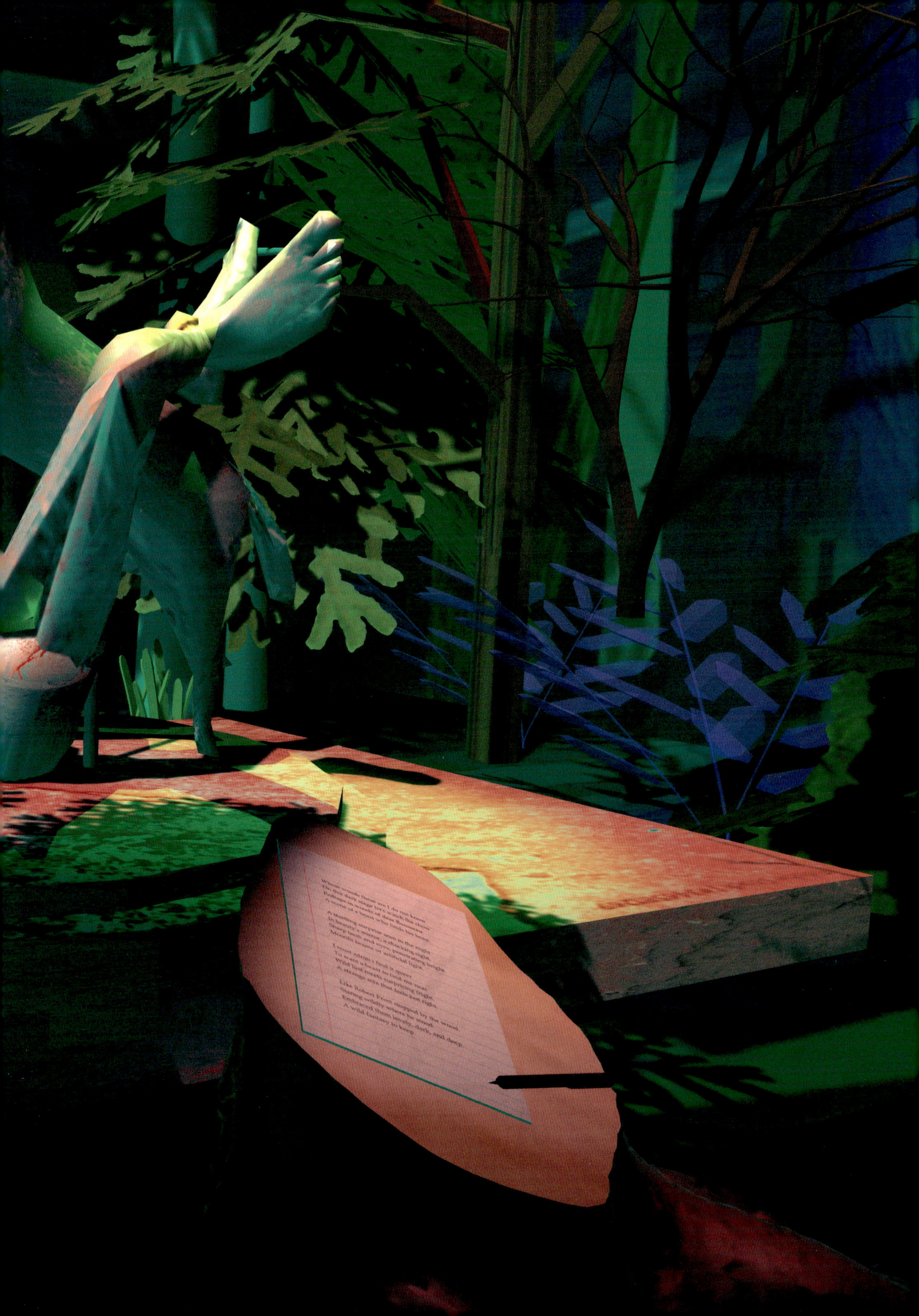
Whose woods these are I do not know
On this dark stage let's watch the show
Perhaps in woods of dear Rousseau

A startling surprise seen in the night
In beauty's mirror, a shocking sight
Sharp teeth and eyes, penetrating bright
Moonlit beams or artificial light

I must admit I find it queer
To want a beast to find me near
Wild lust meets surprising fright
A strange mix that feels just right

Like Robert Frost stopped by the wood
Staring wildly where he stood
Embraced them lovely, dark, and deep
A wild fantasy to keep

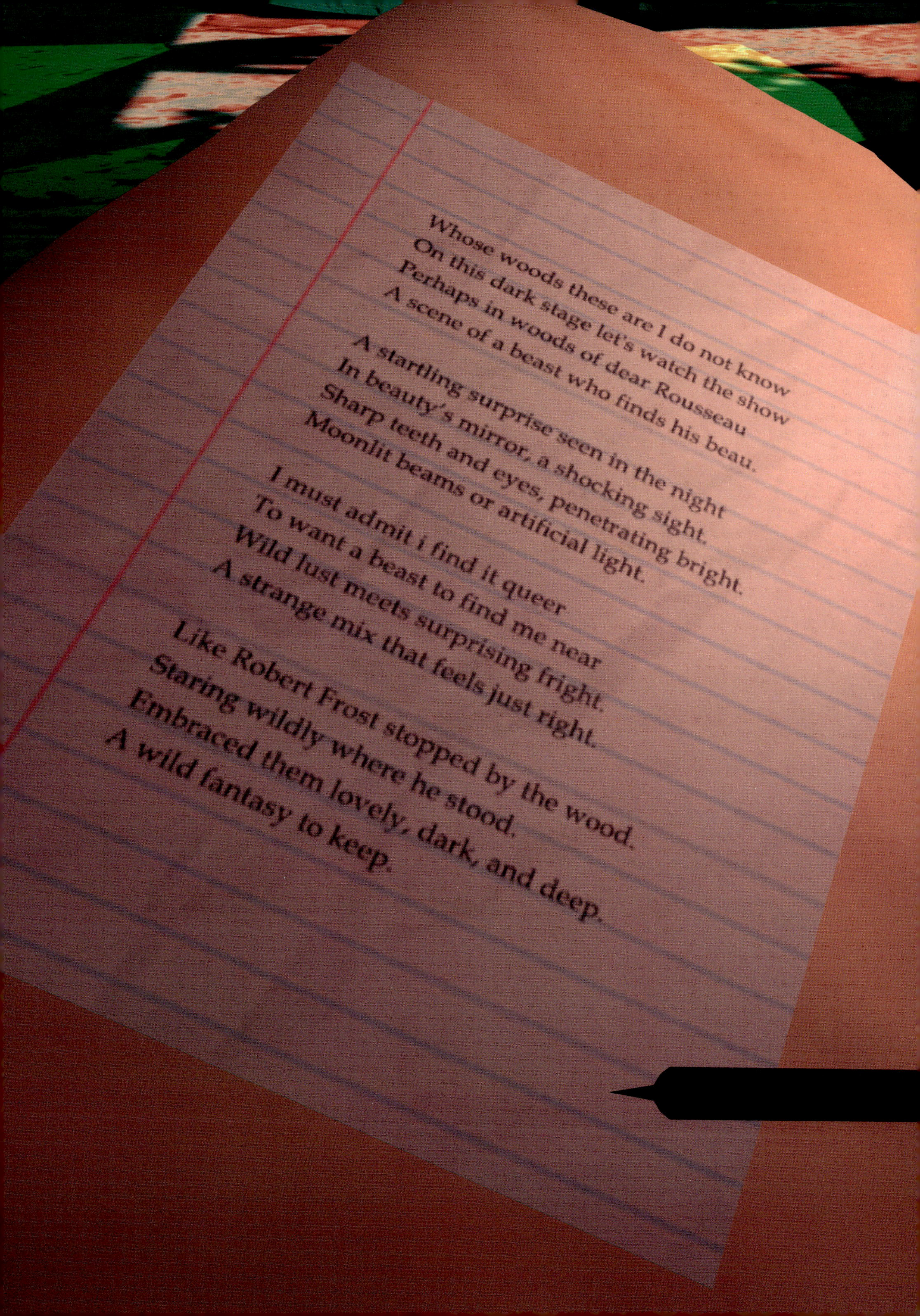

Whose woods these are I do not know
On this dark stage let's watch the show
Perhaps in woods of dear Rousseau
A scene of a beast who finds his beau.

A startling surprise seen in the night
In beauty's mirror, a shocking sight.
Sharp teeth and eyes, penetrating bright.
Moonlit beams or artificial light.

I must admit i find it queer
To want a beast to find me near
Wild lust meets surprising fright.
A strange mix that feels just right.

Like Robert Frost stopped by the wood.
Staring wildly where he stood.
Embraced them lovely, dark, and deep.
A wild fantasy to keep.

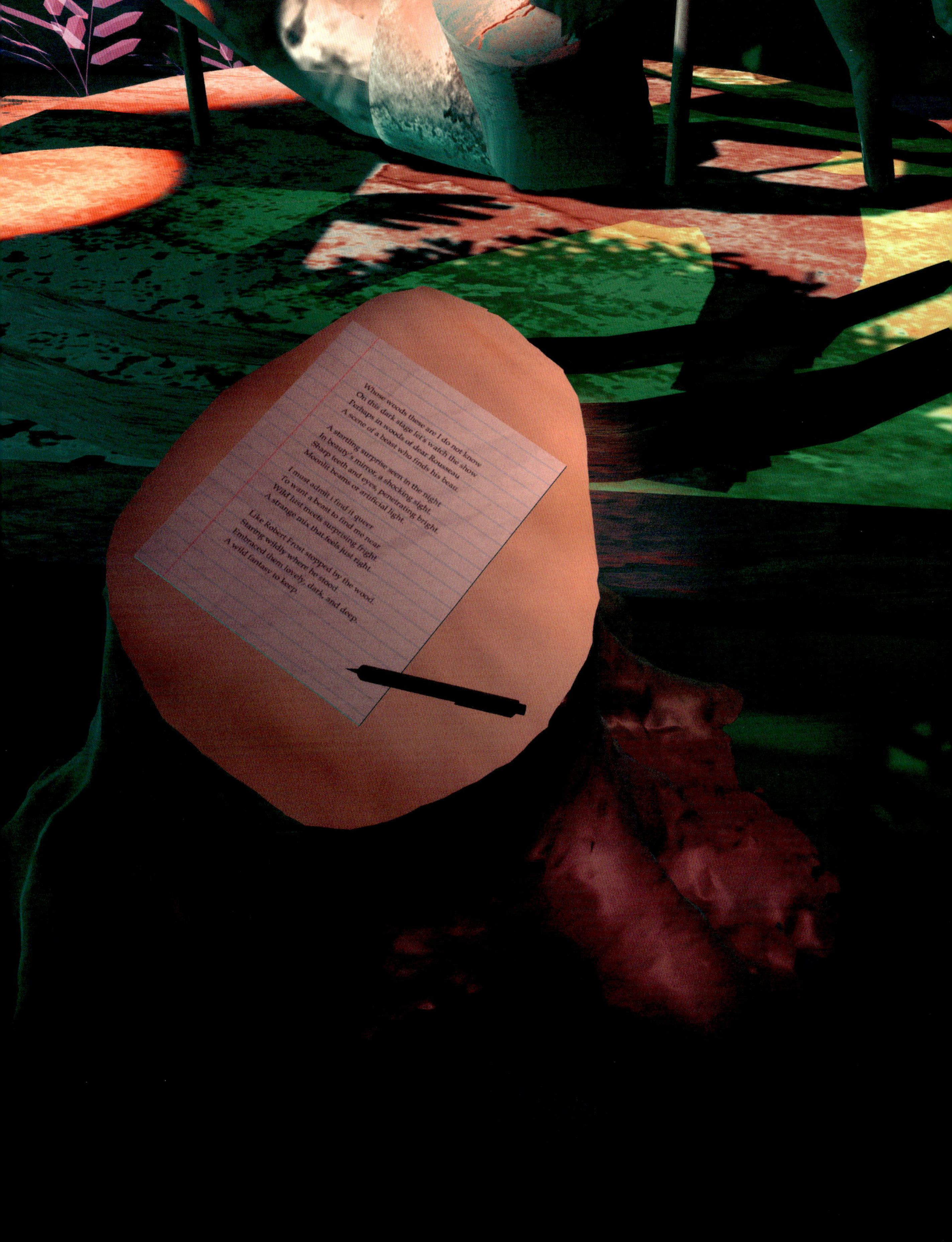
Whose woods these are I do not know
On this dark stage let's watch the show
Perhaps in woods of dear Rousseau
A scene of a beast who finds his beau.
A startling surprise seen in the night
In beauty's mirror, a shocking sight.
Sharp teeth and eyes, penetrating bright.
Moonlit beams or artificial light.
I must admit I find it queer
To want a beast to find me near
Wild lust meets surprising fright
A strange mix that feels just right.
Like Robert Frost stopped by the wood.
Staring wildly where he stood
Embraced them lovely, dark, and deep.
A wild fantasy to keep.

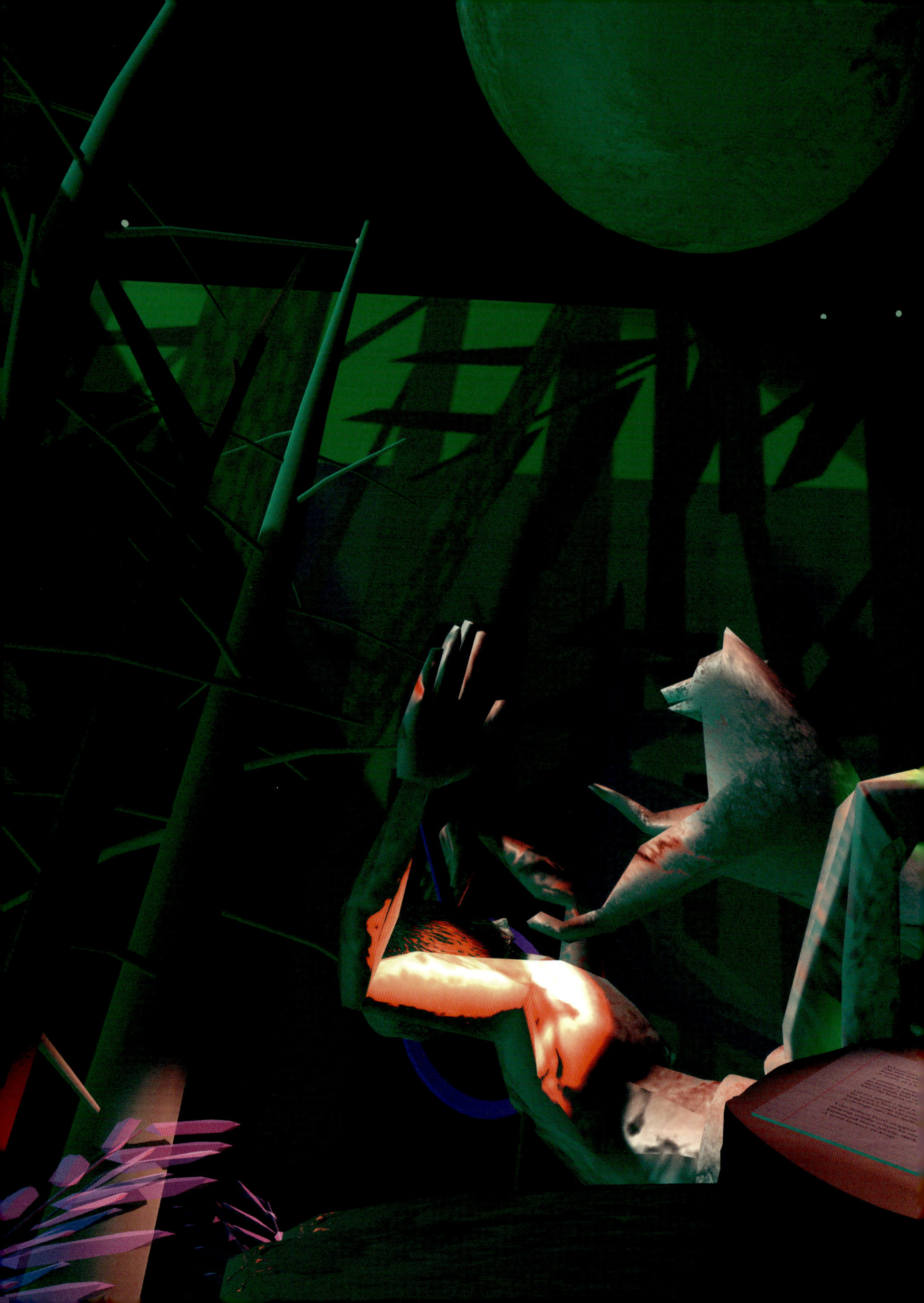

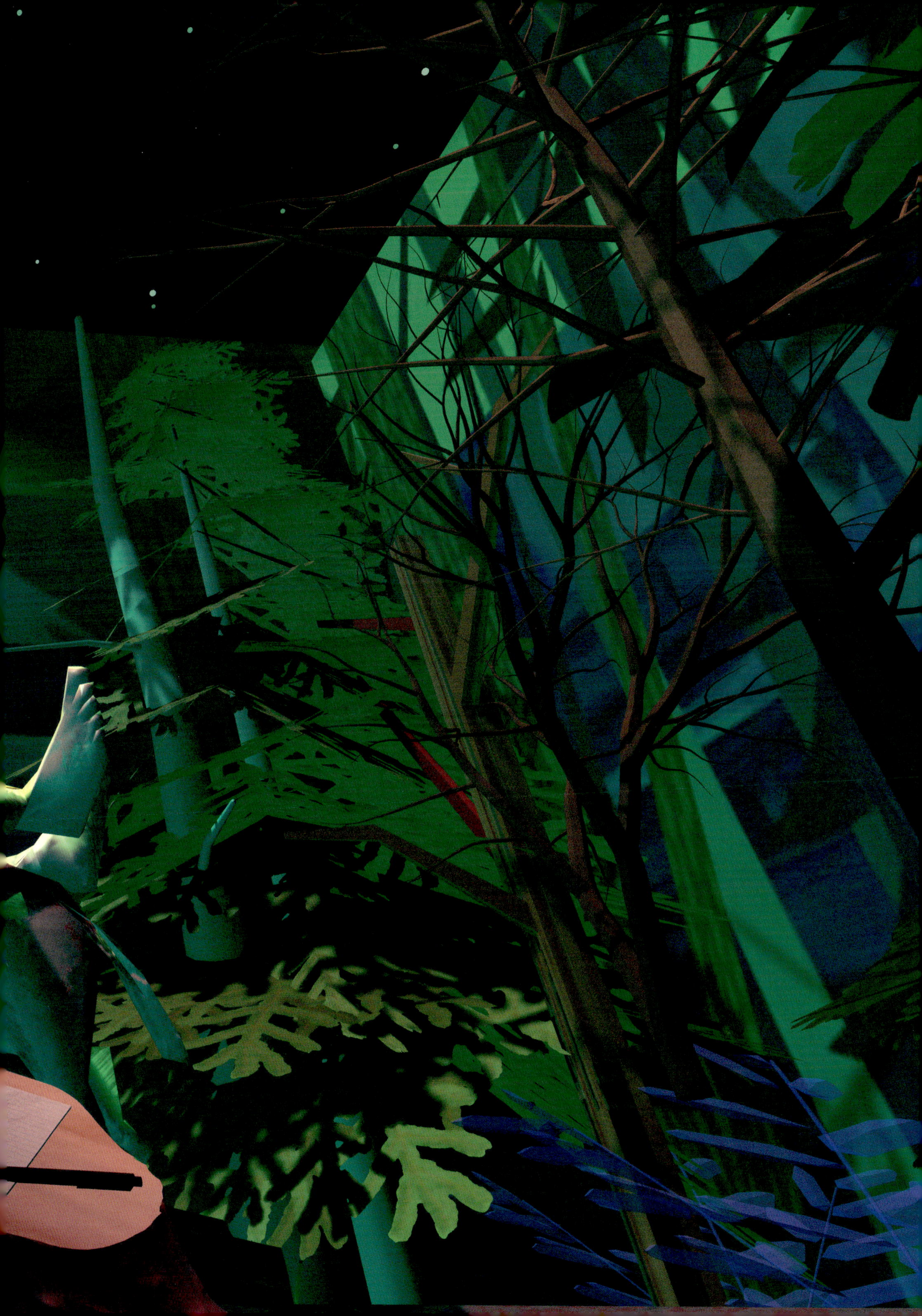

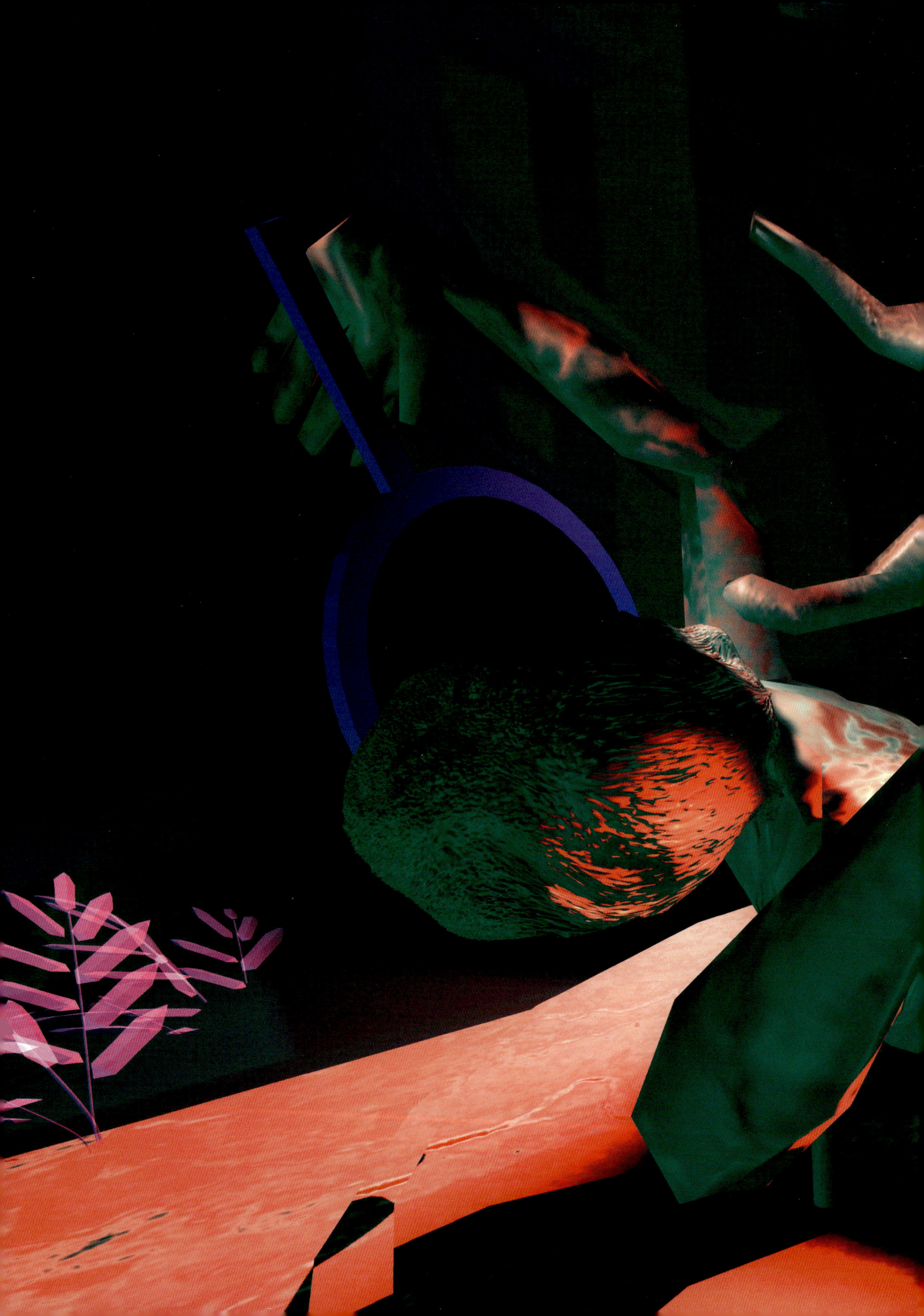

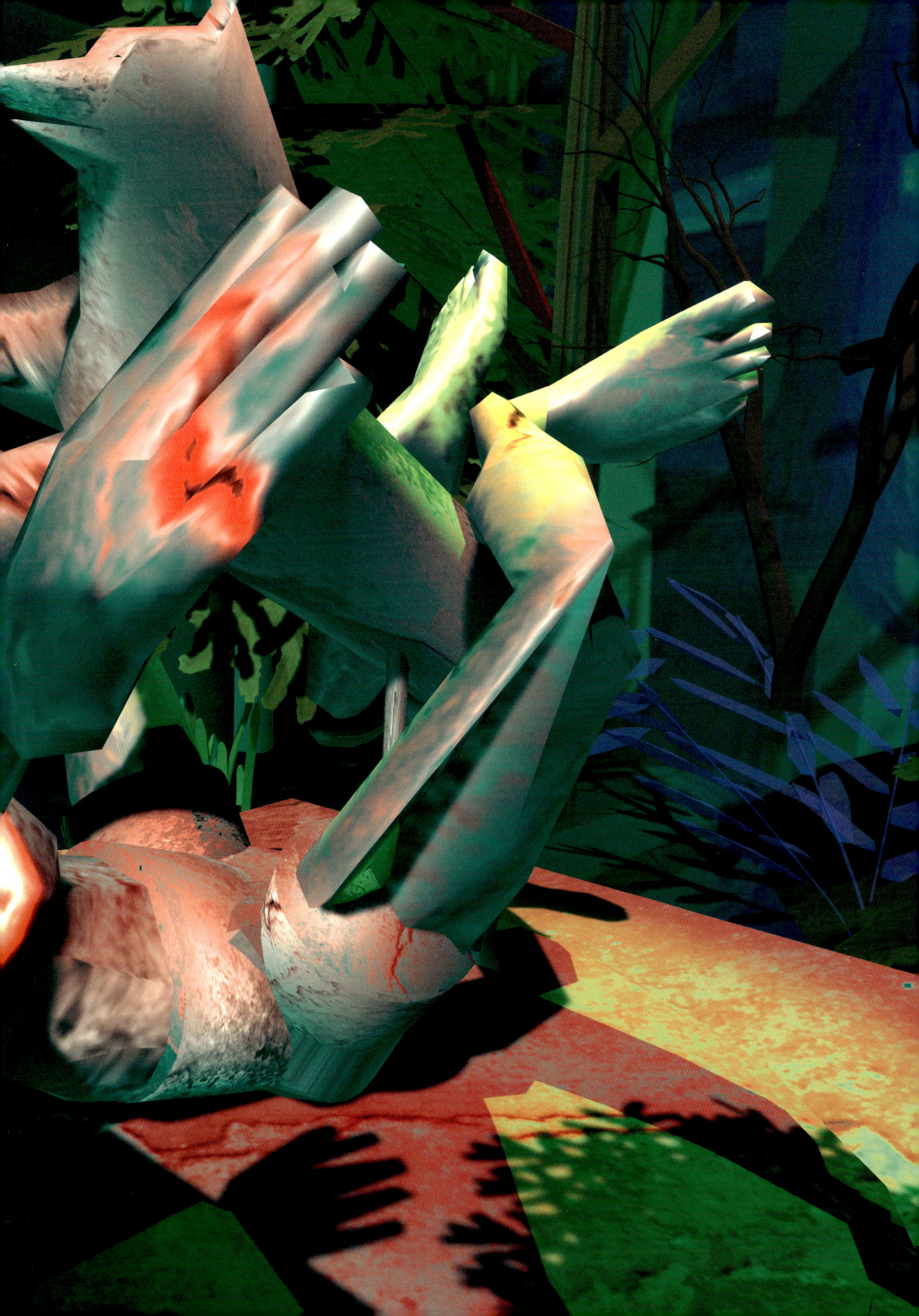

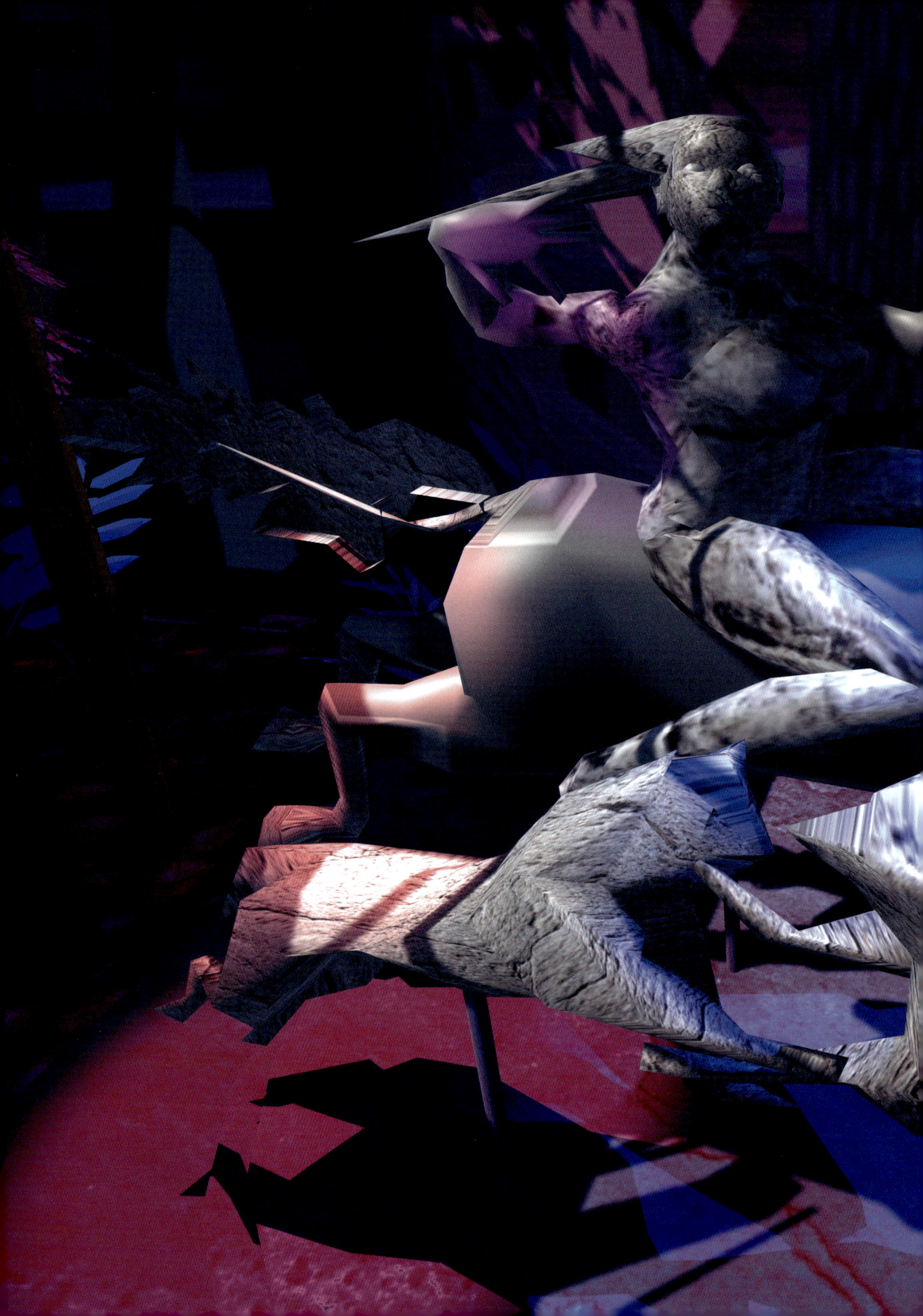

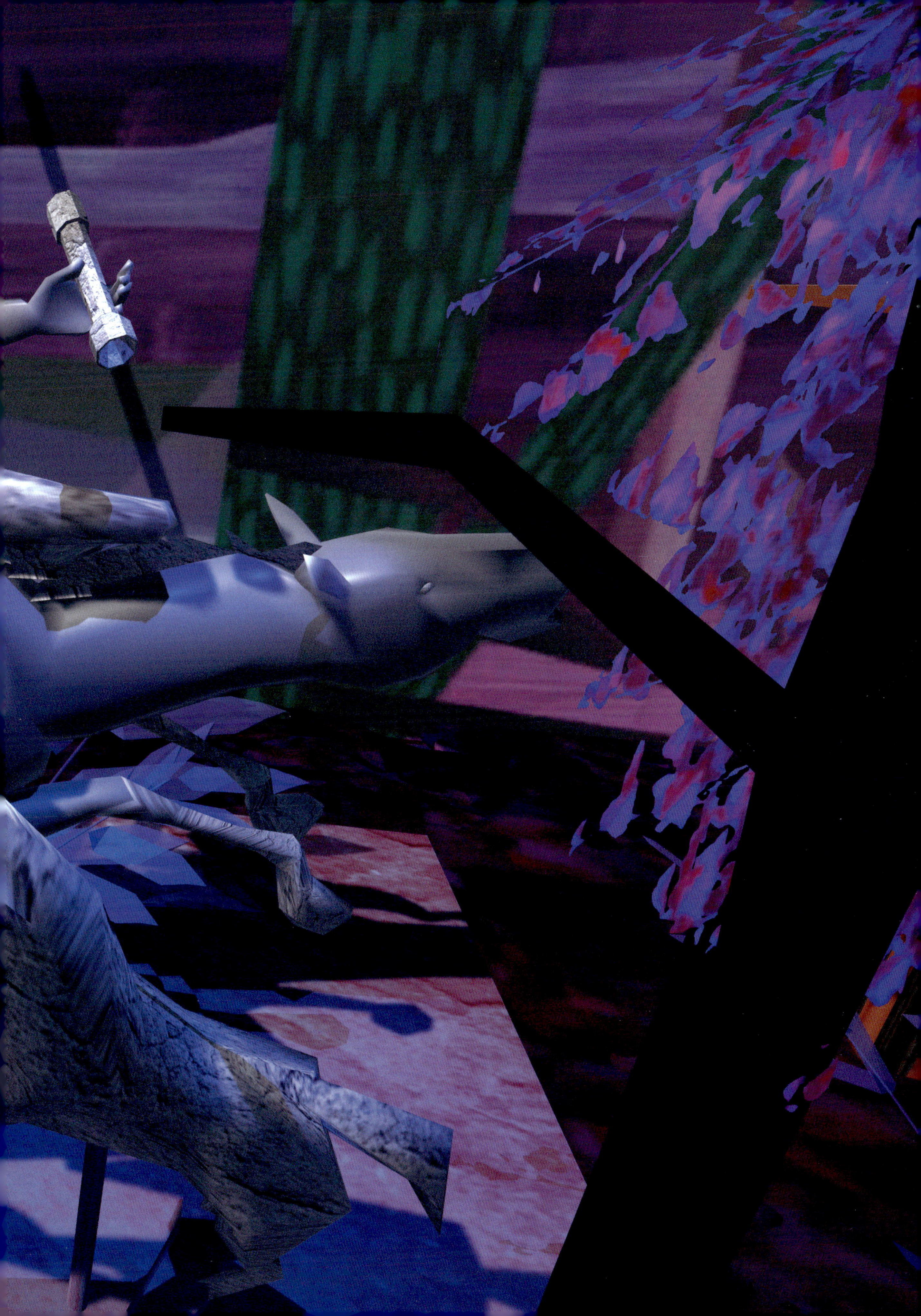

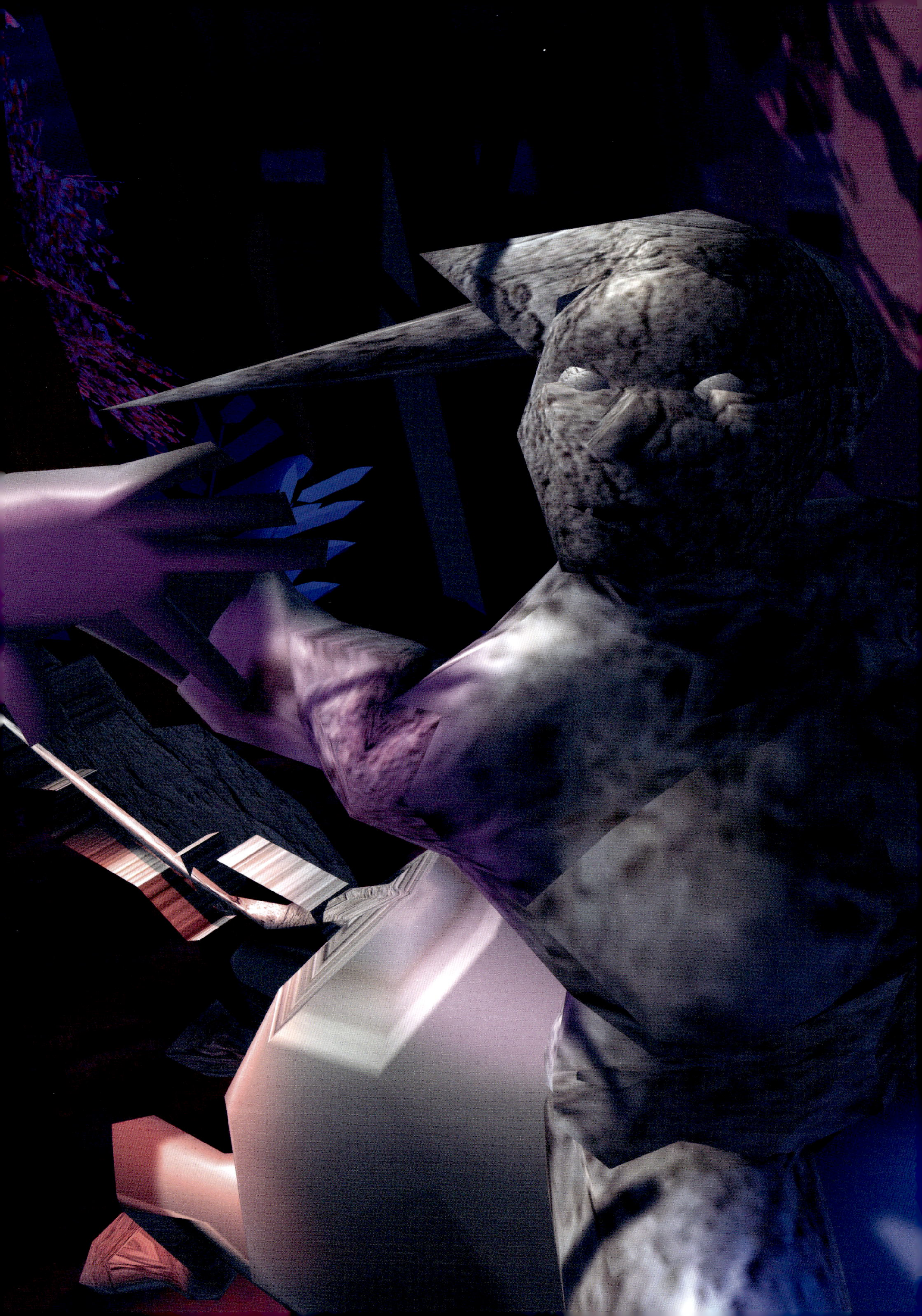

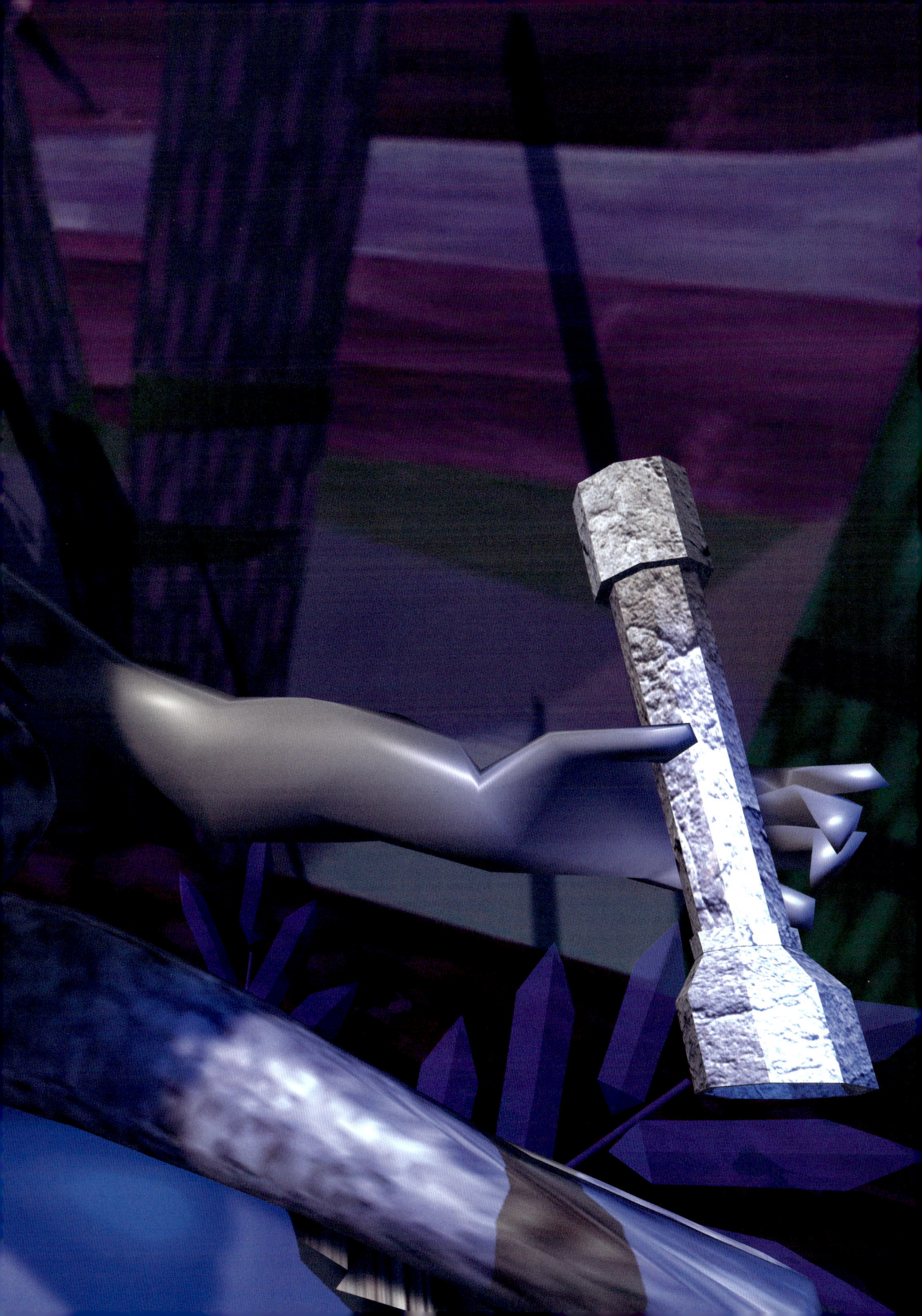

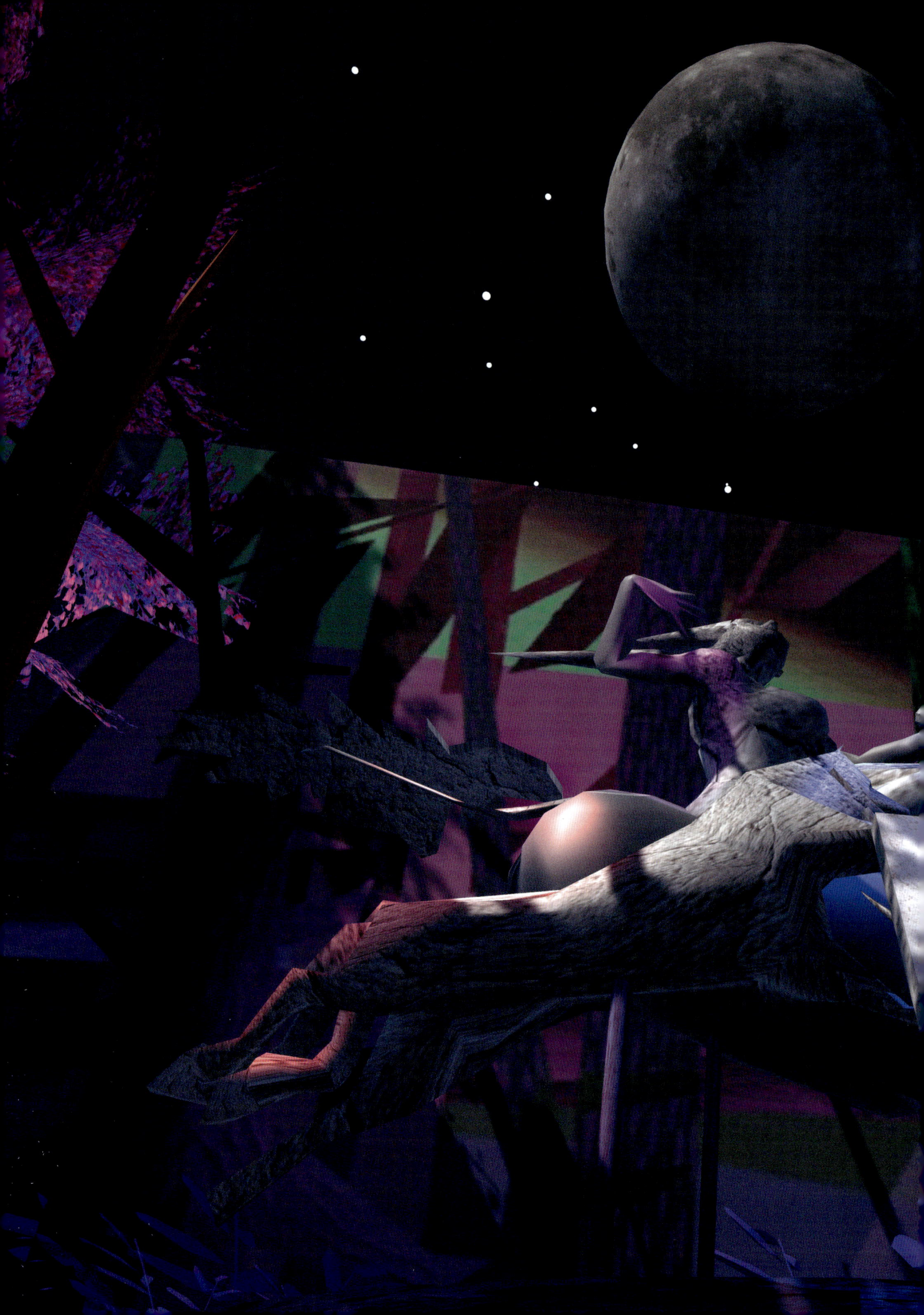

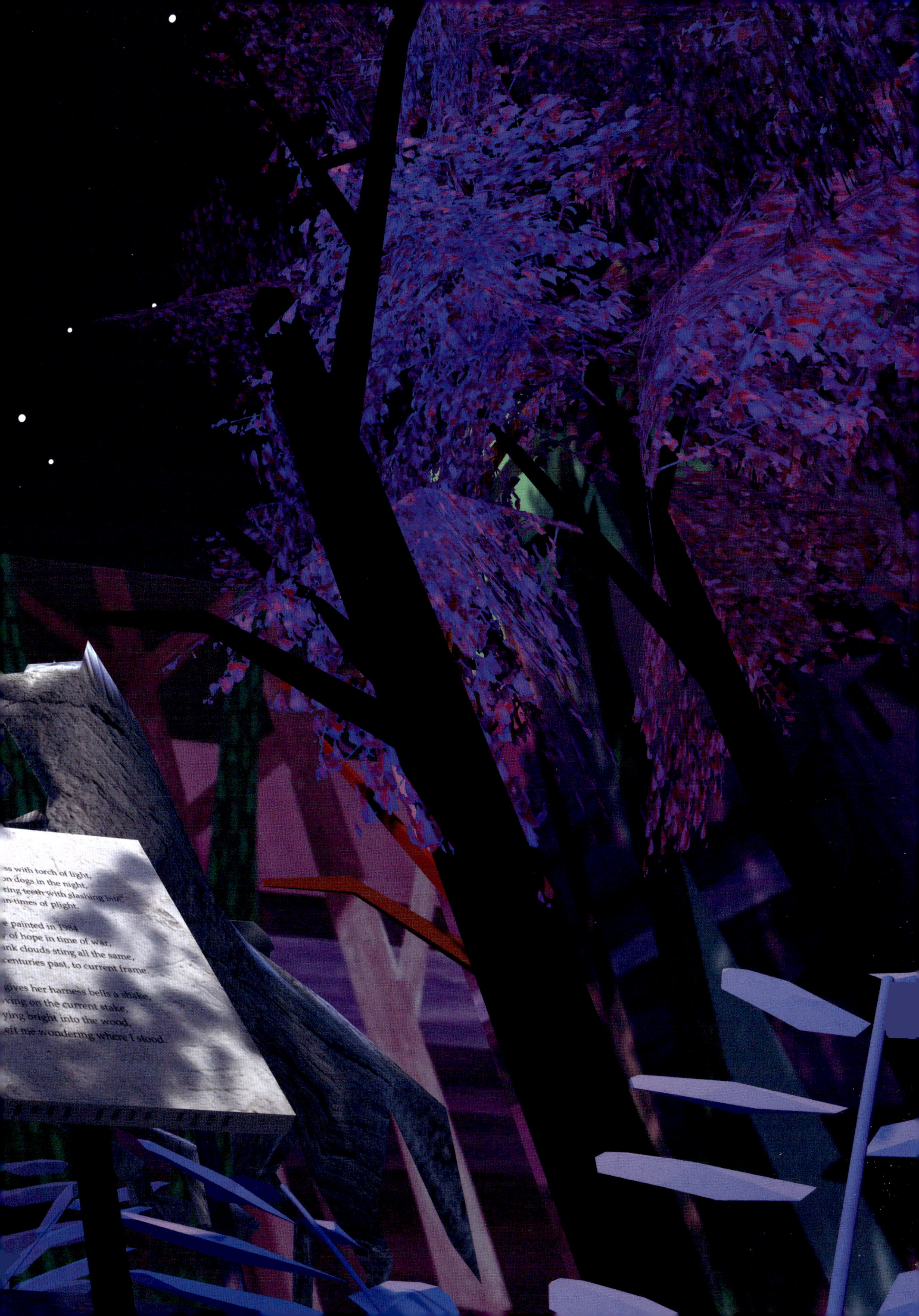
ss with torch of light,
on dogs in the night,
ring teeth with slashing bite,
in times of plight.
e painted in 1984
of hope in time of war,
nk clouds sting all the same,
centuries past, to current frame.
gives her harness bells a shake,
ving on the current stake,
ying bright into the wood,
eft me wondering where I stood.

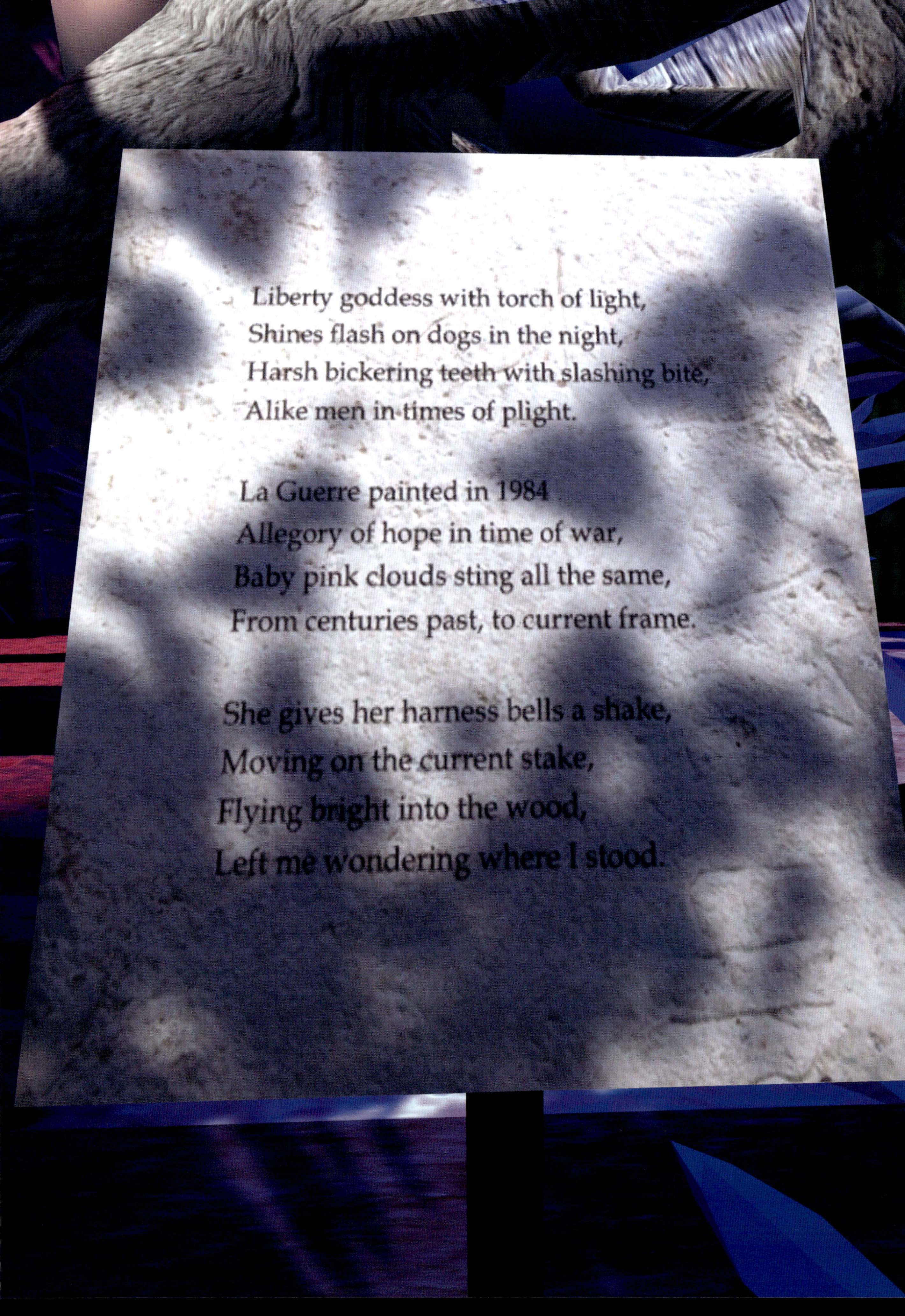
Liberty goddess with torch of light,
Shines flash on dogs in the night,
Harsh bickering teeth with slashing bite,
Alike men in times of plight.

La Guerre painted in 1984
Allegory of hope in time of war,
Baby pink clouds sting all the same,
From centuries past, to current frame.

She gives her harness bells a shake,
Moving on the current stake,
Flying bright into the wood,
Left me wondering where I stood.

p. · S. 90–96

LA GUERRE DES CHIENS

Render Stills of Virtual Reality · 2022

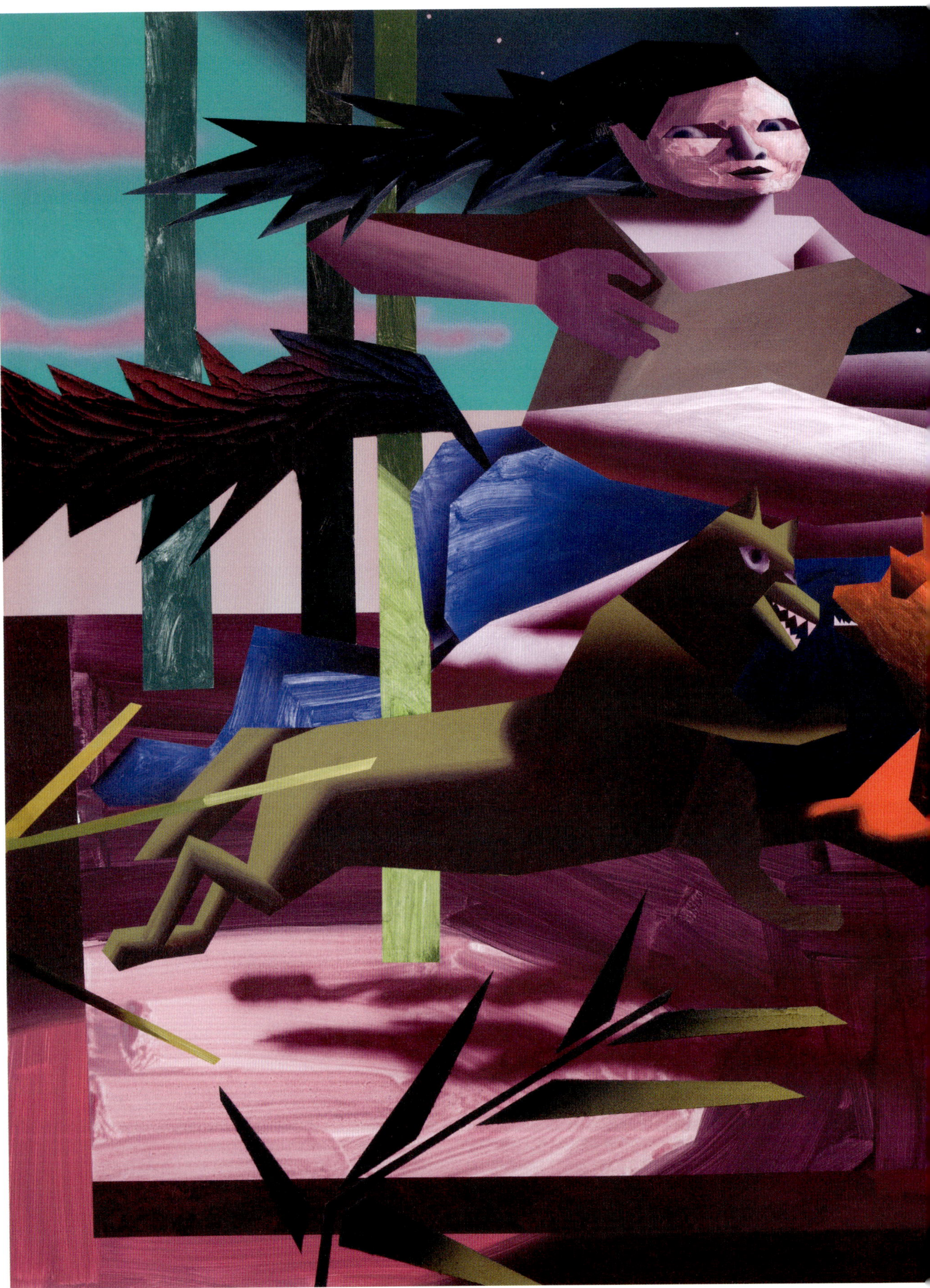

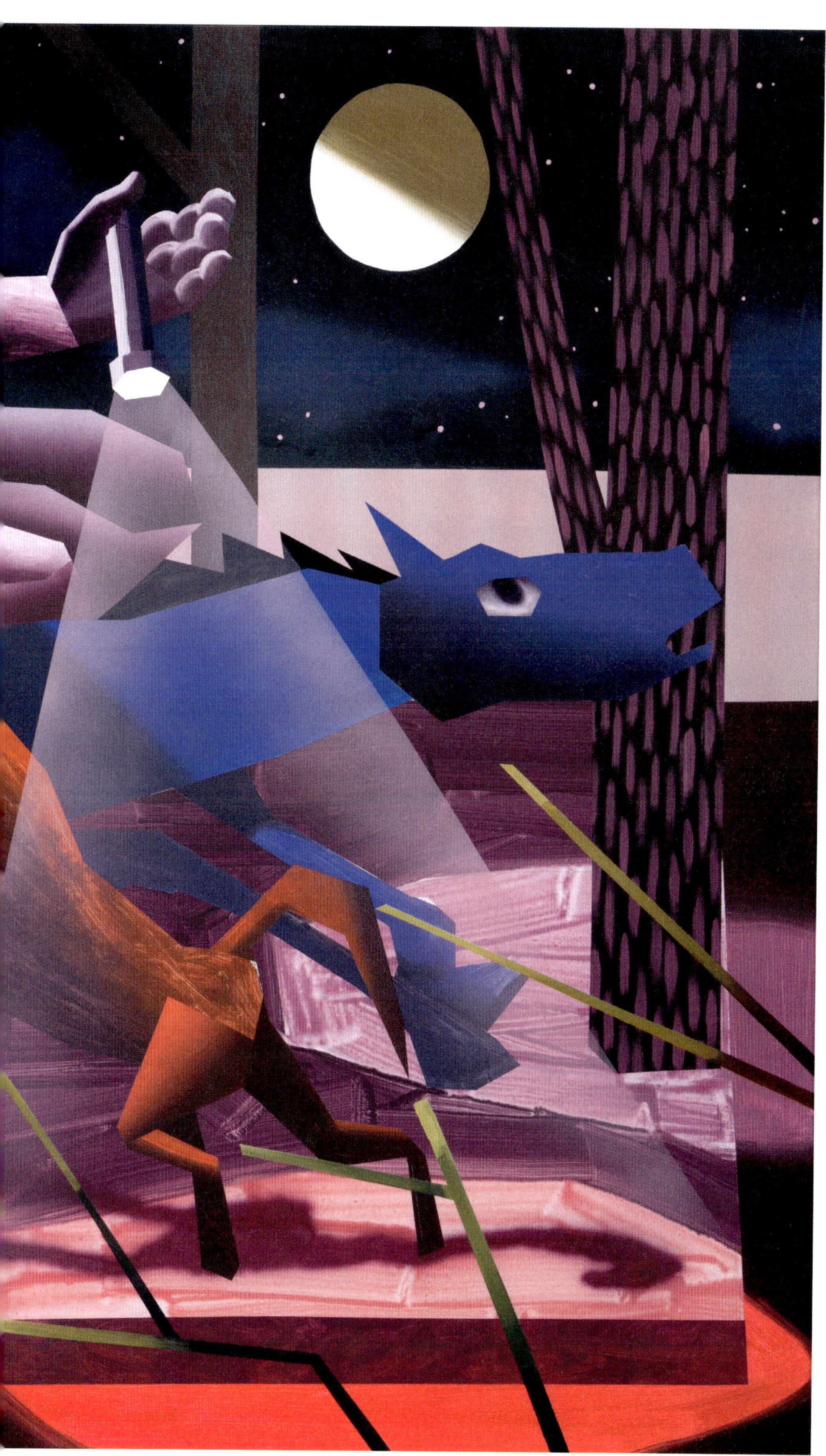

LA GUERRE DES CHIENS
2022 · 175 × 250 cm

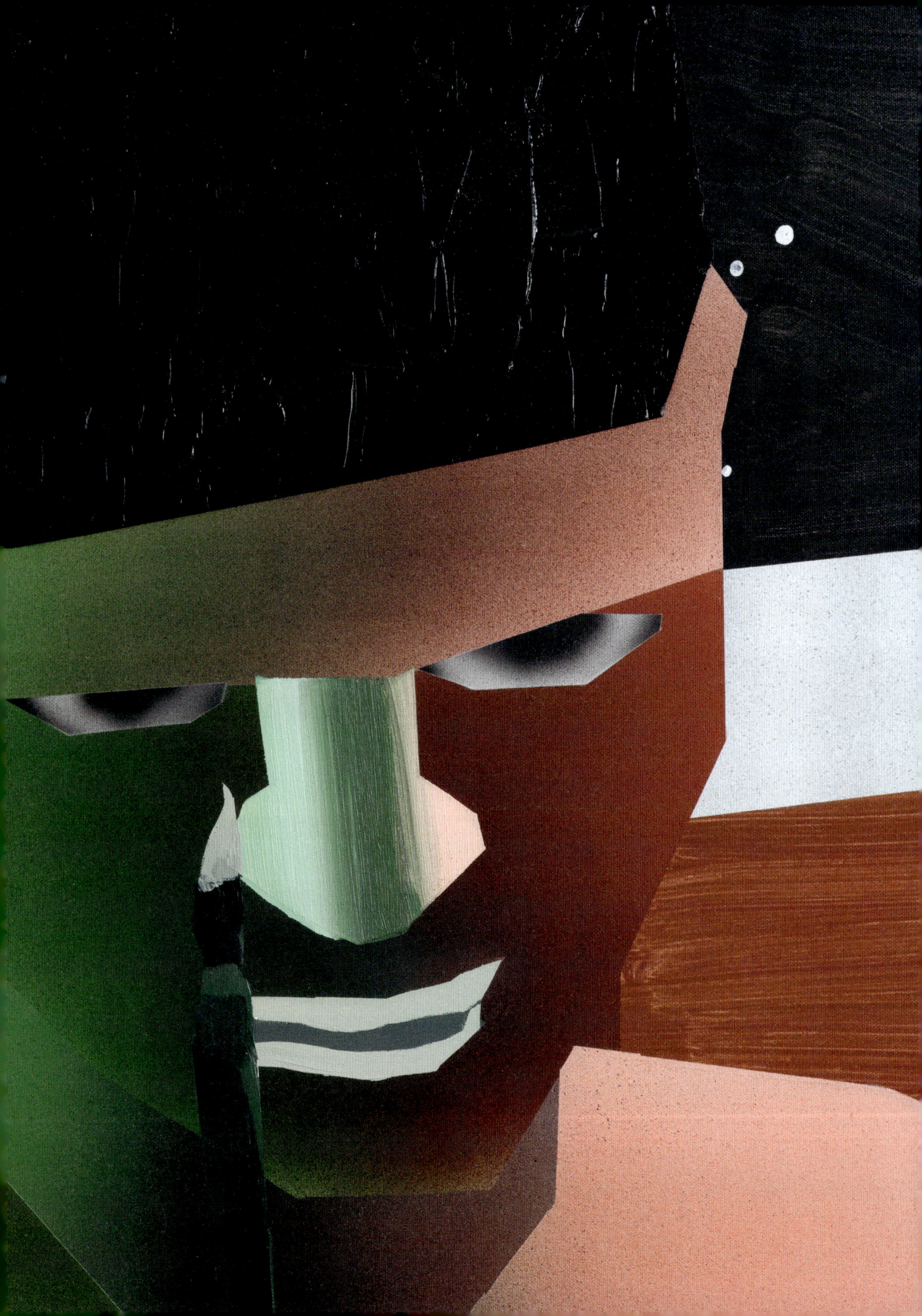

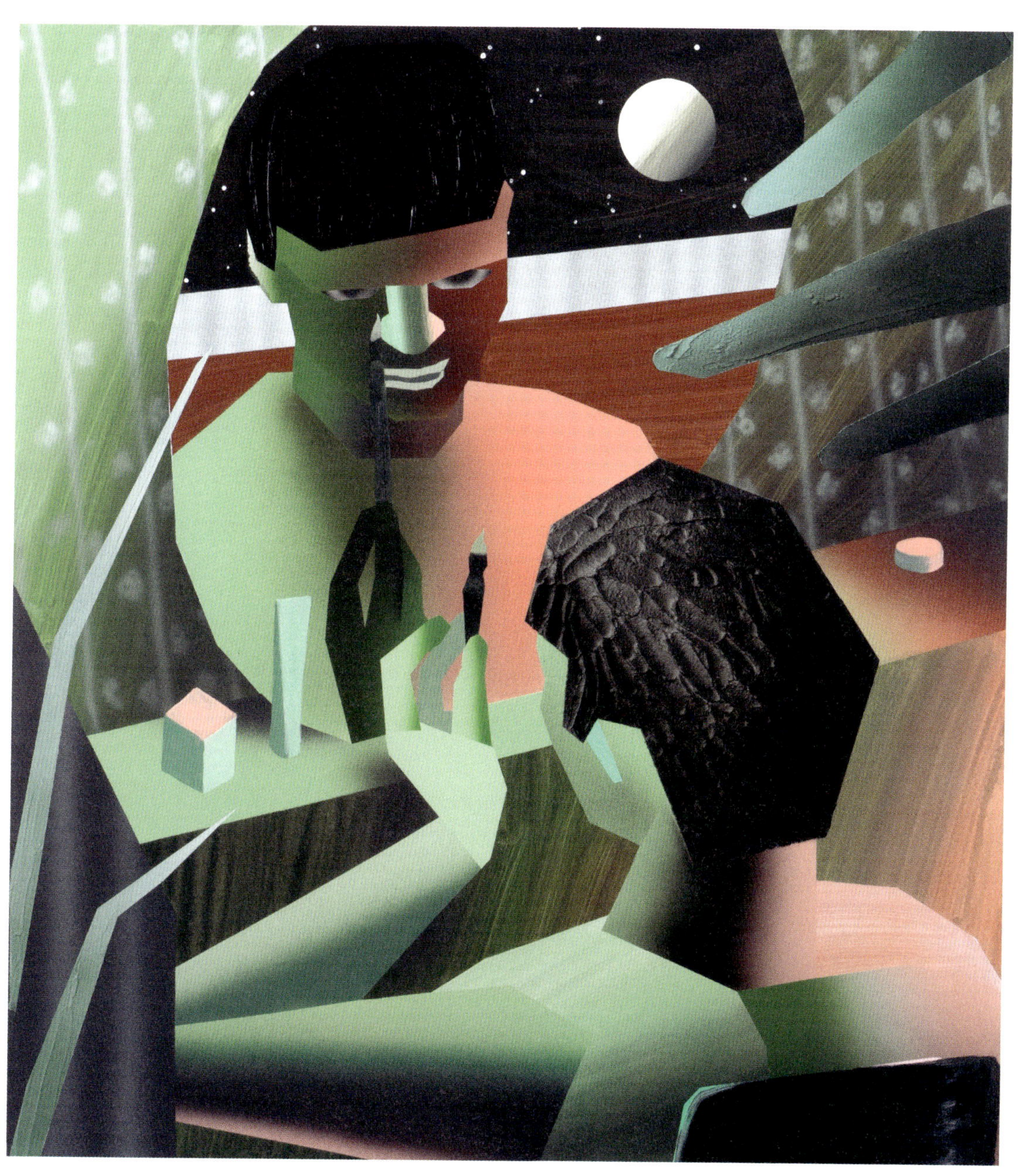

MAKEUP BRUSH 2021 · 120 × 100 cm

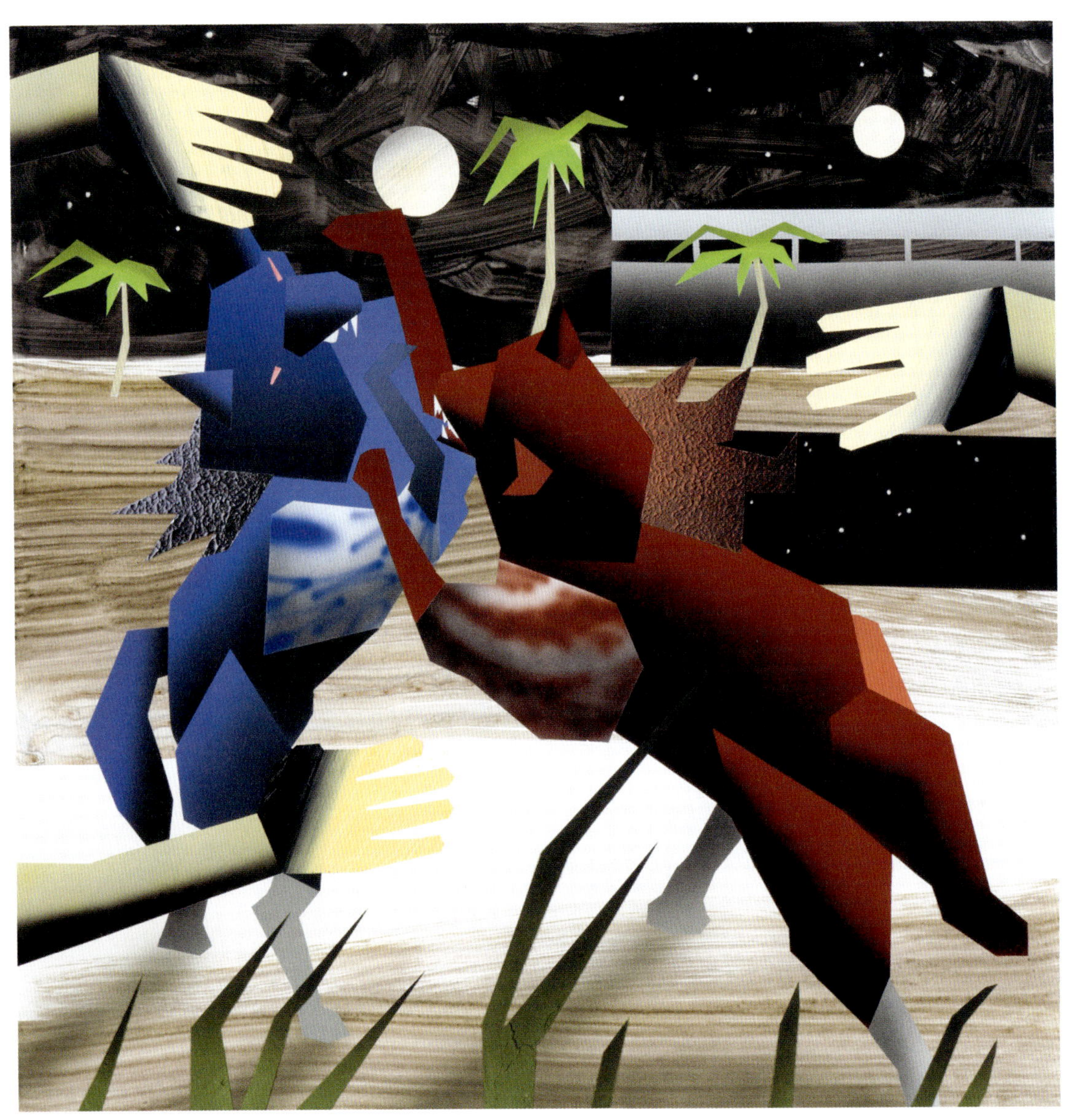

DOG FIGHT 2021 · 110 × 110 cm

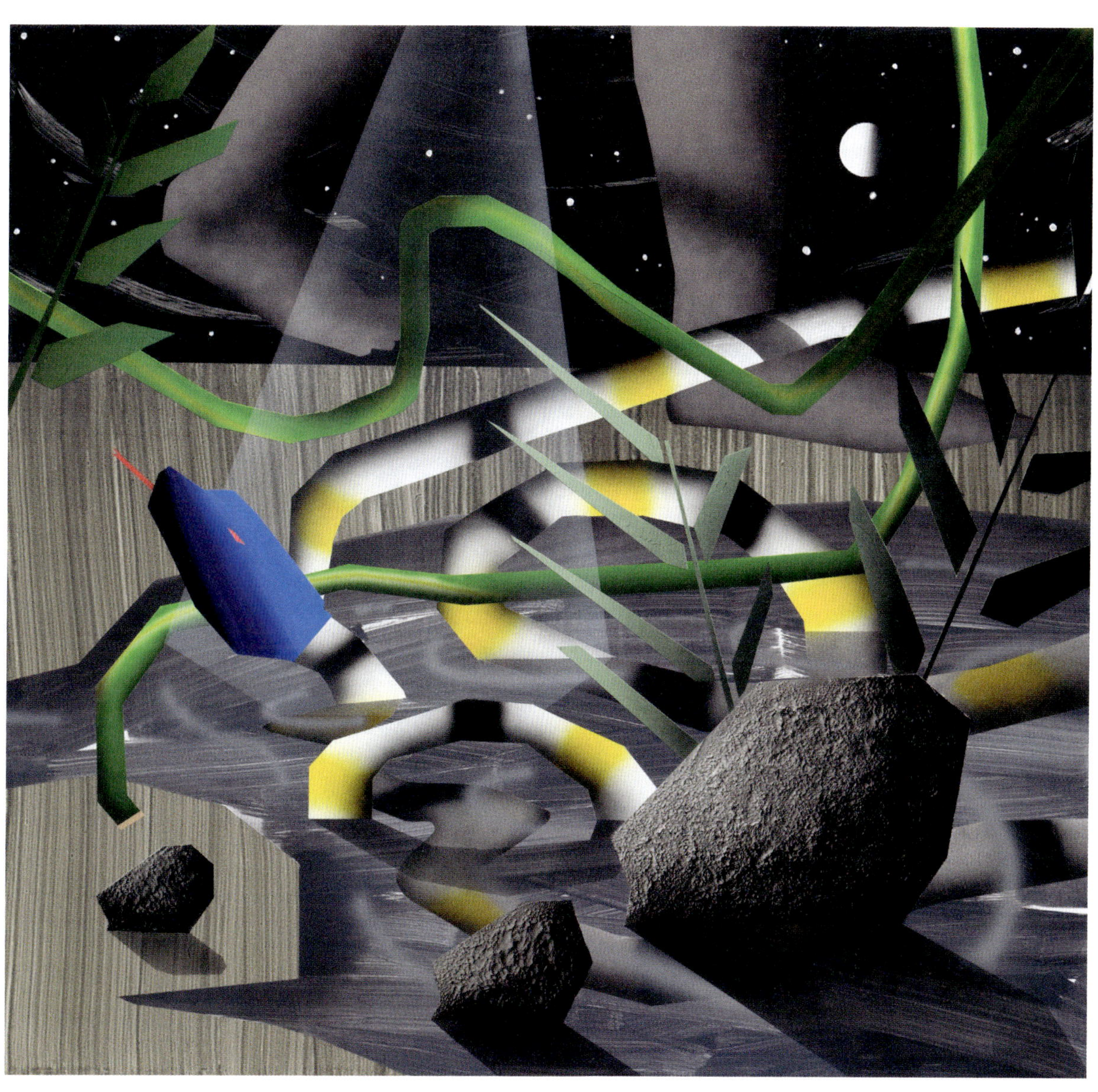

SNAKE PUDDLE 2021 · 160 × 148 cm

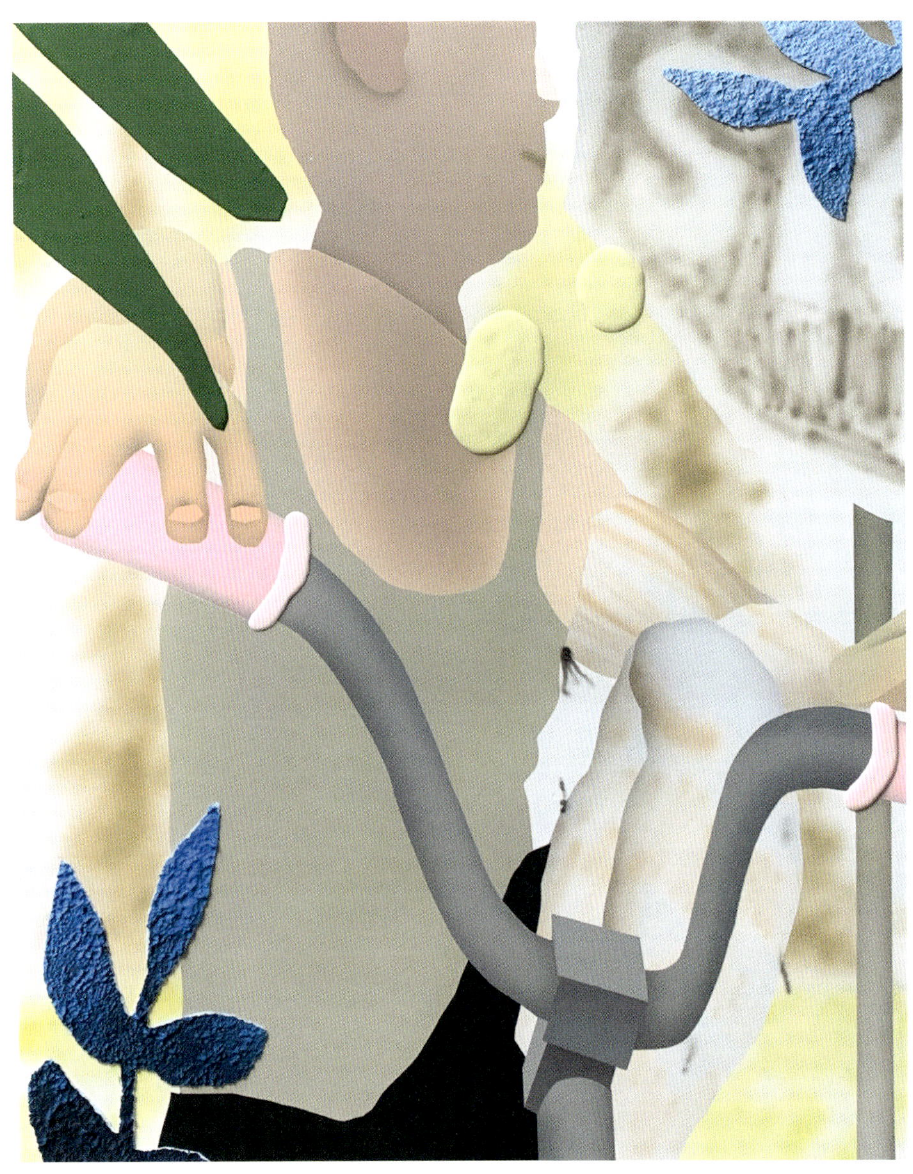

BIKER 2019 · 77 × 60 cm

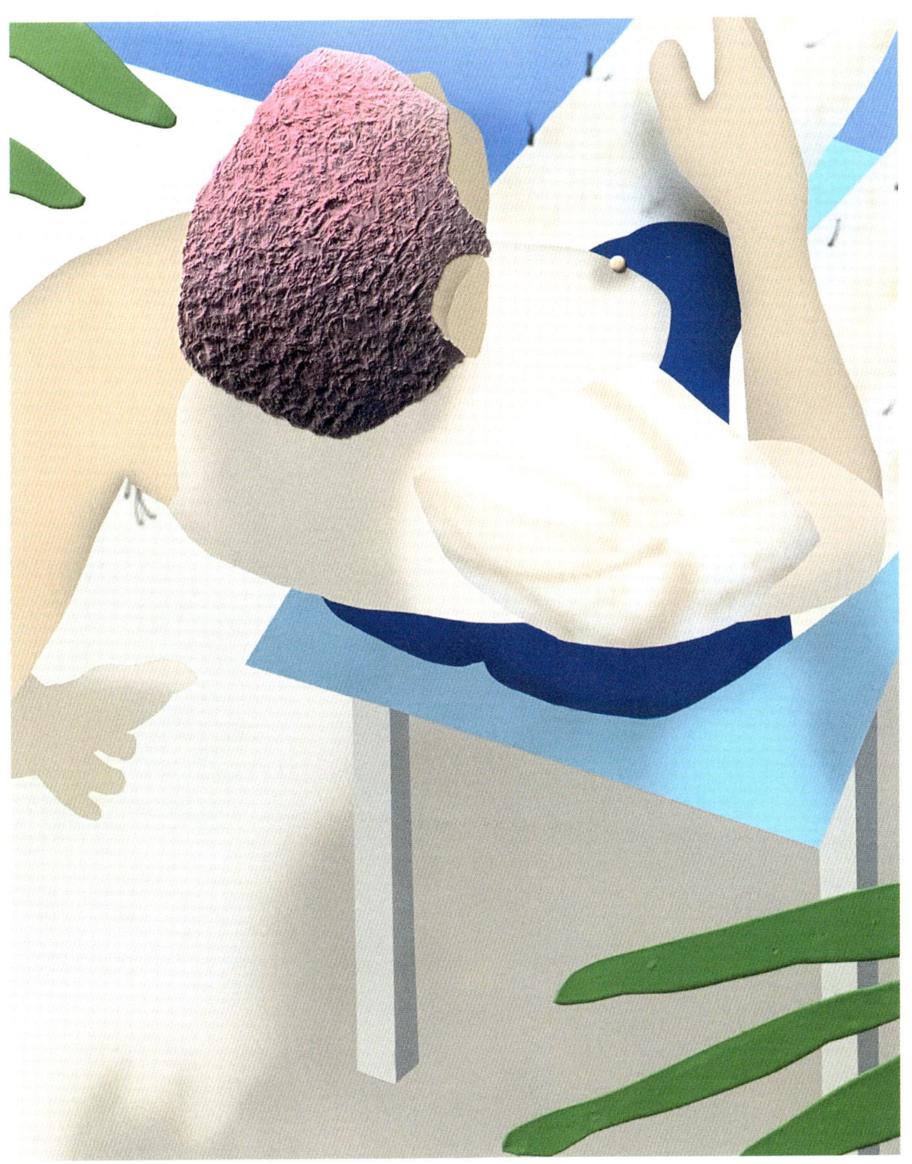

POOLSIDE 2019 · 75 × 60 cm

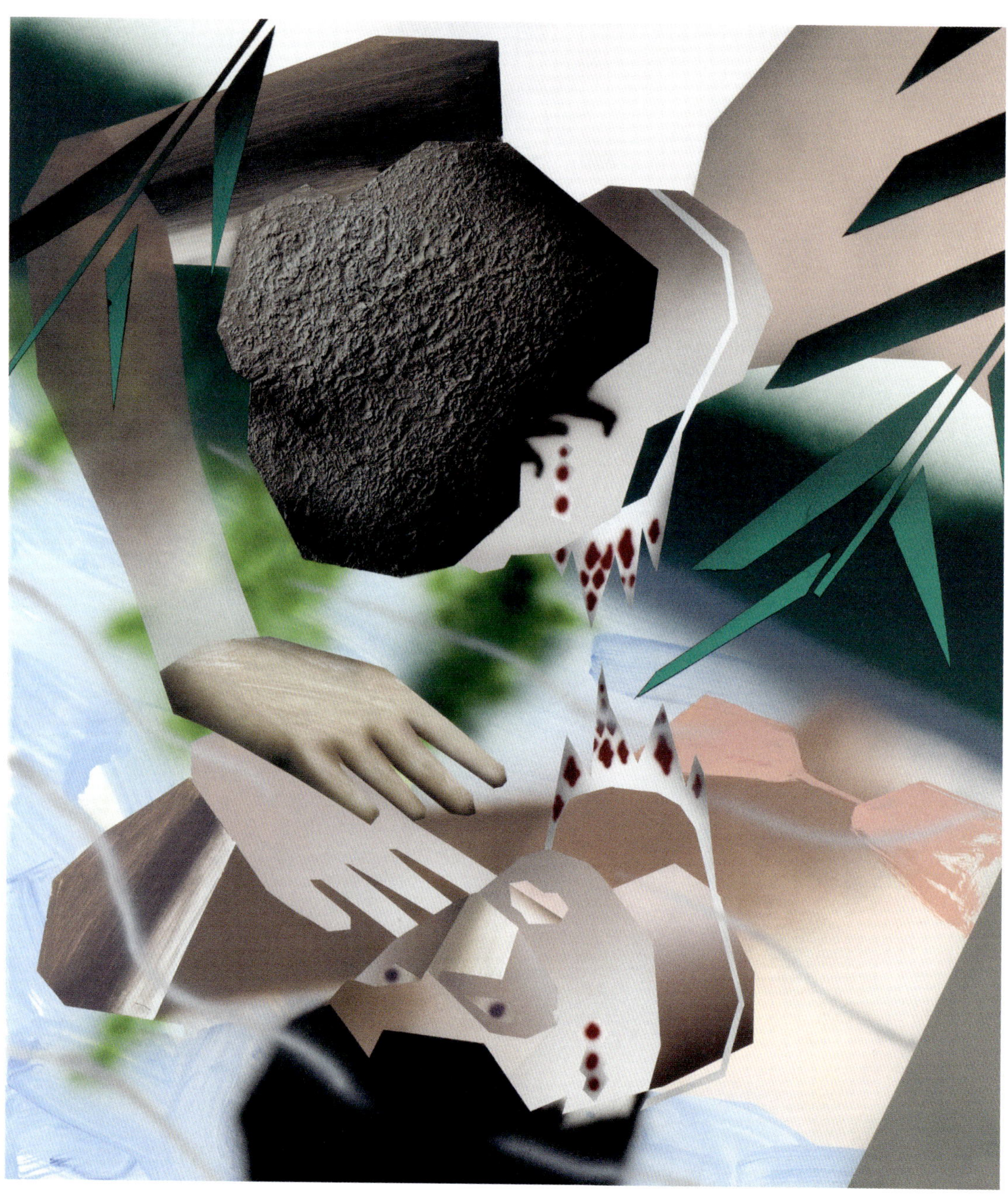

ELIZABETH TAYLOR'S REFLECTION 2021 · 120 × 100 cm

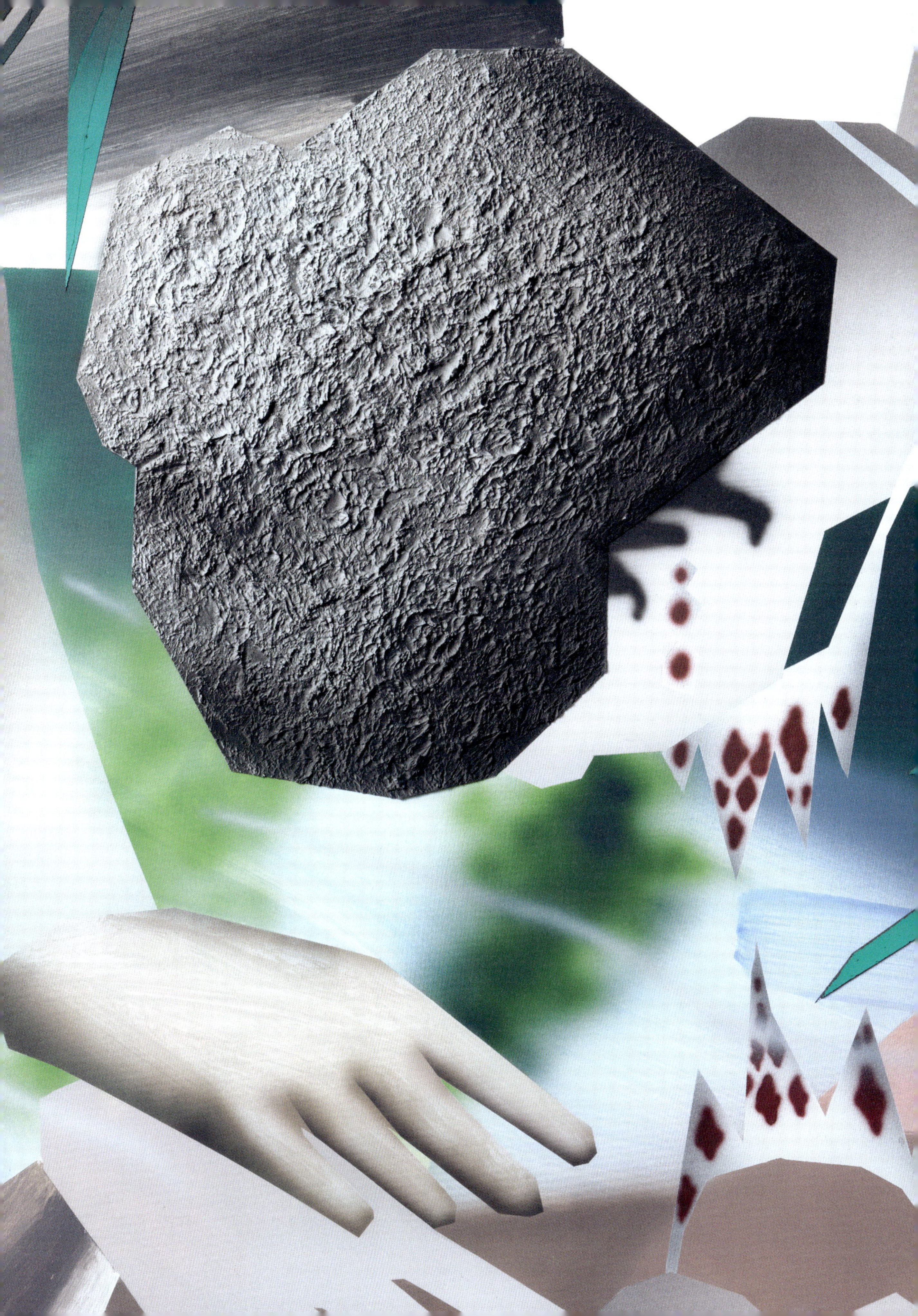

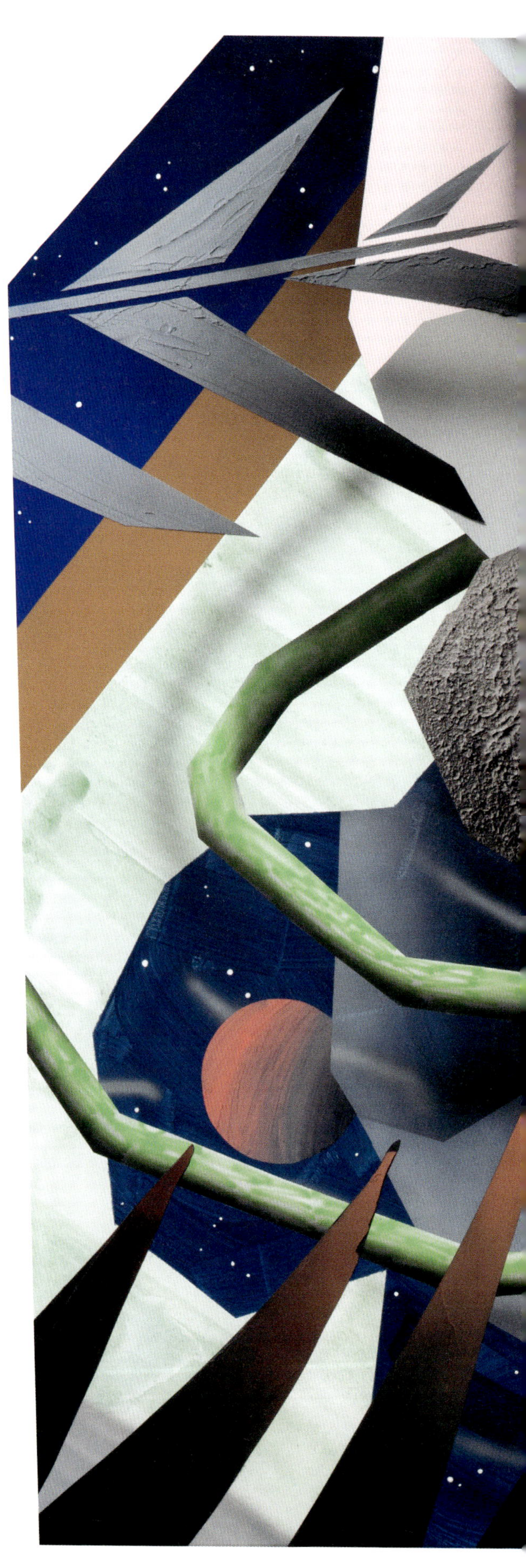

MOONGAZING WITH GARDEN HOSE
2021 · 195 × 219 cm

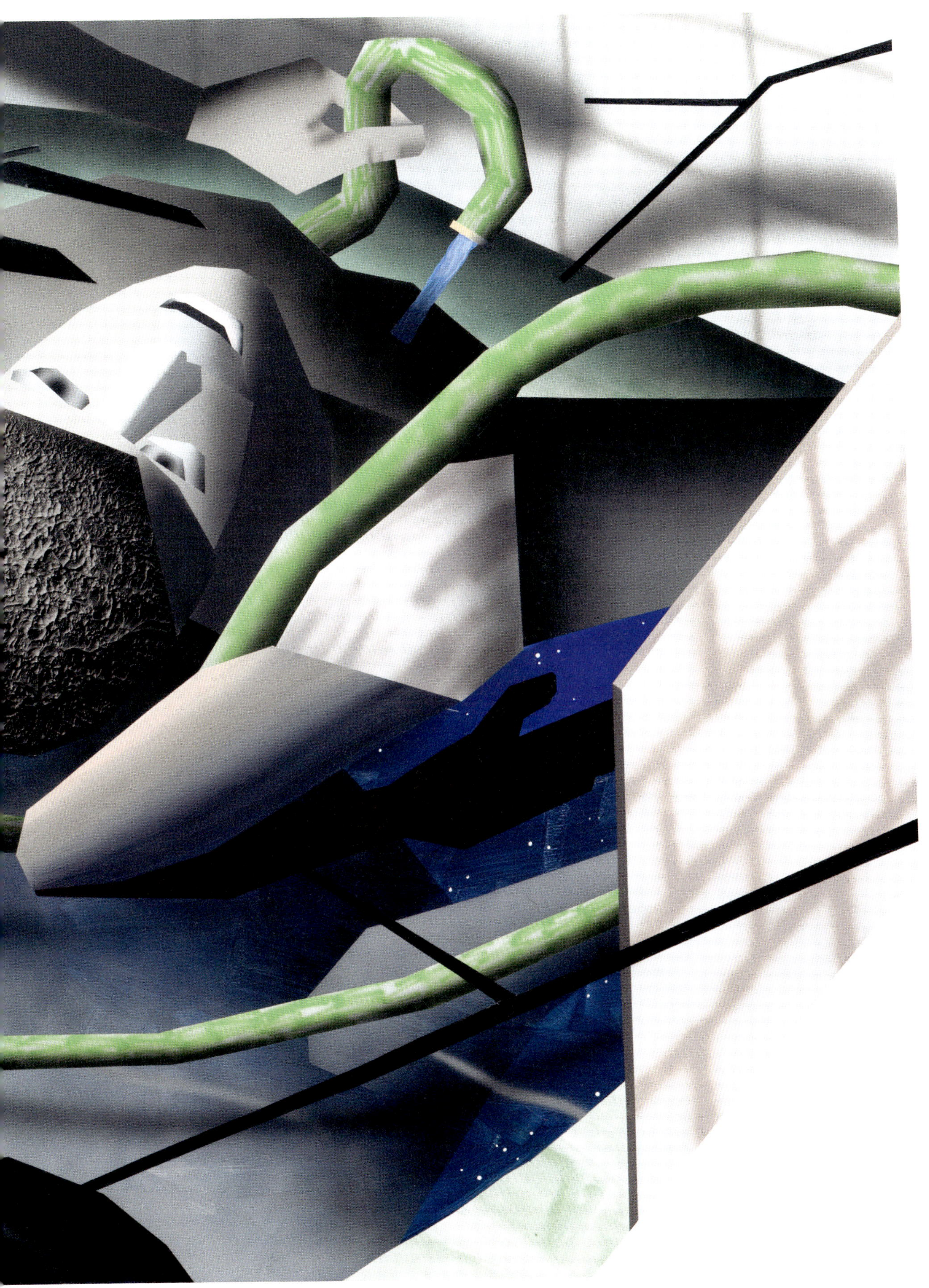

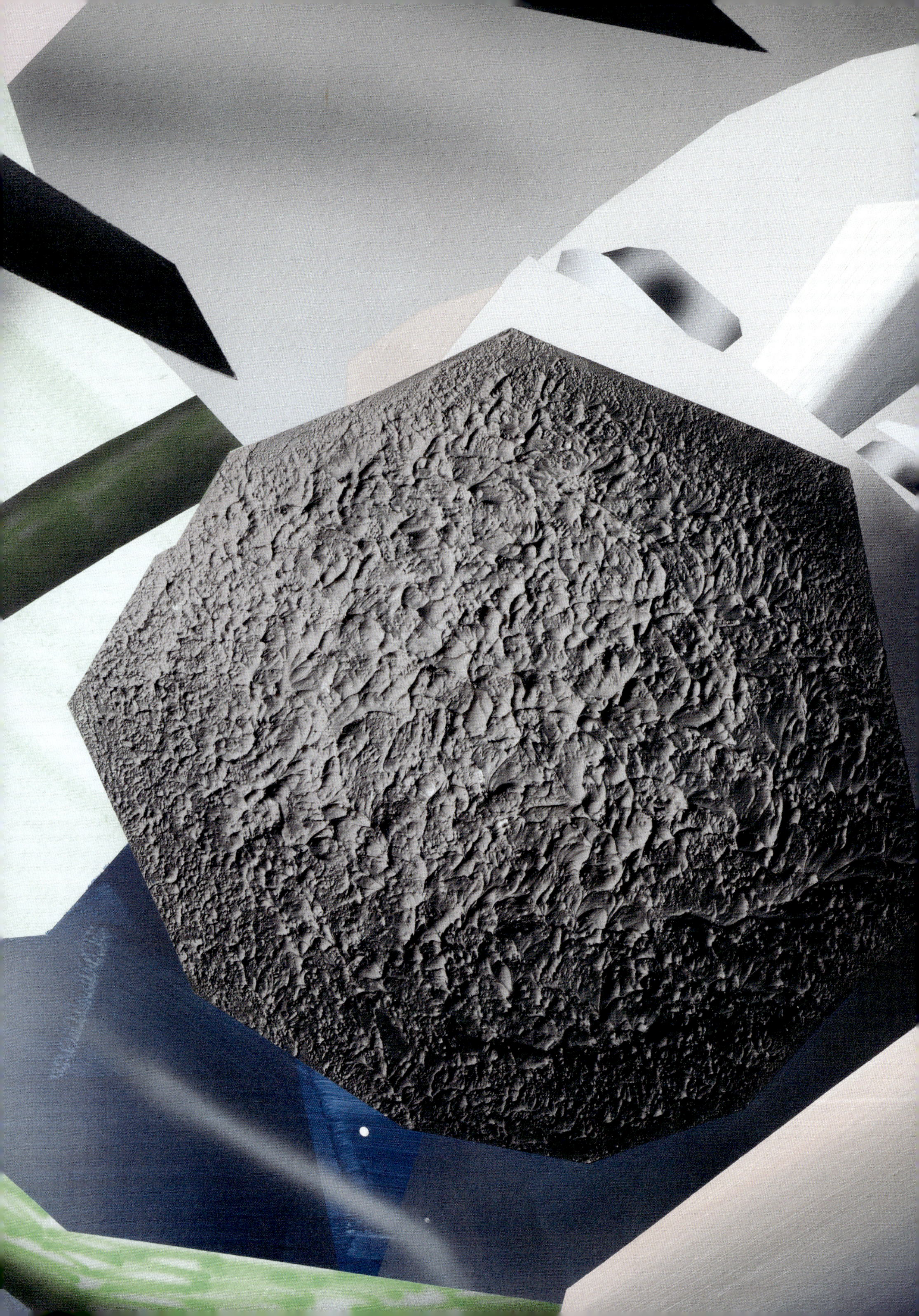

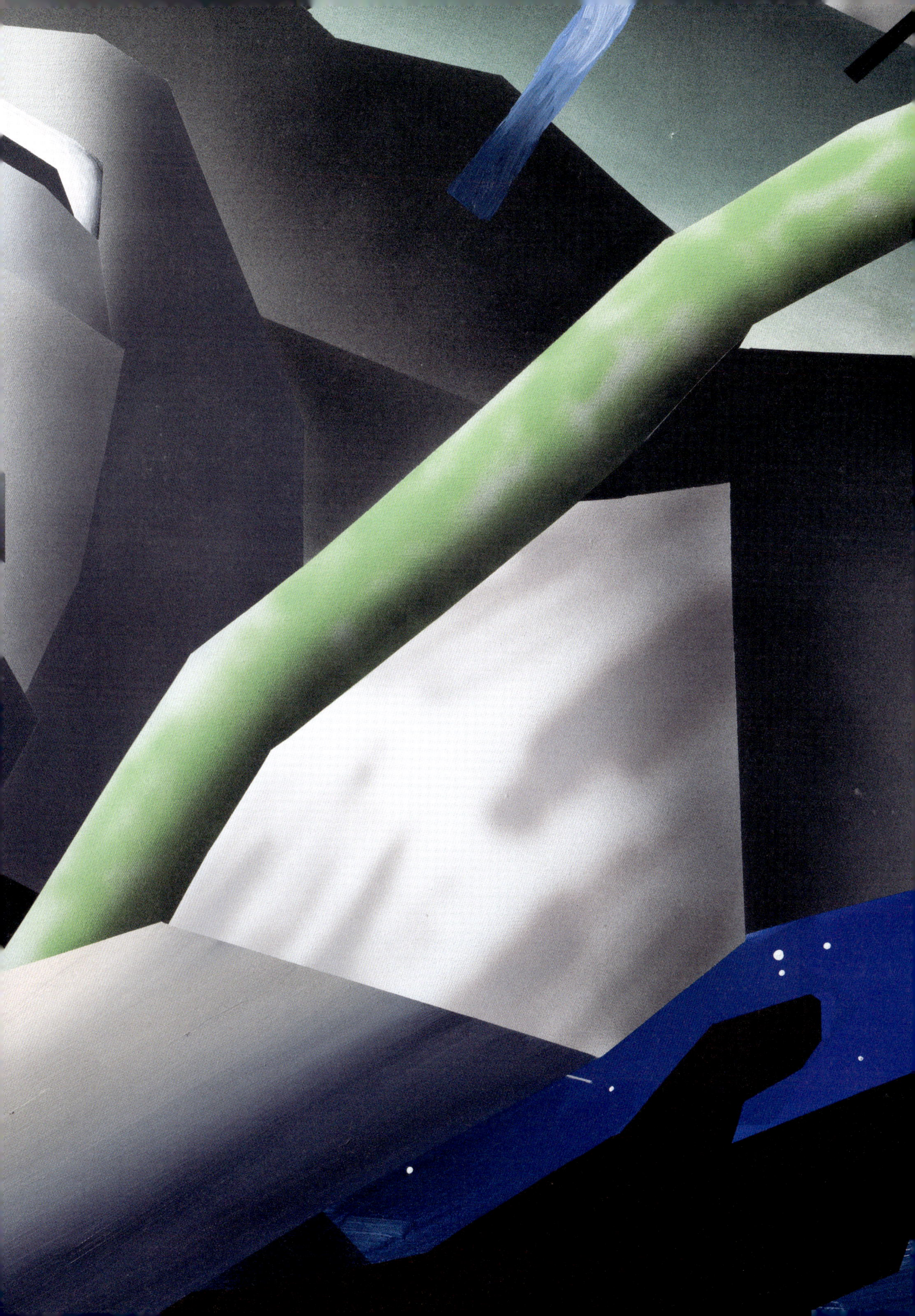

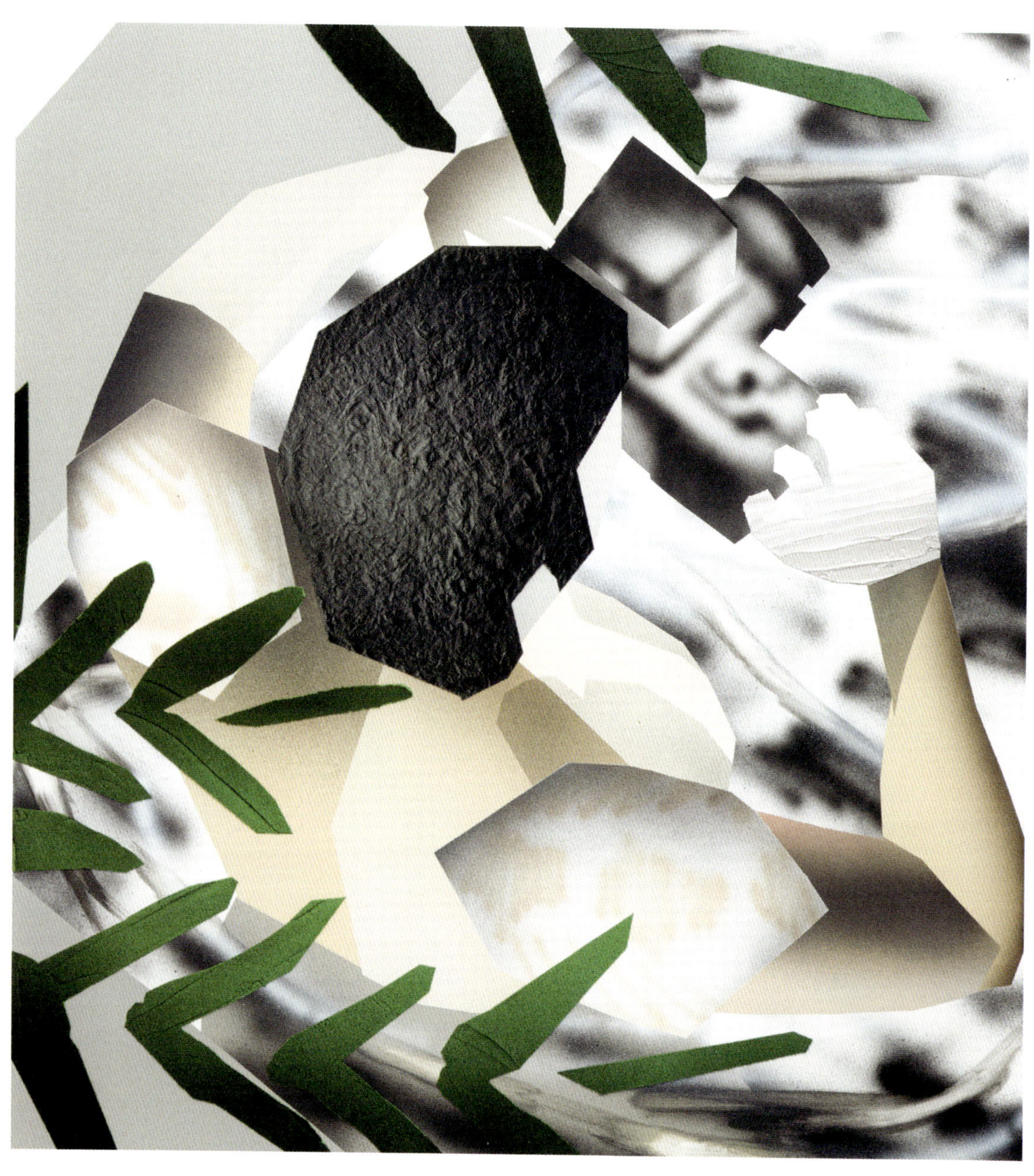

PHOTOGRAPHER IN DARK POOL 2020 · 74 × 80 cm

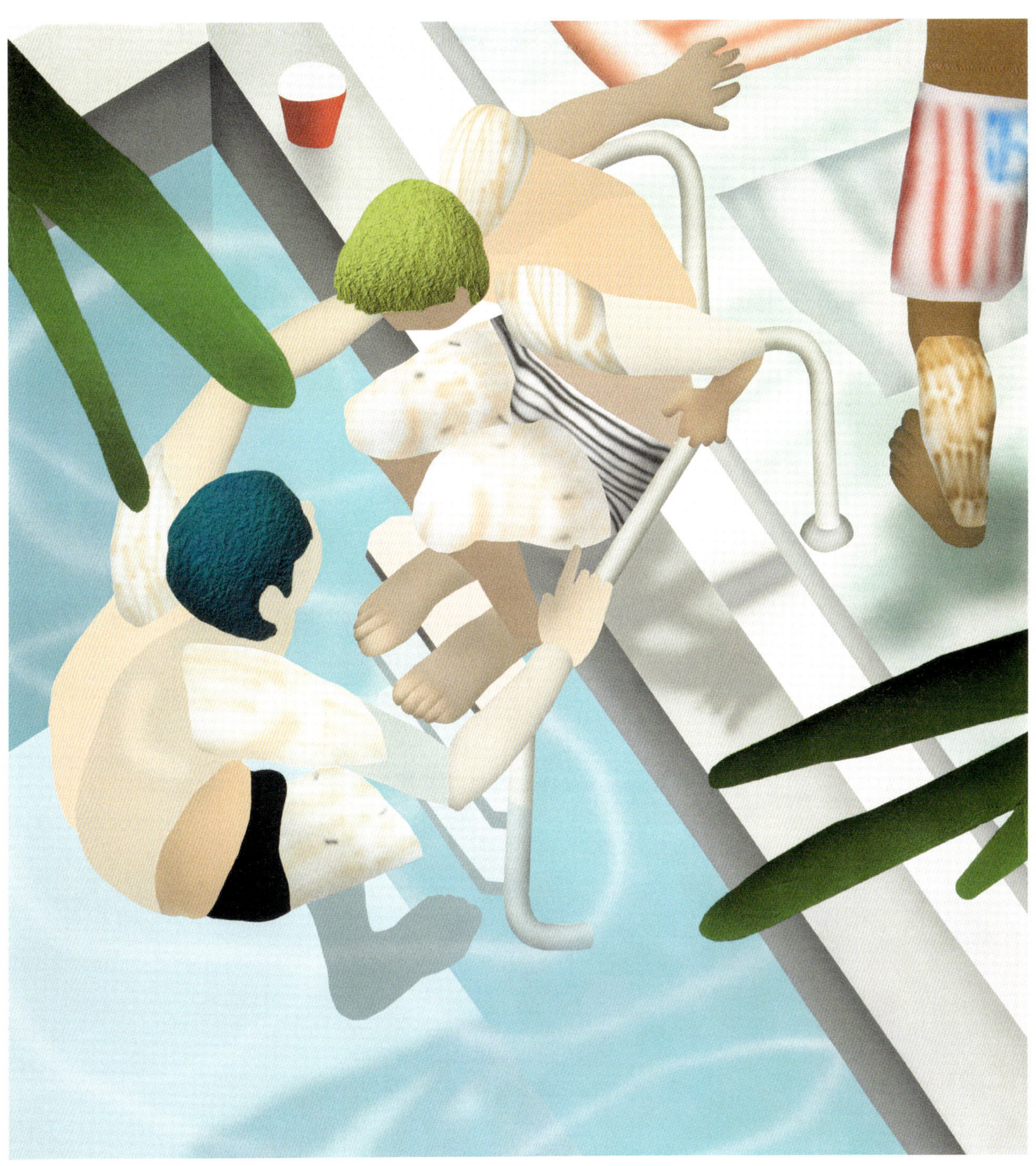

SWIMMING POOL 2020 · 200 × 185 cm

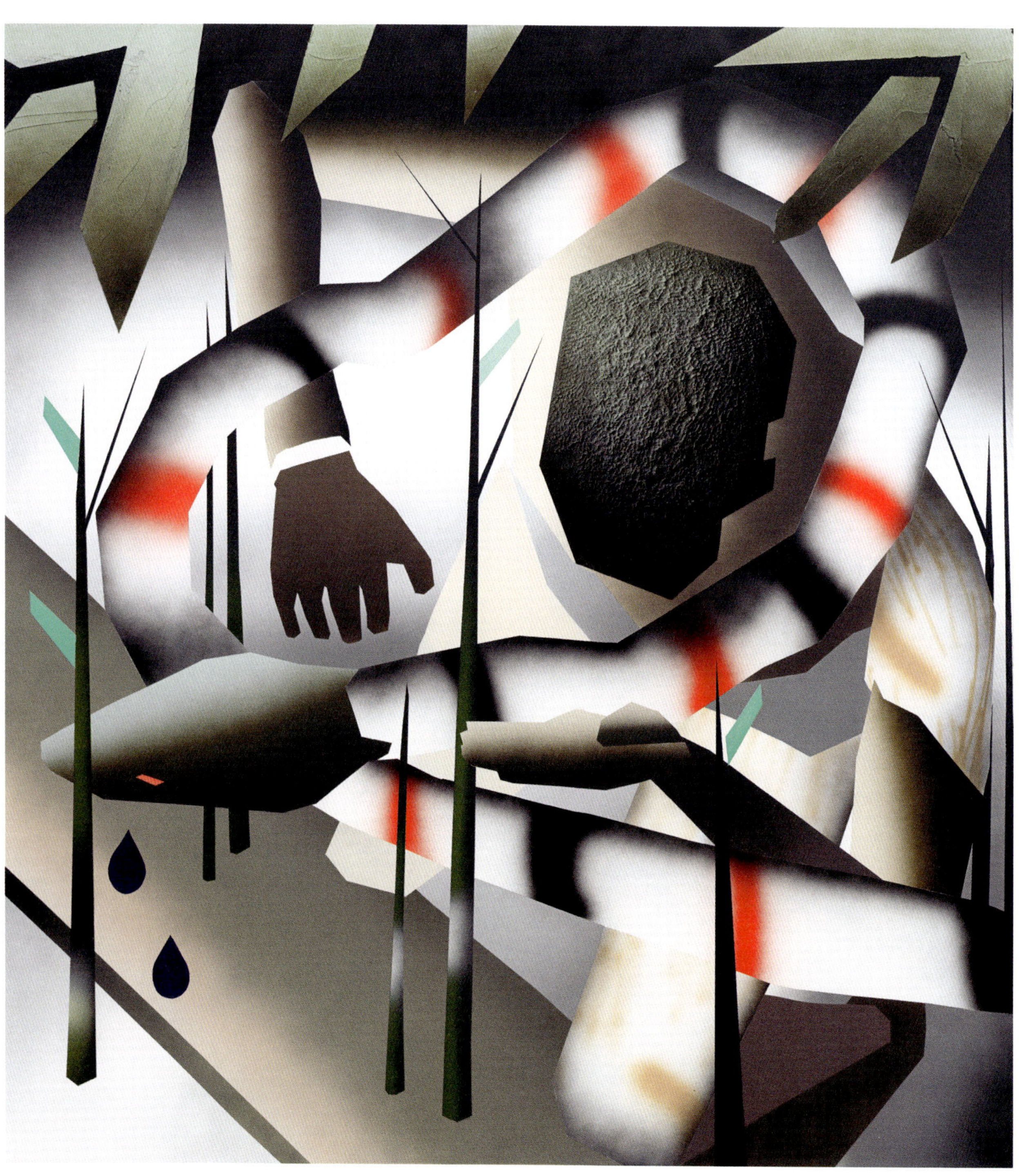

HOWLING SNAKE 2020 · 200 × 185 cm

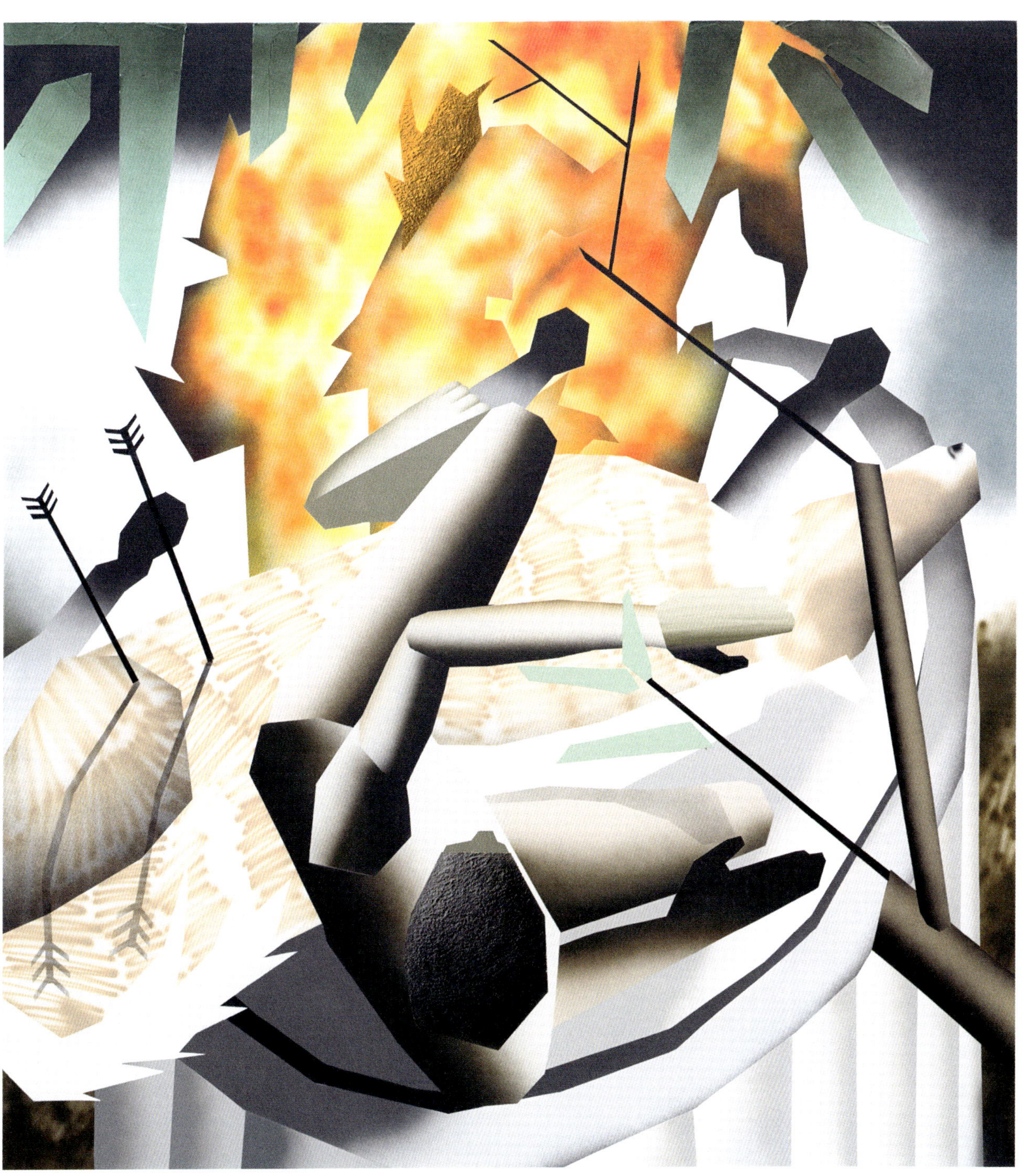

VISION OF MONUMENT AFLAME 2020 · 200 × 185 cm

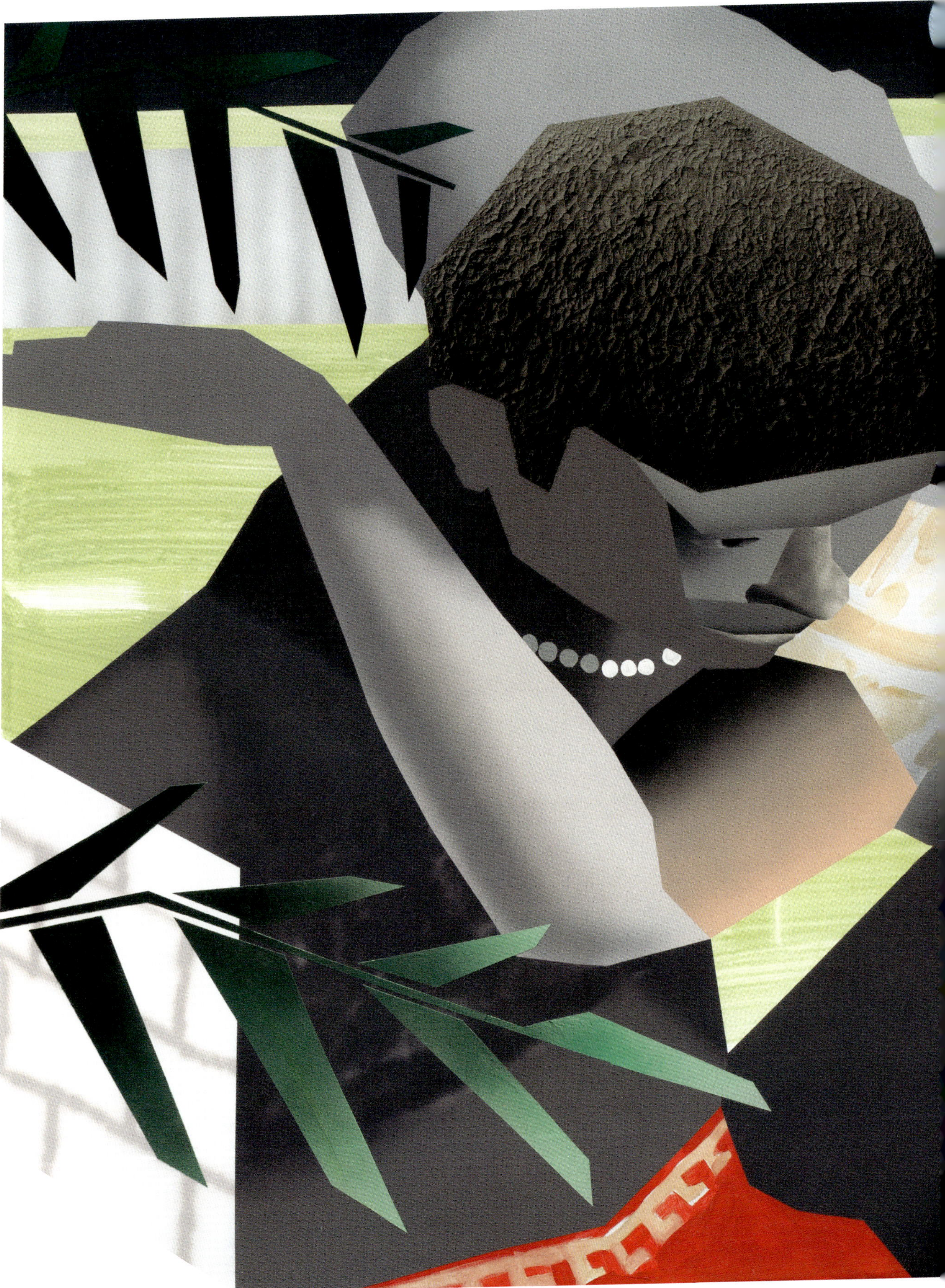

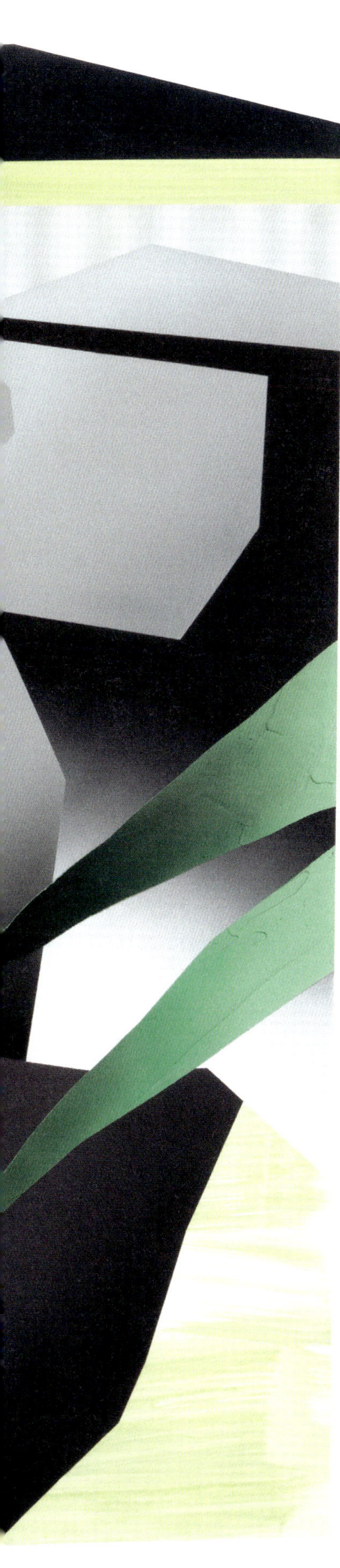

BOY WITH PEARL NECKLACE
2021 · 198,5 × 211 cm

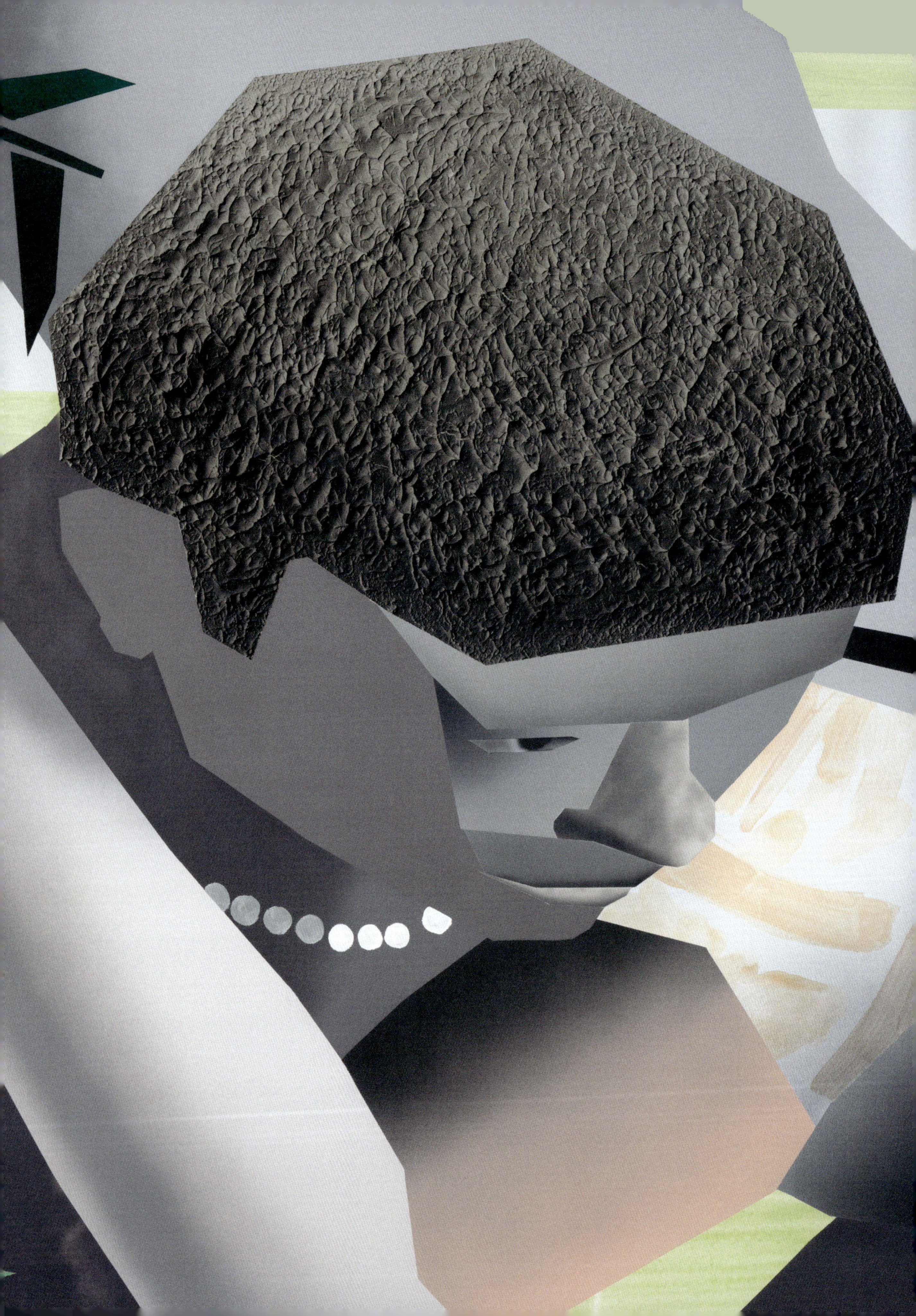

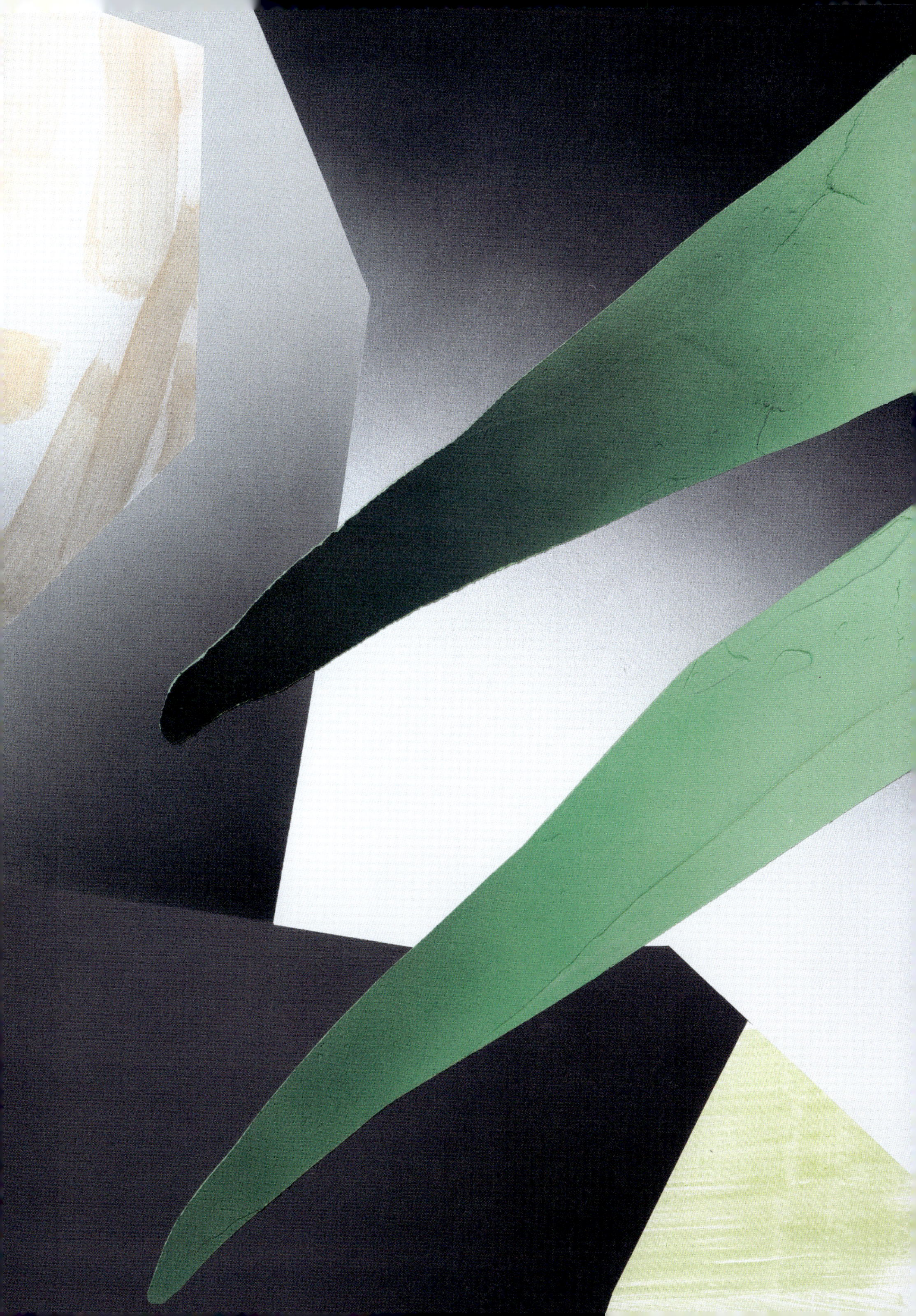

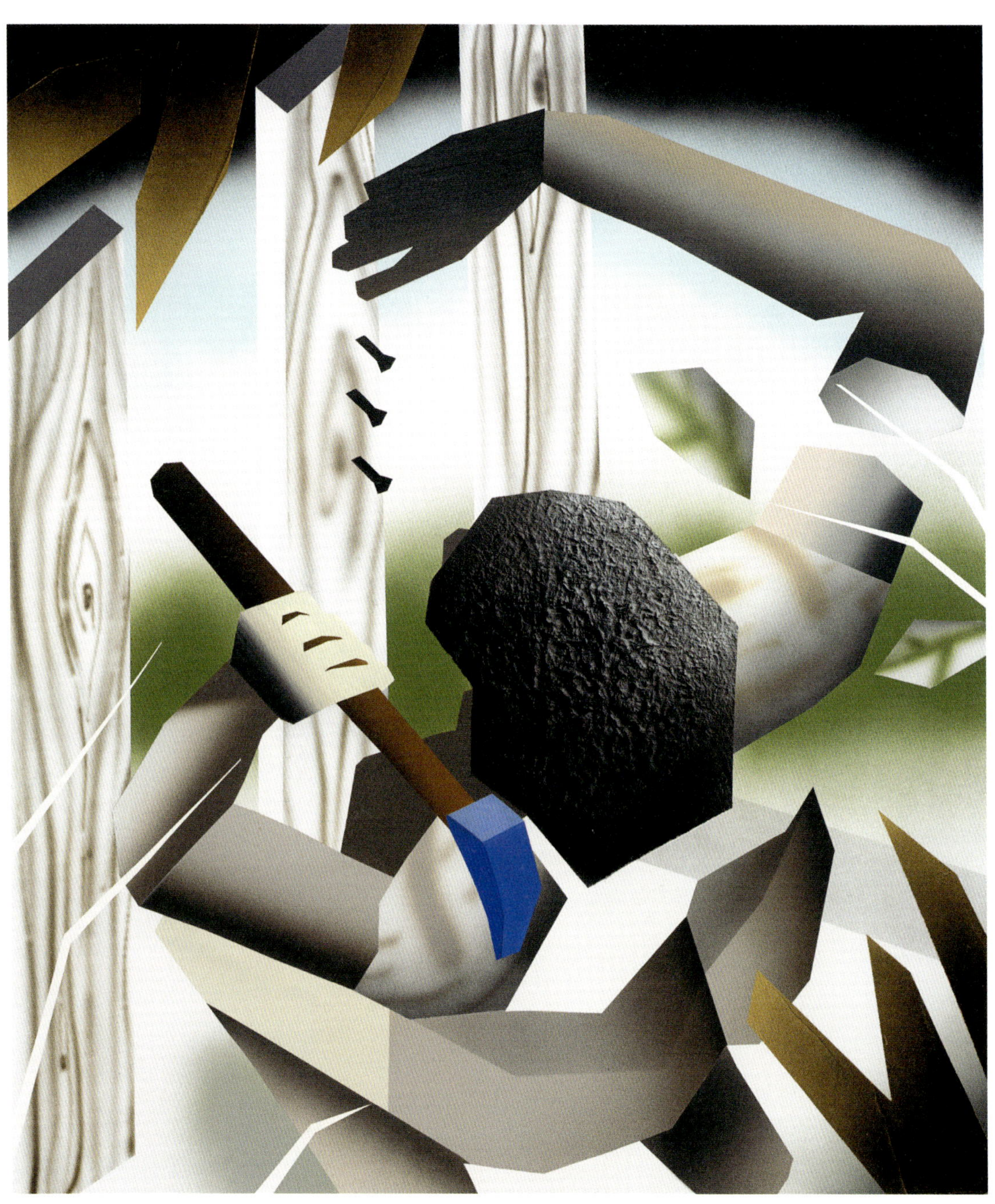

BUILDING ROOMS YET TO COME 2020 · 107 × 122 cm

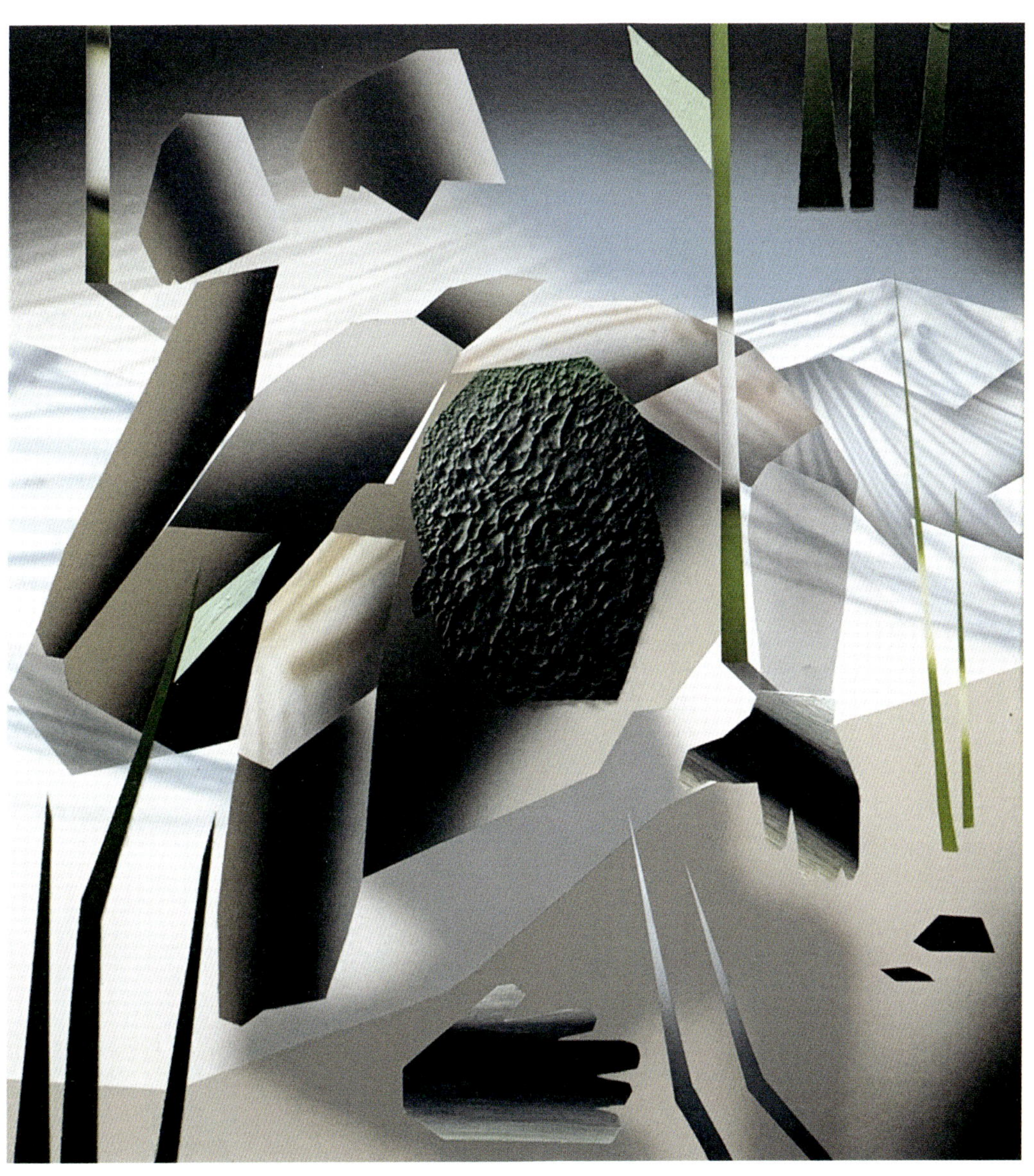

GROWTH IN POND WATERS 2020 · 60 × 65 cm

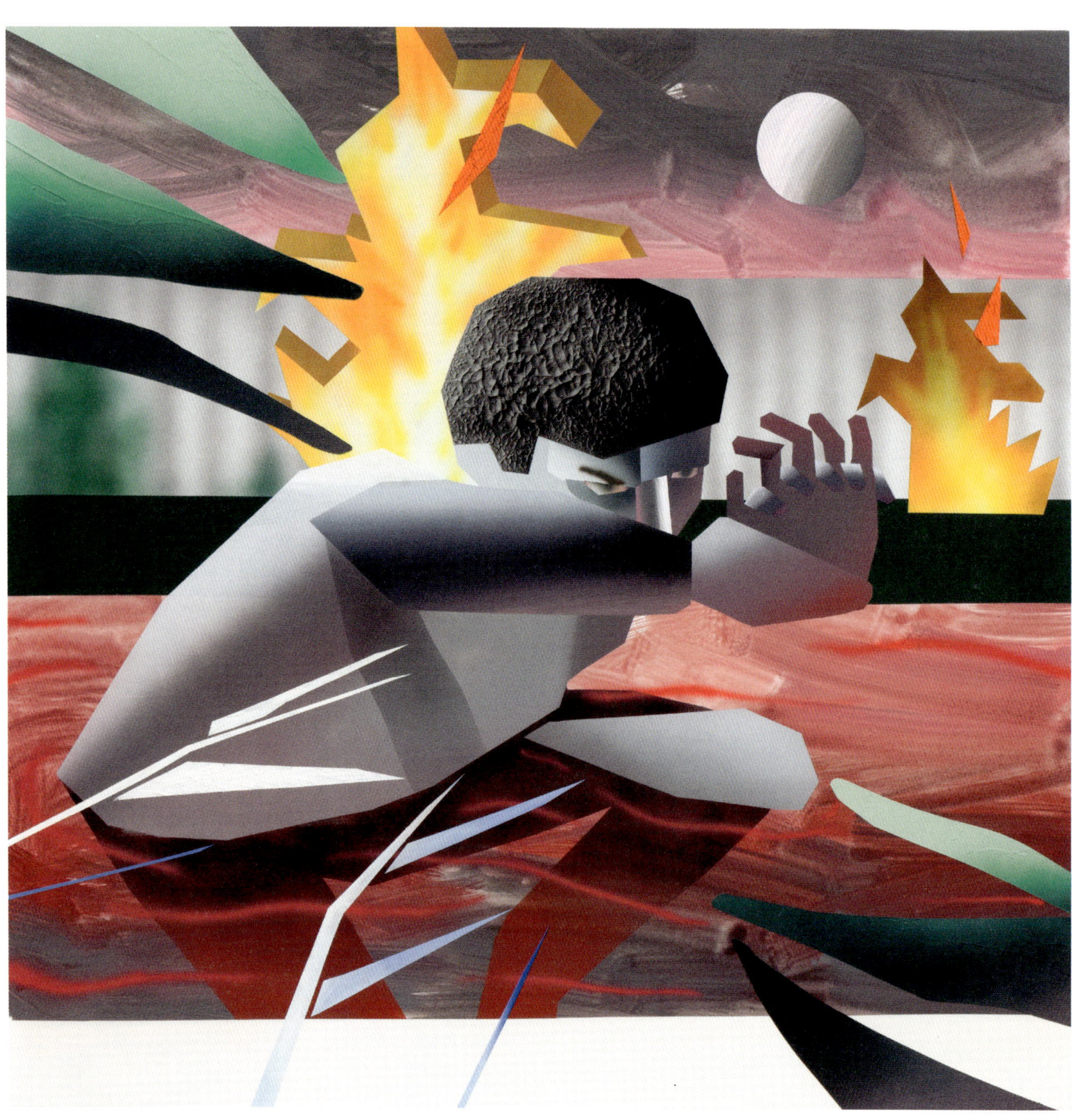

FALLEN ANGEL 2021 · 197 × 200 cm

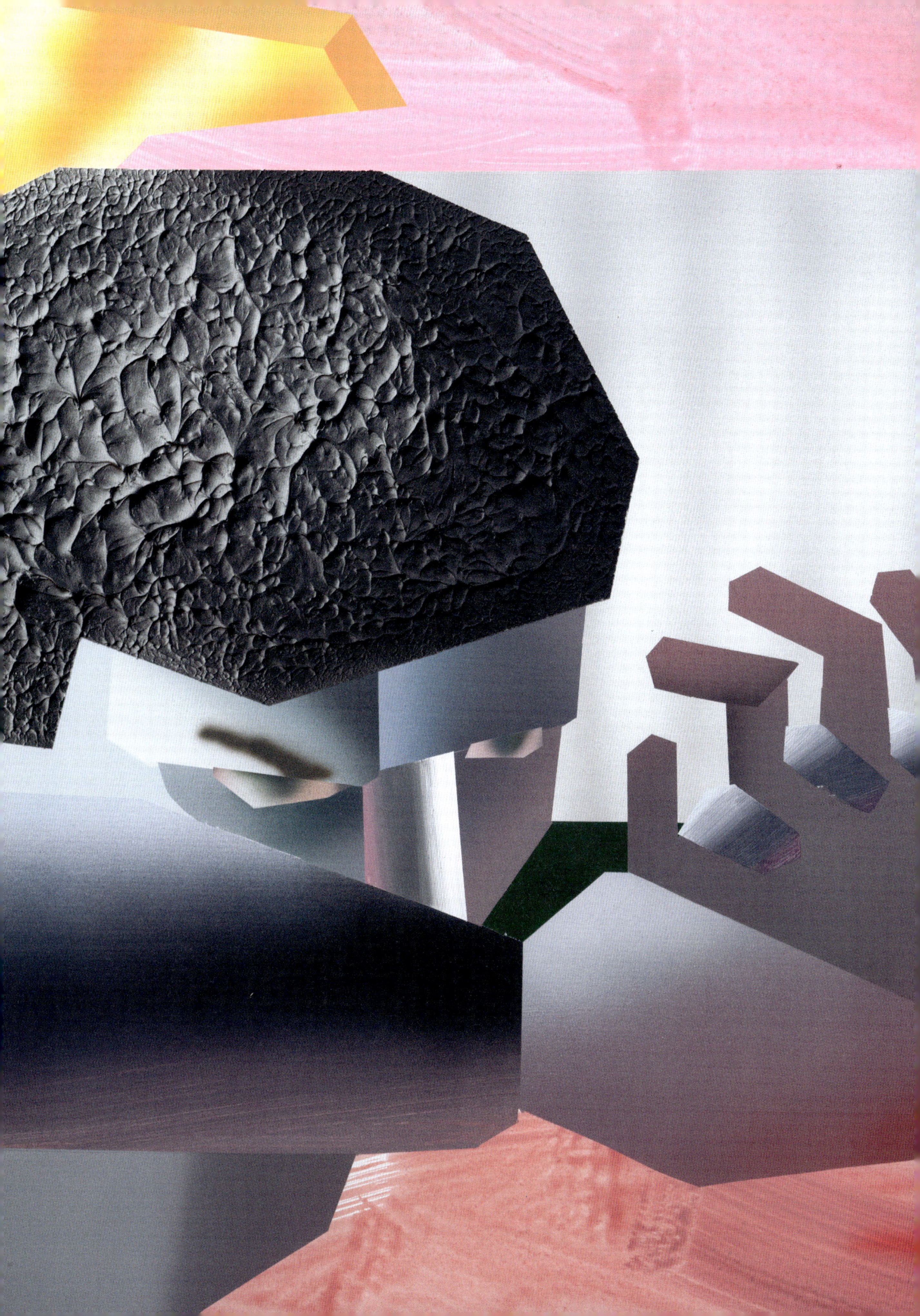

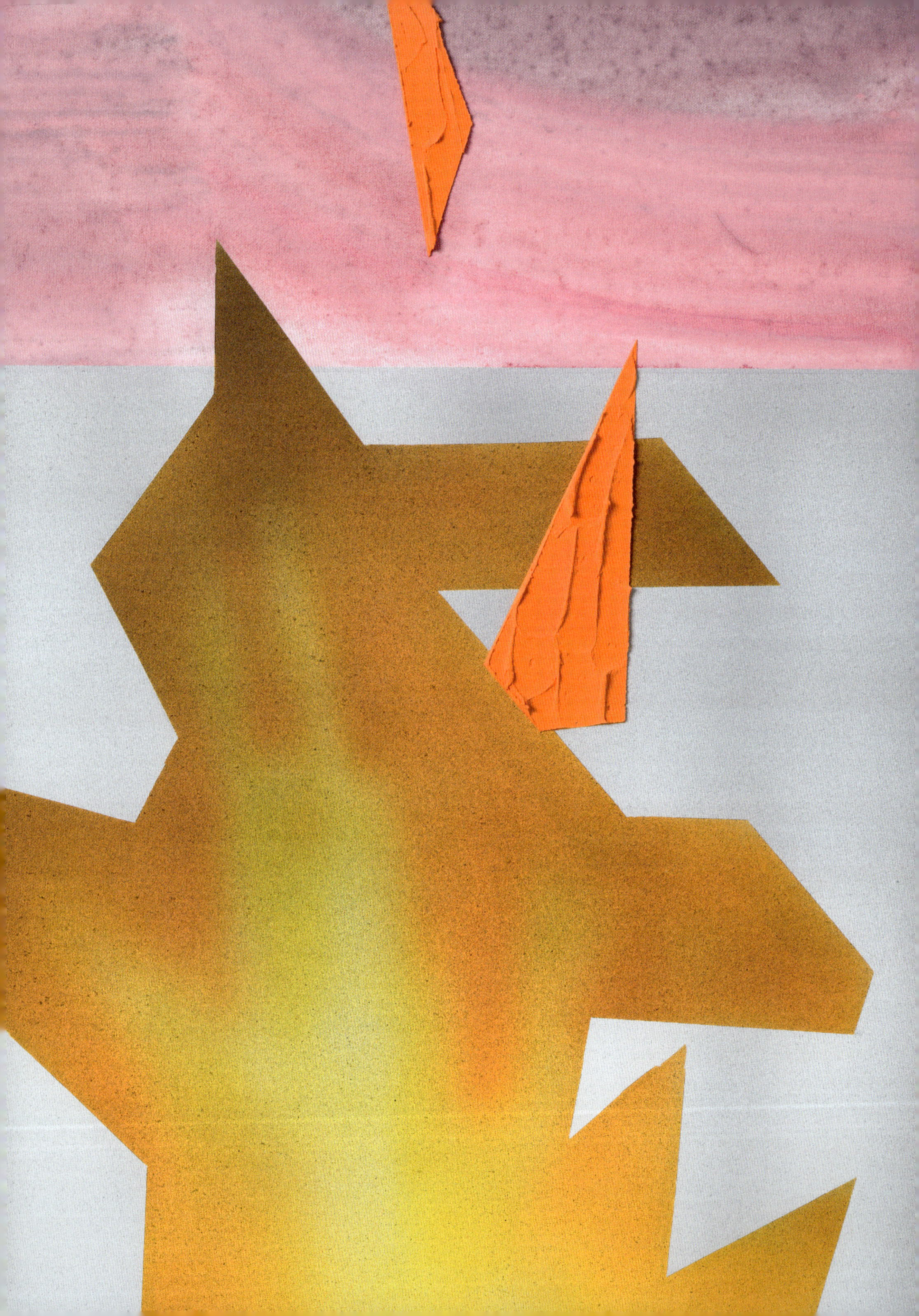

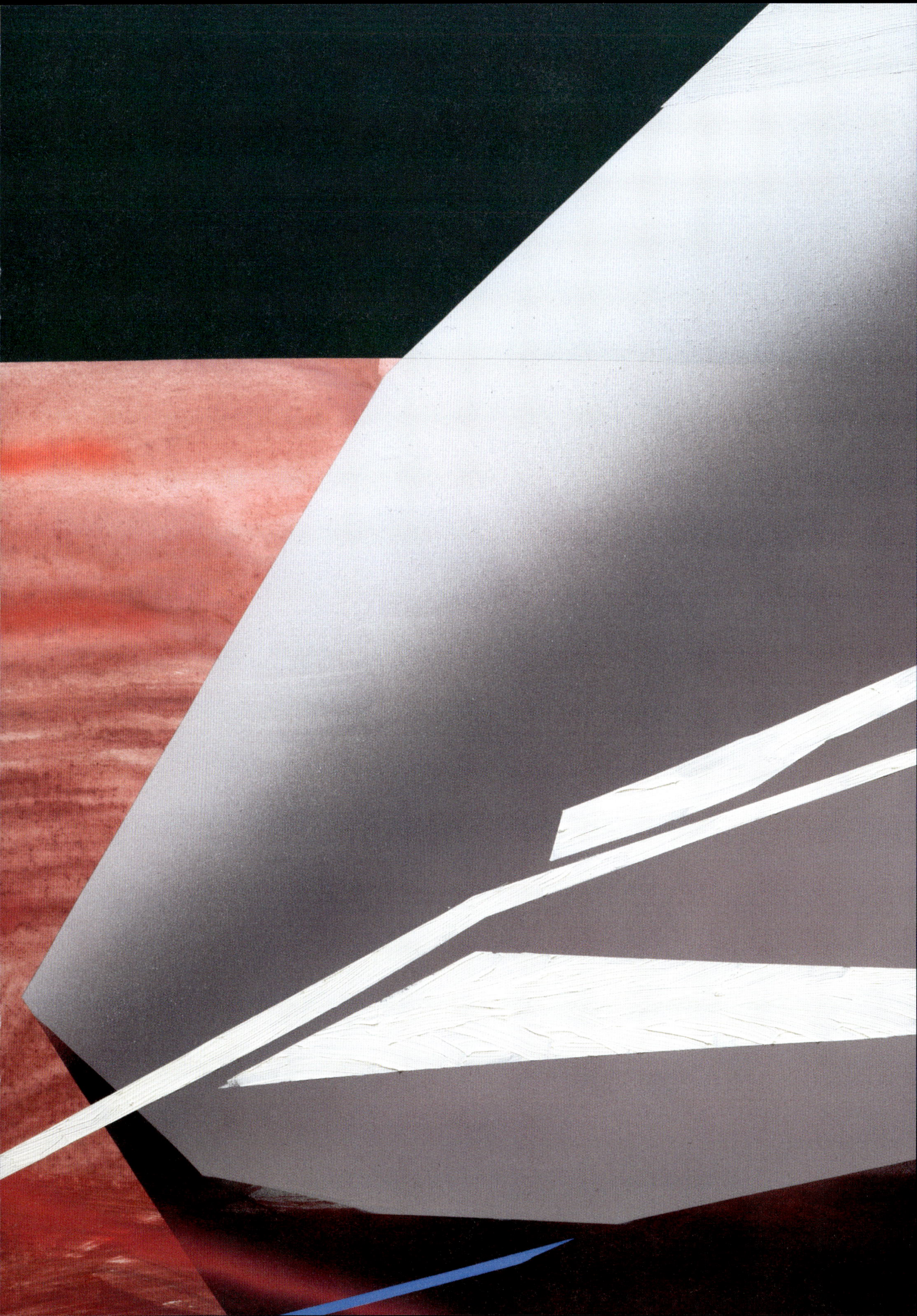

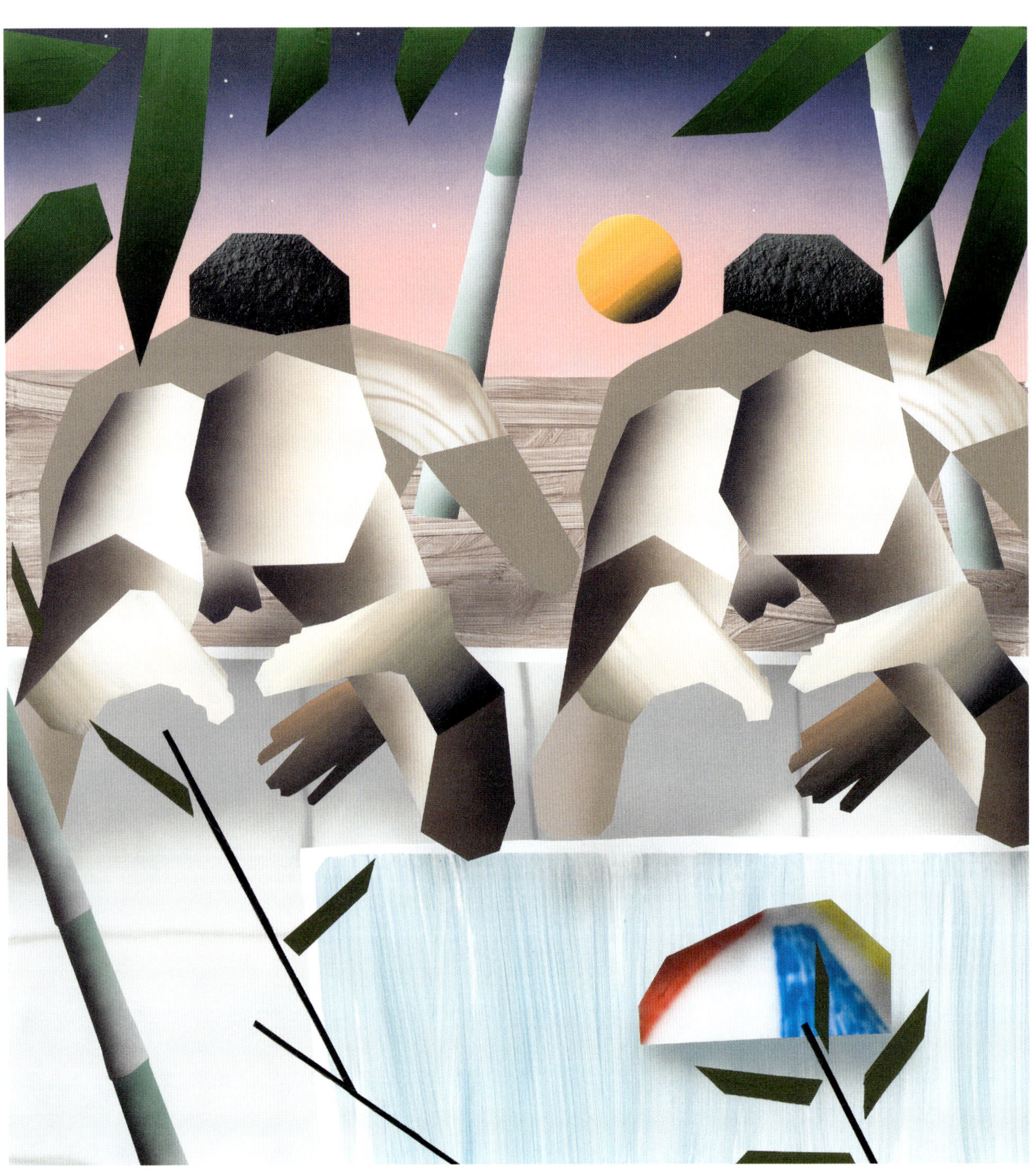

MOONRISE 2021 · 200 × 180 cm

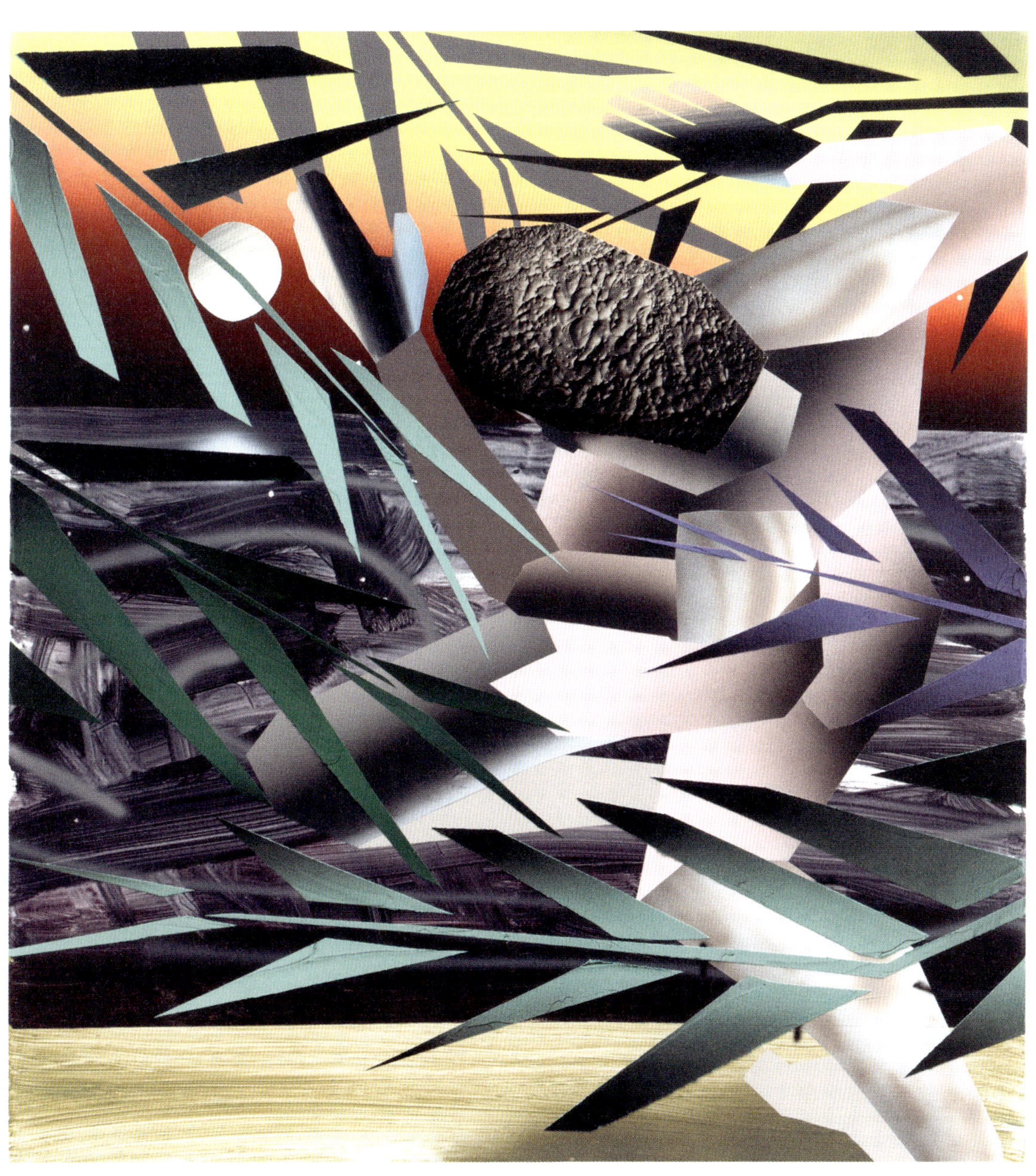

MOONLIT LAKE 2020 · 90 × 83 cm

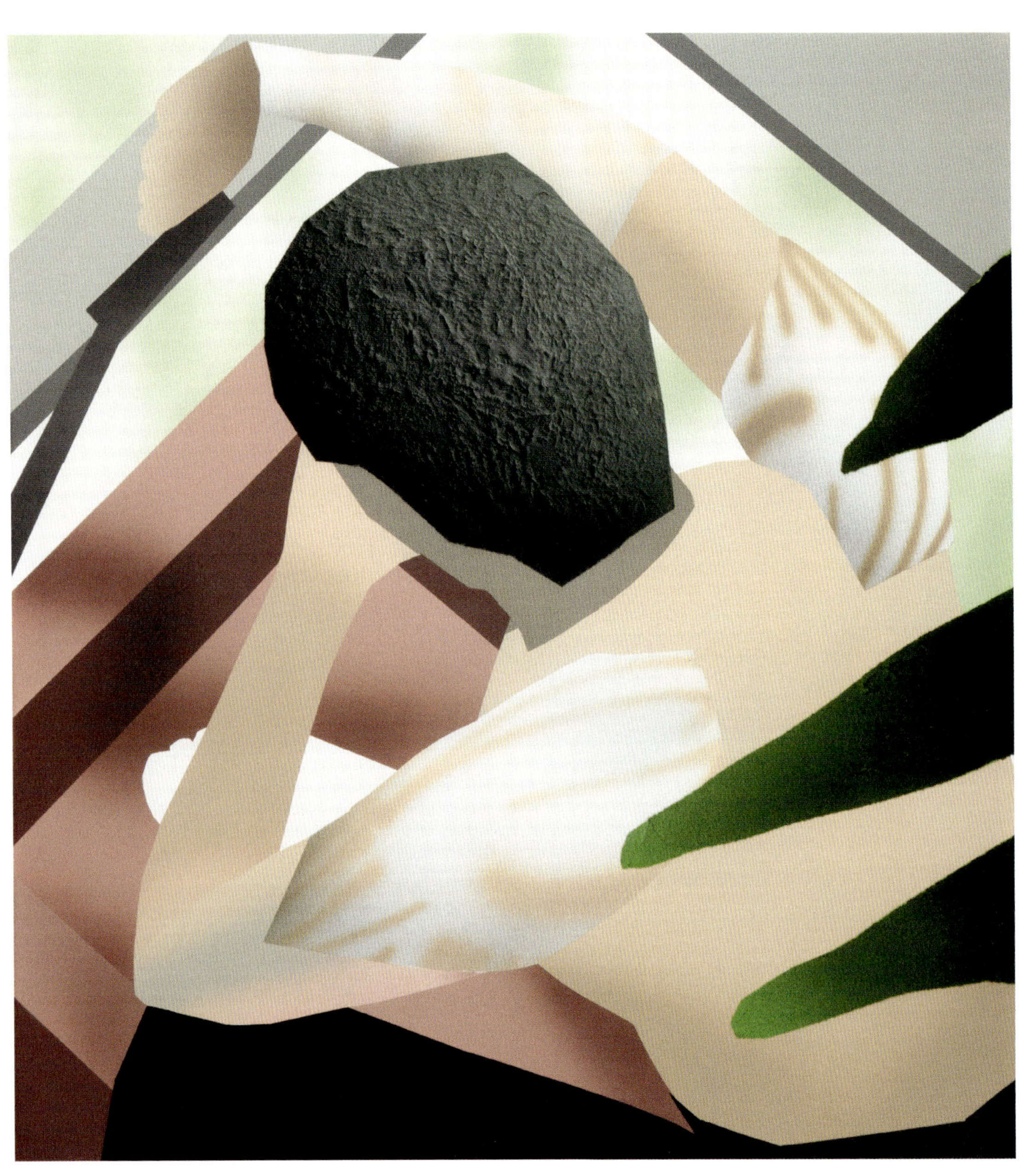

RED WAGON 2020 · 80 × 74 cm

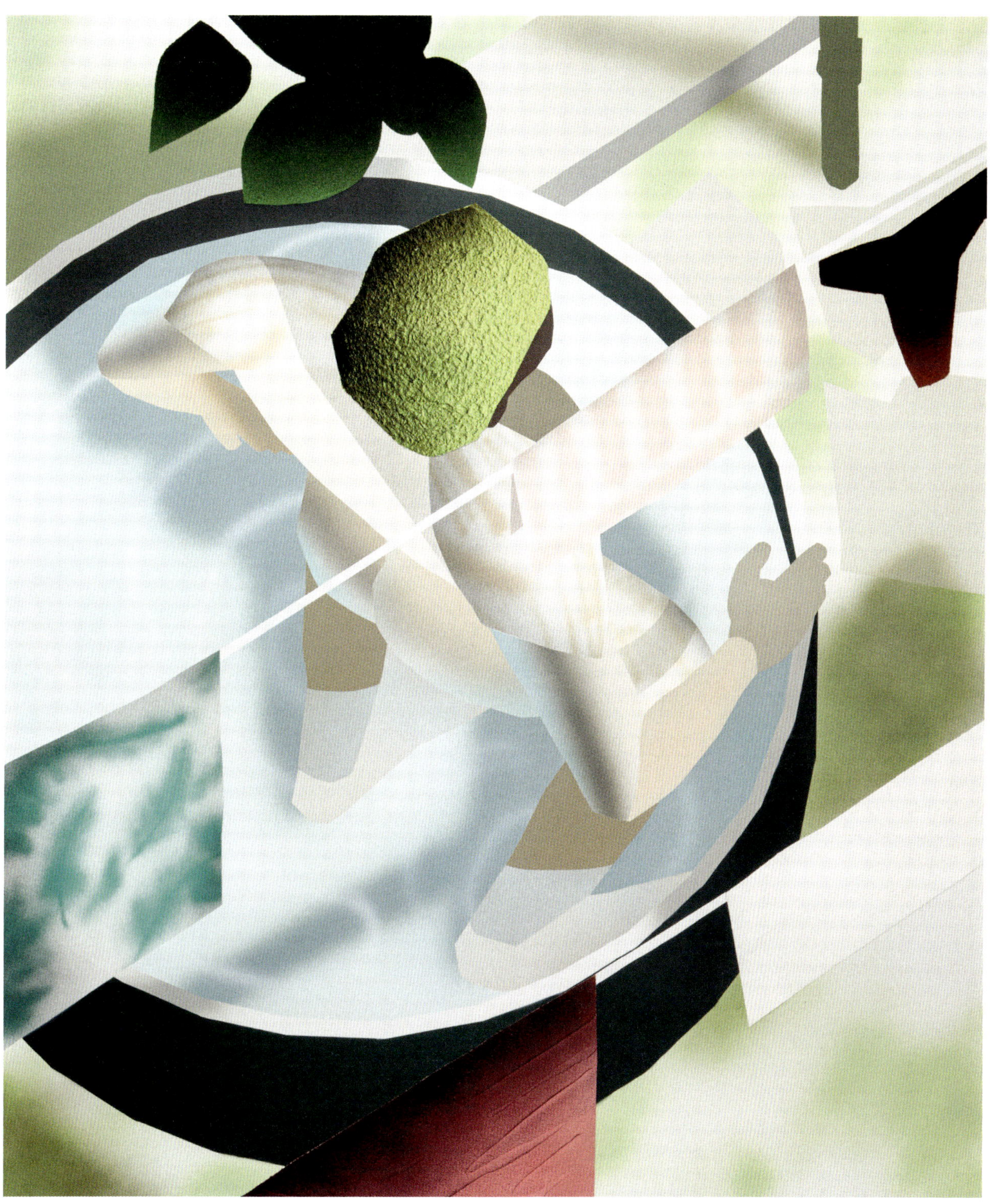

WASH LINE 2020 · 180 × 150 cm

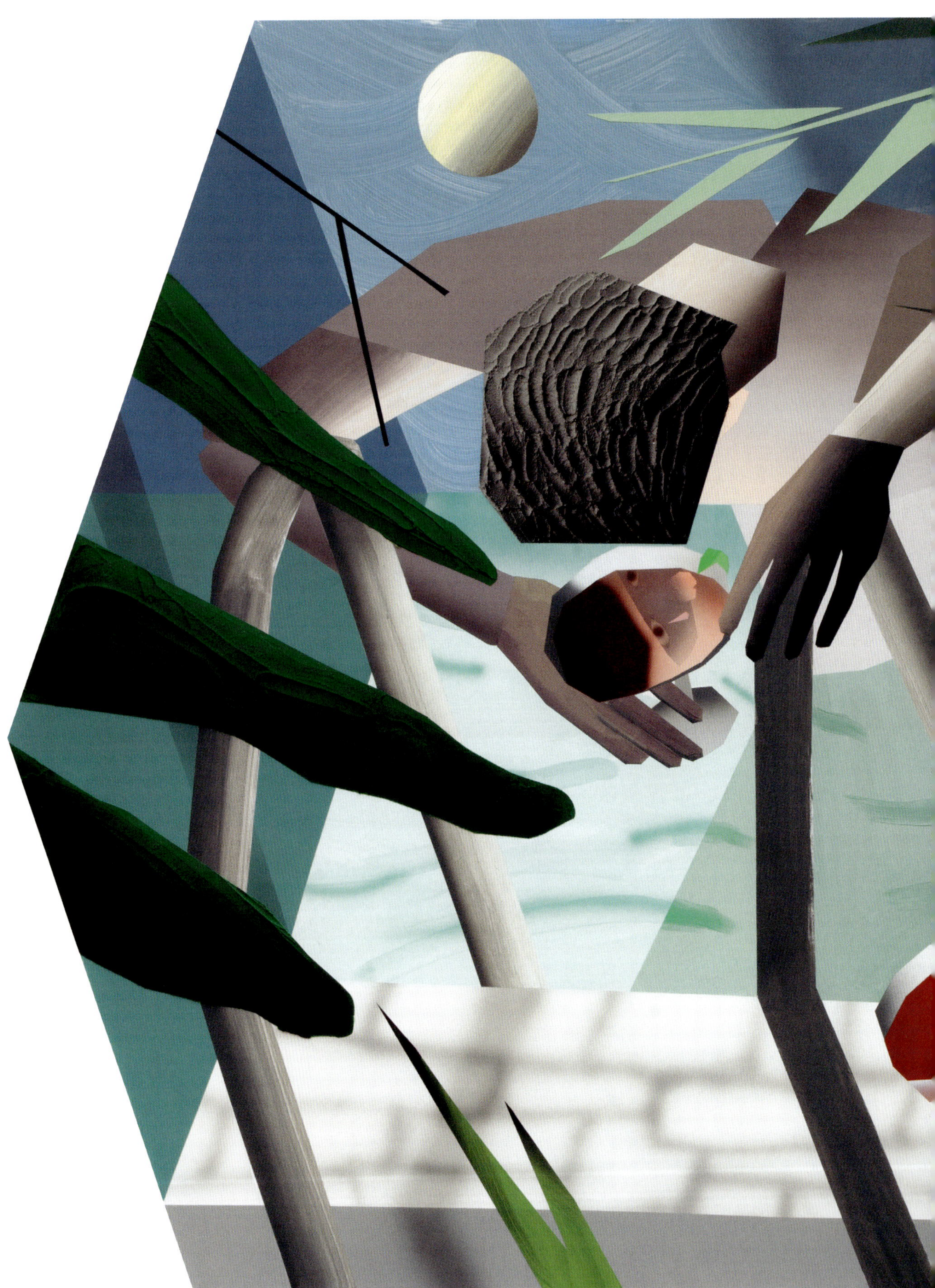

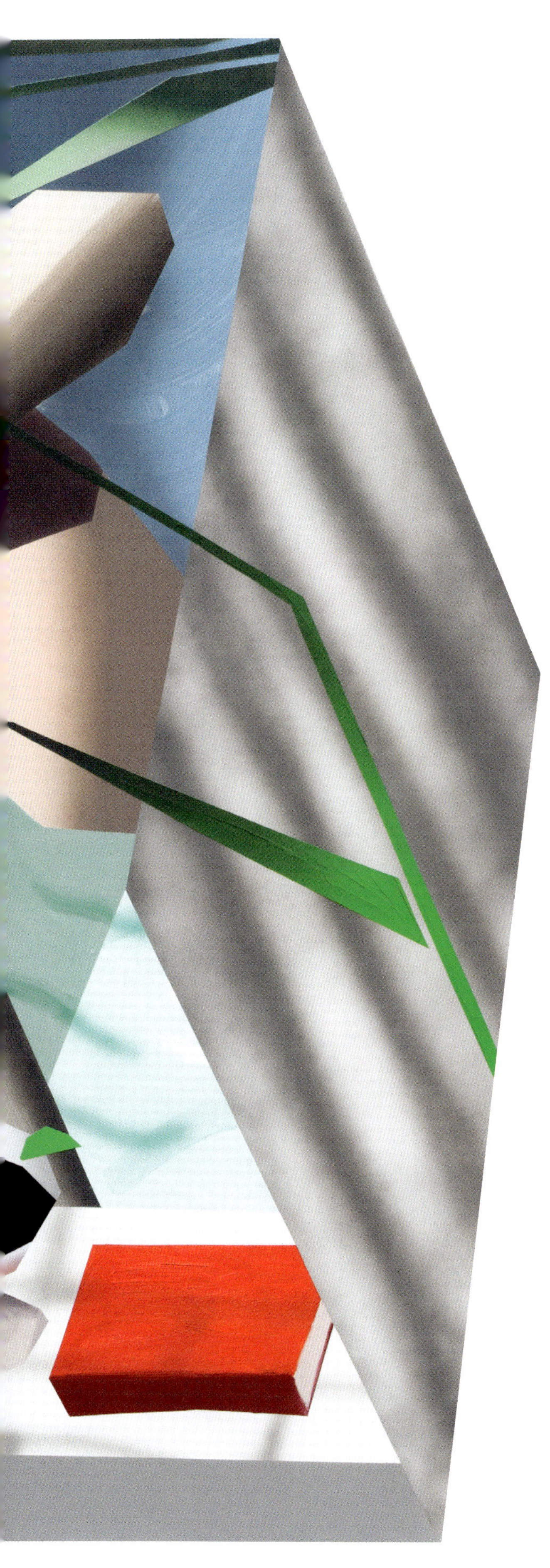

POOLSIDE COCKTAIL
2021 · 183,5 × 218 cm

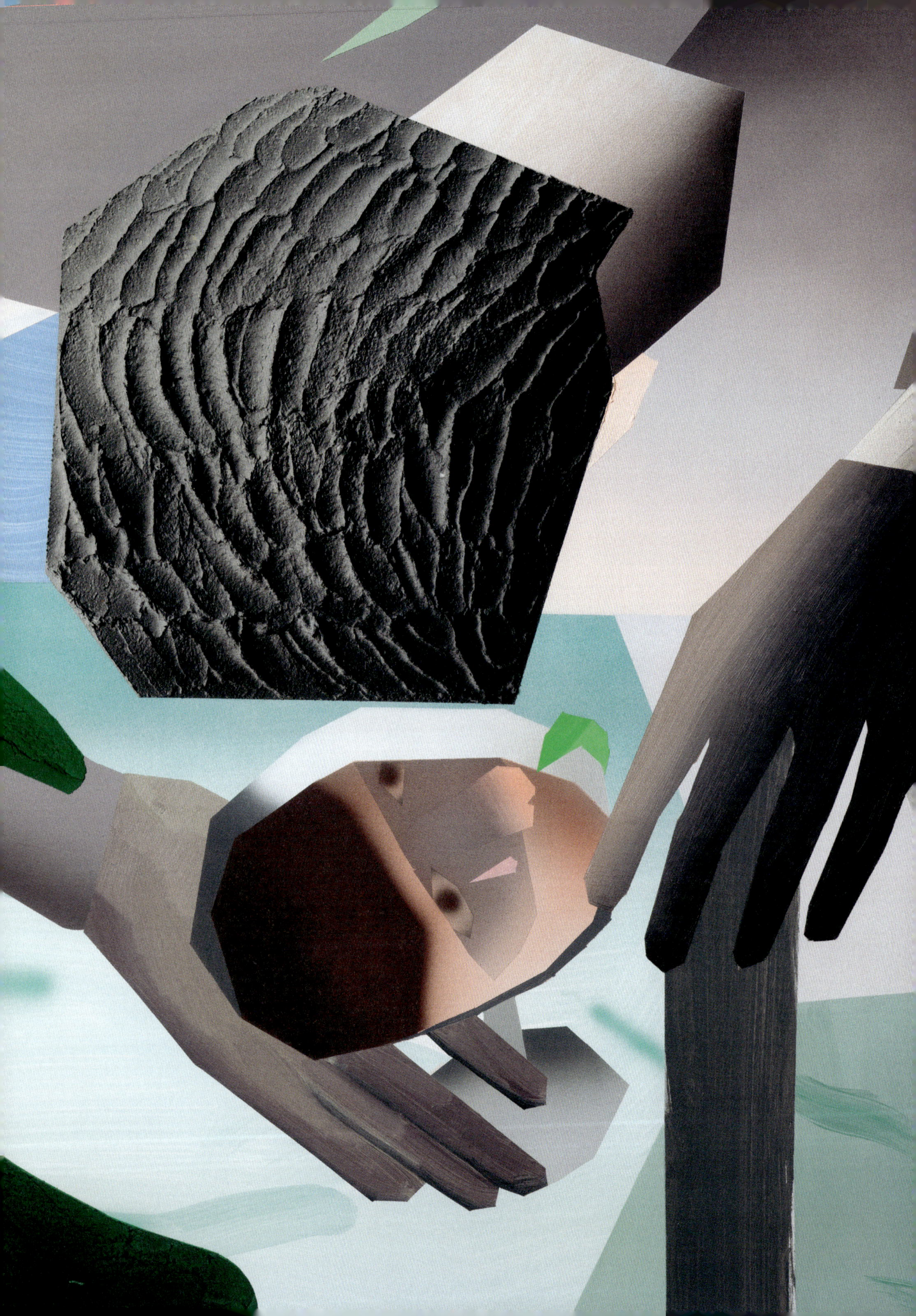

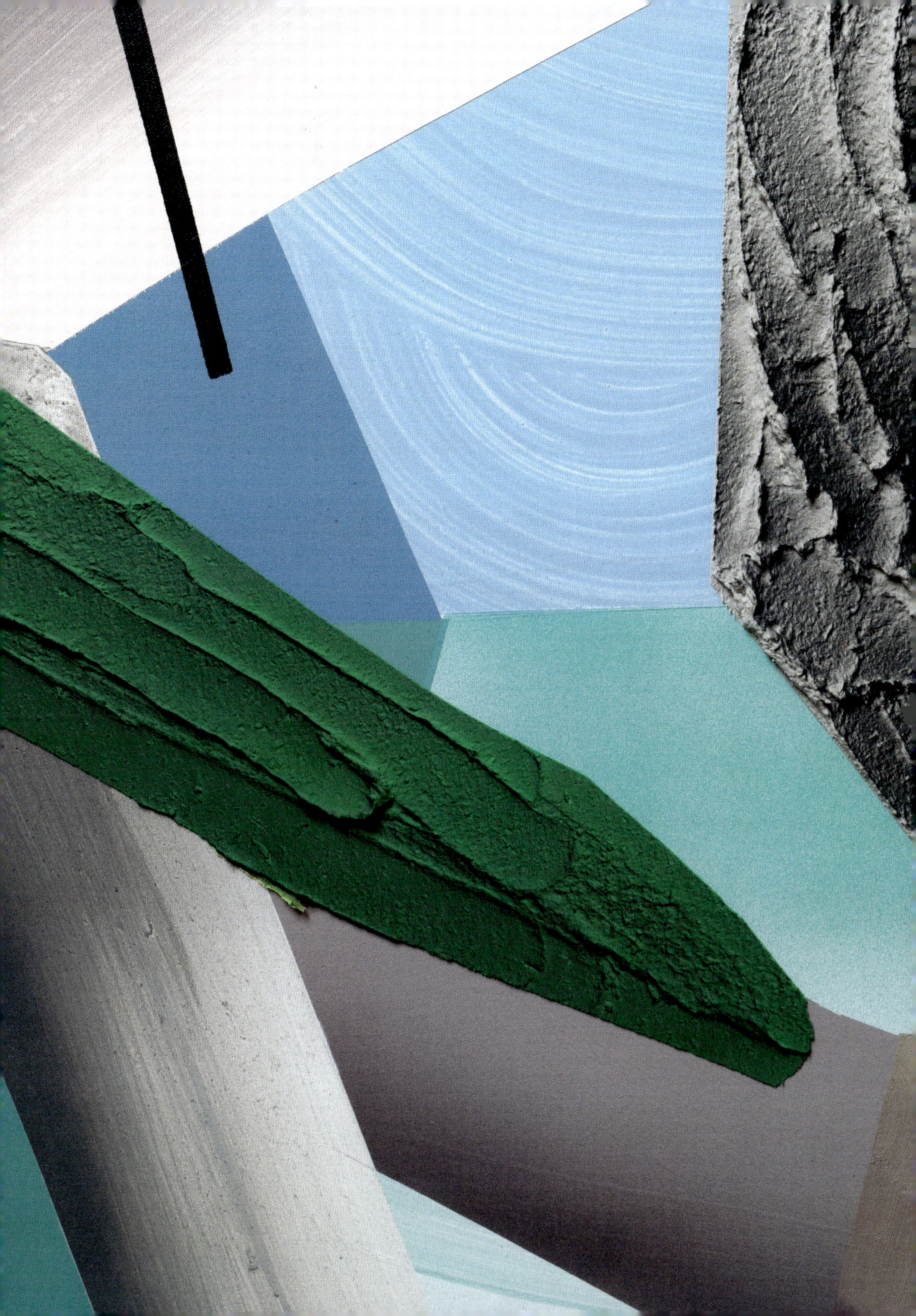

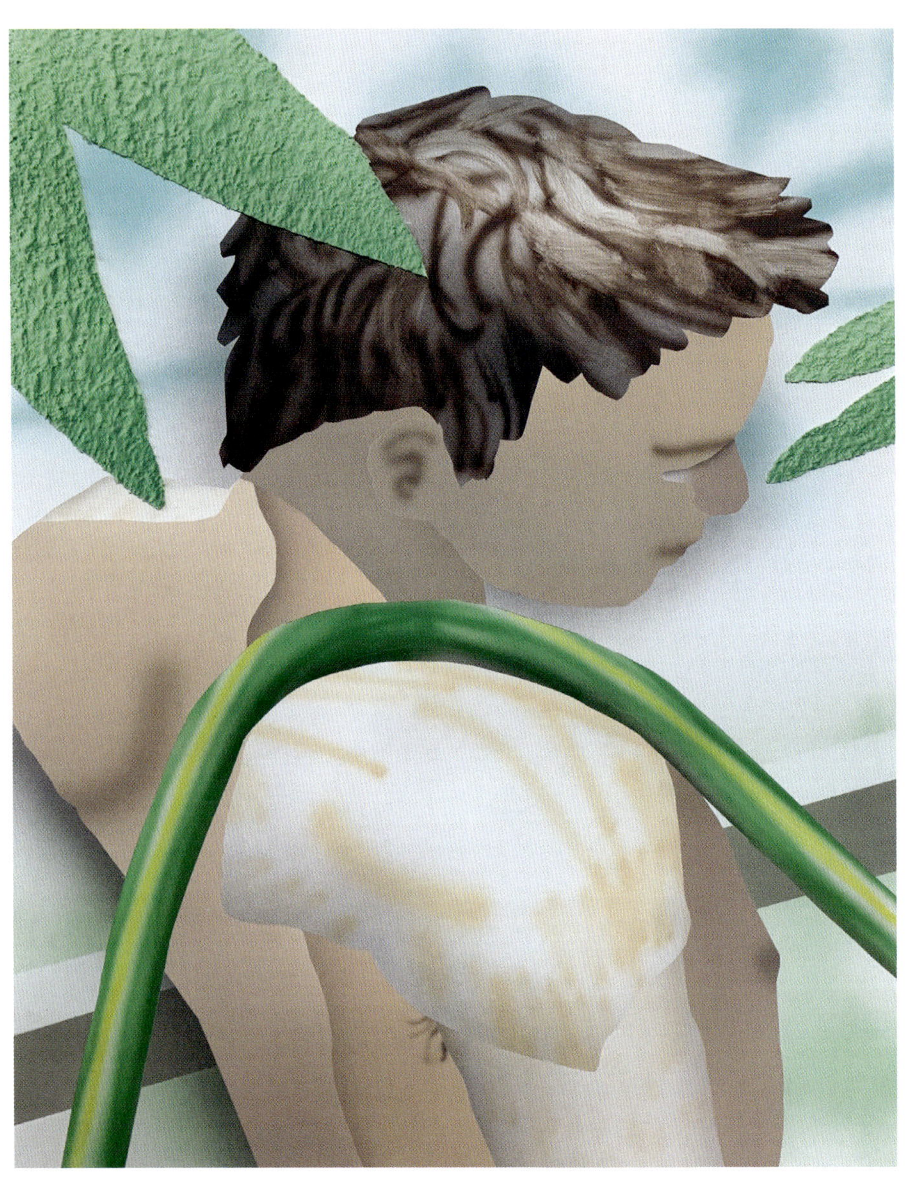

GARDENER 2019 · 75 × 60 cm

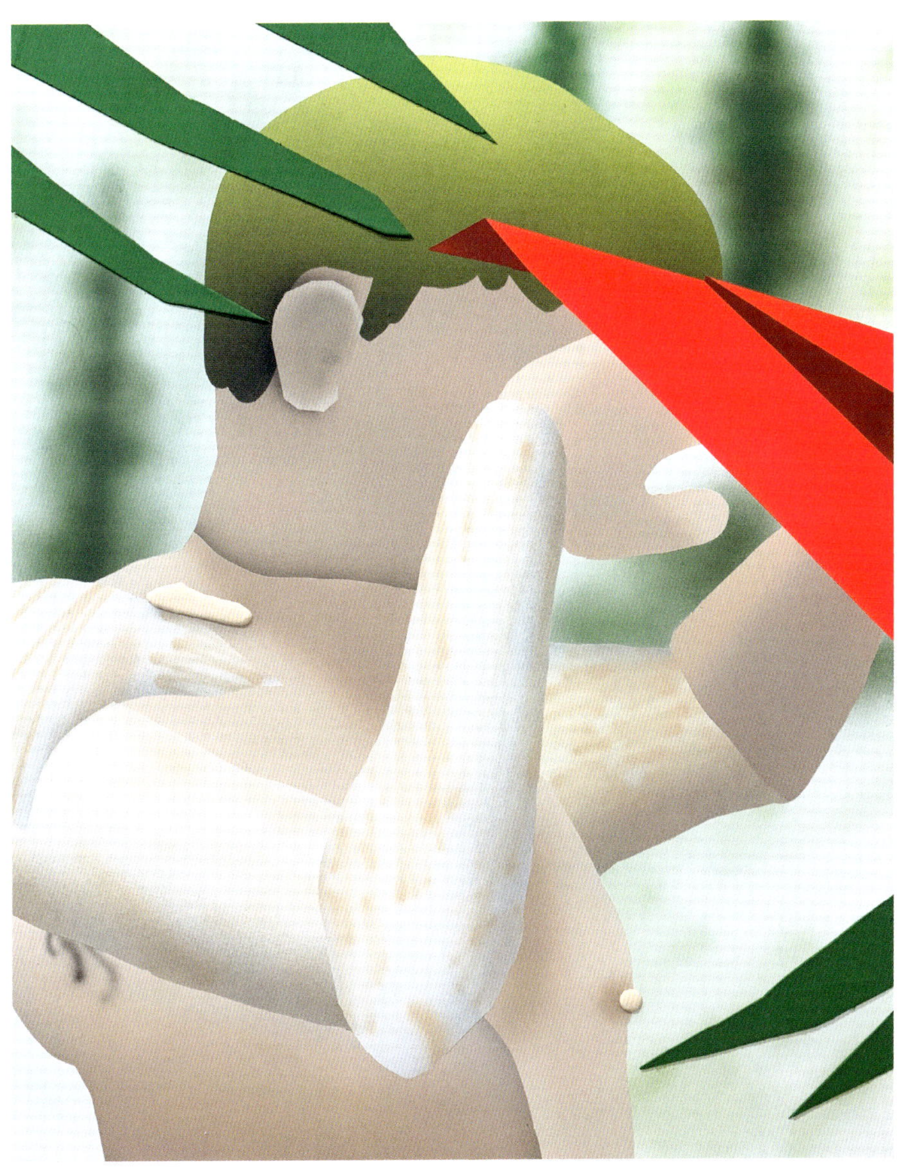

UNDER THE HOOD 2019 · 76 × 60 cm

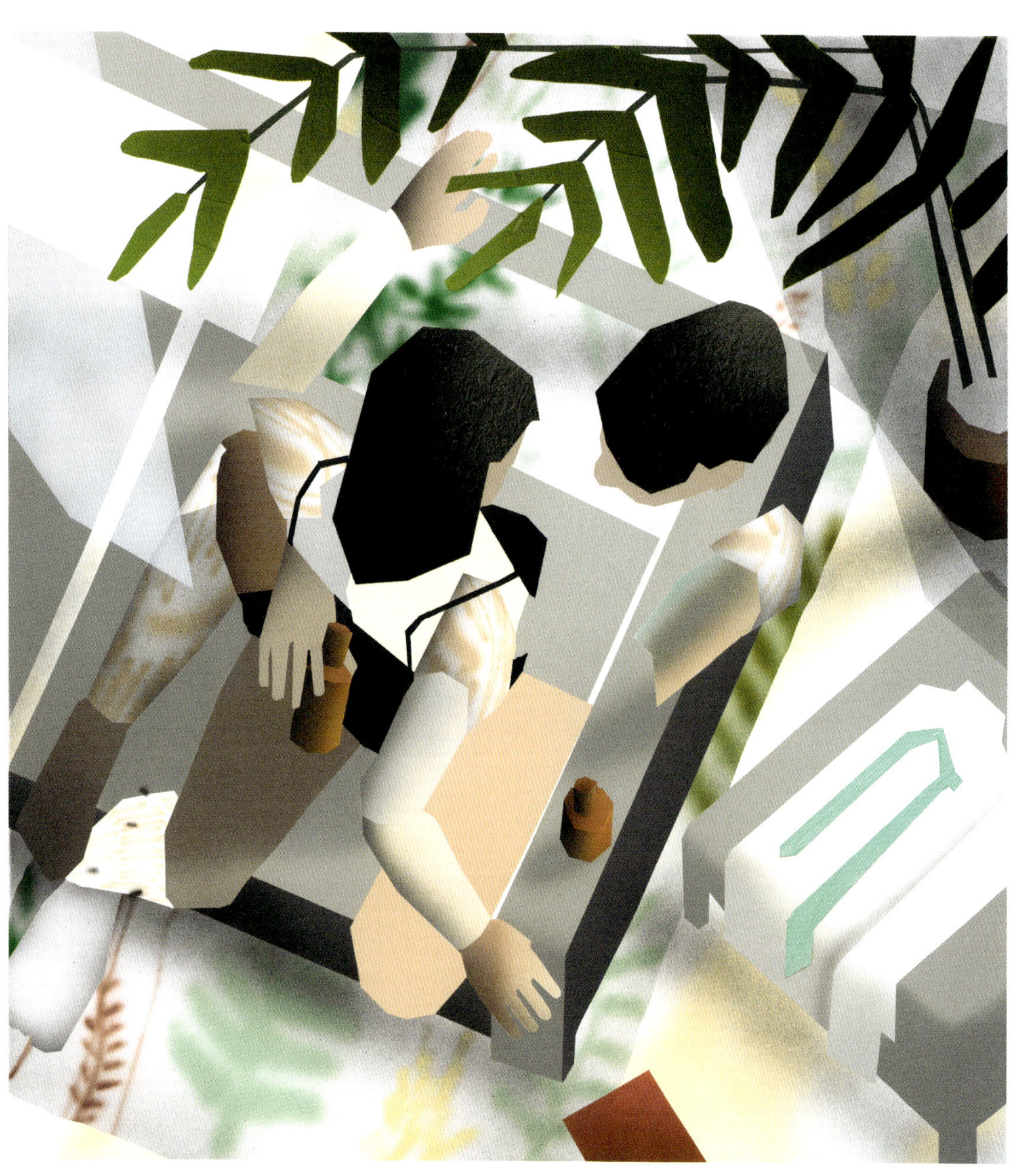

LAP DANCE 2020 · 120 × 110 cm

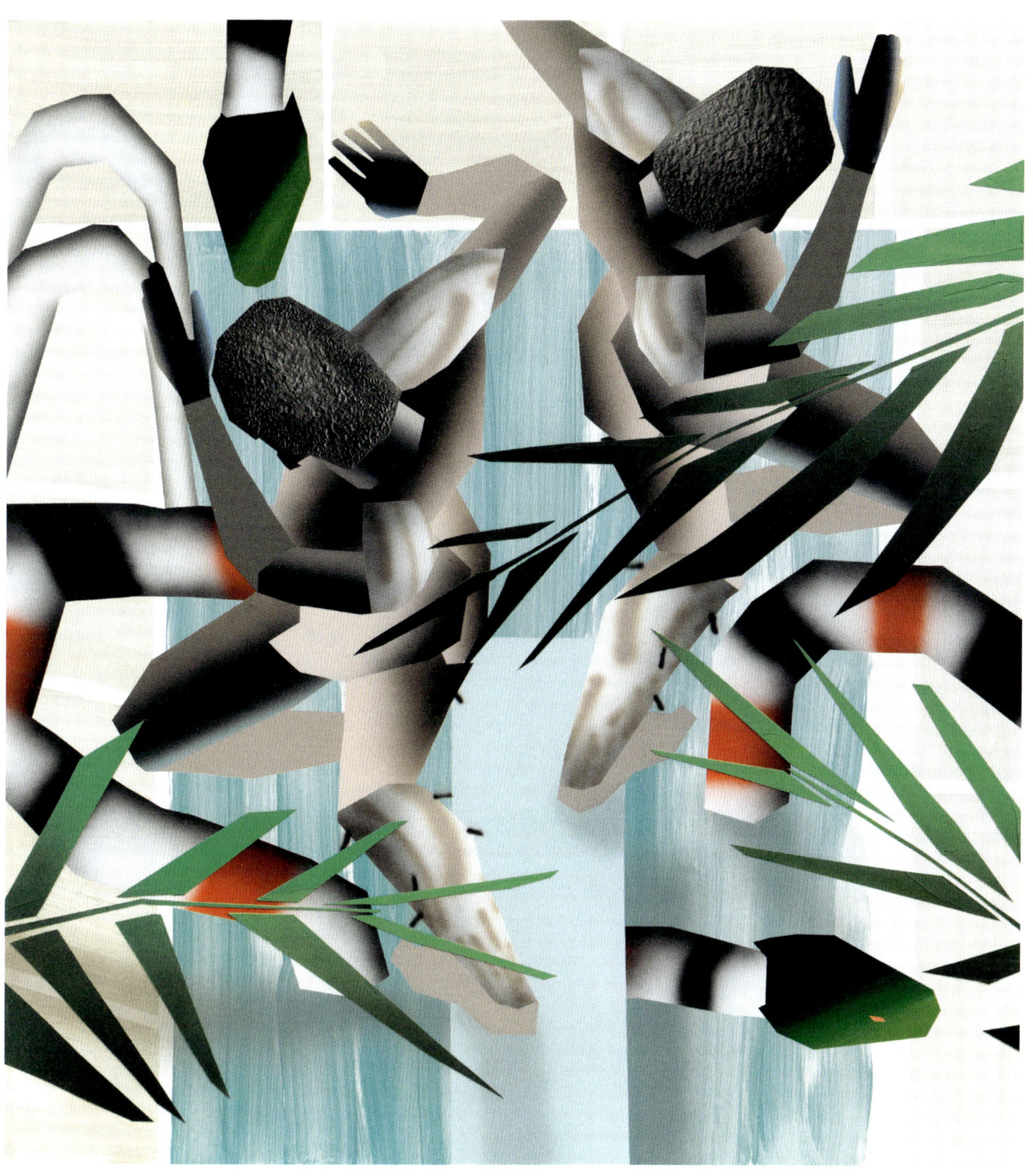

SNAKE POOL 2021 · 200 × 185 cm

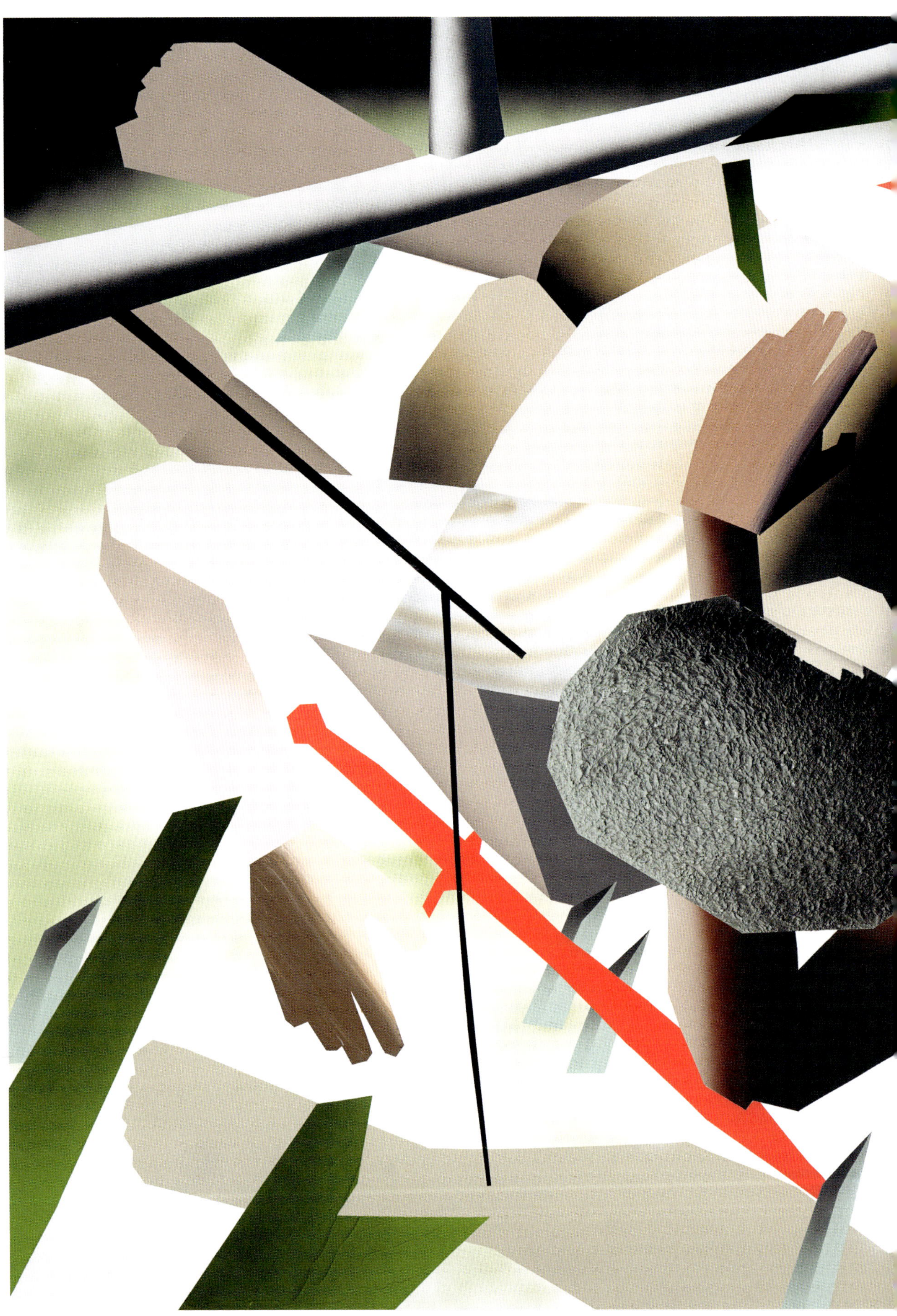

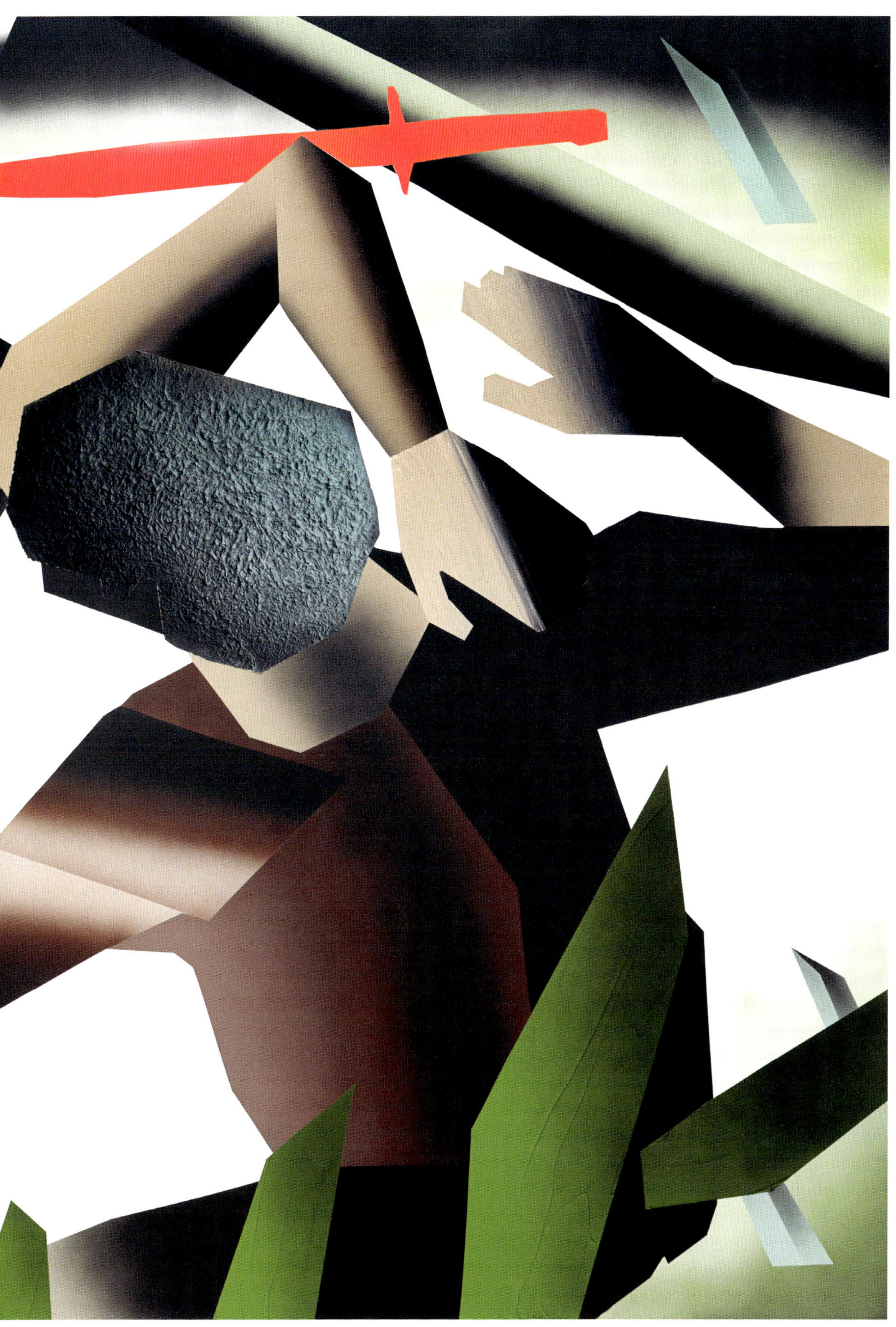

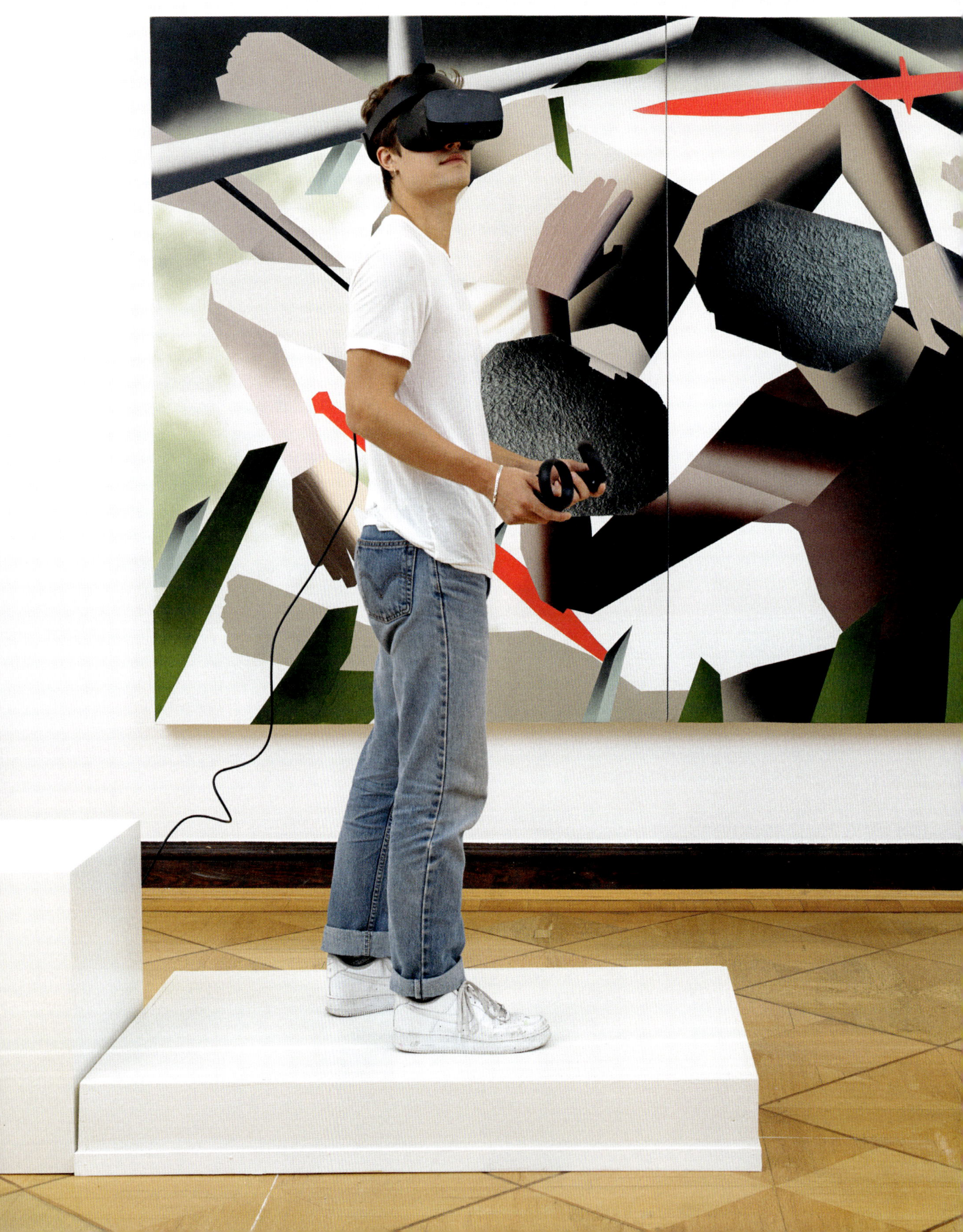

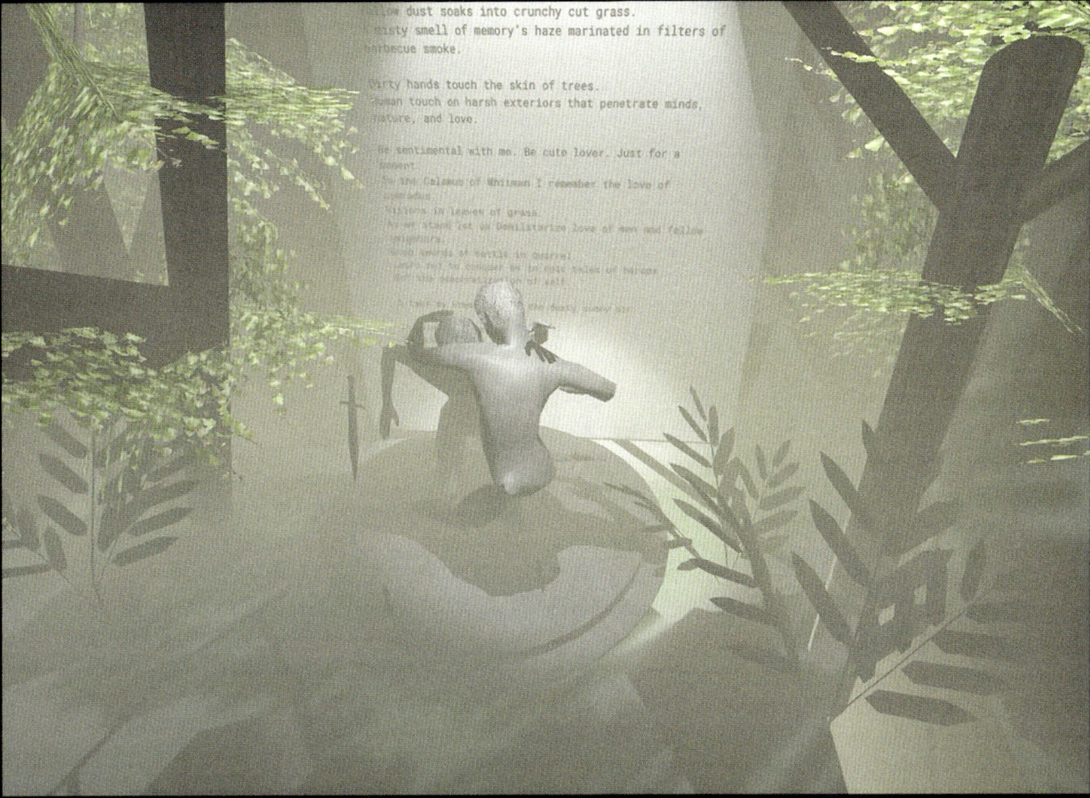

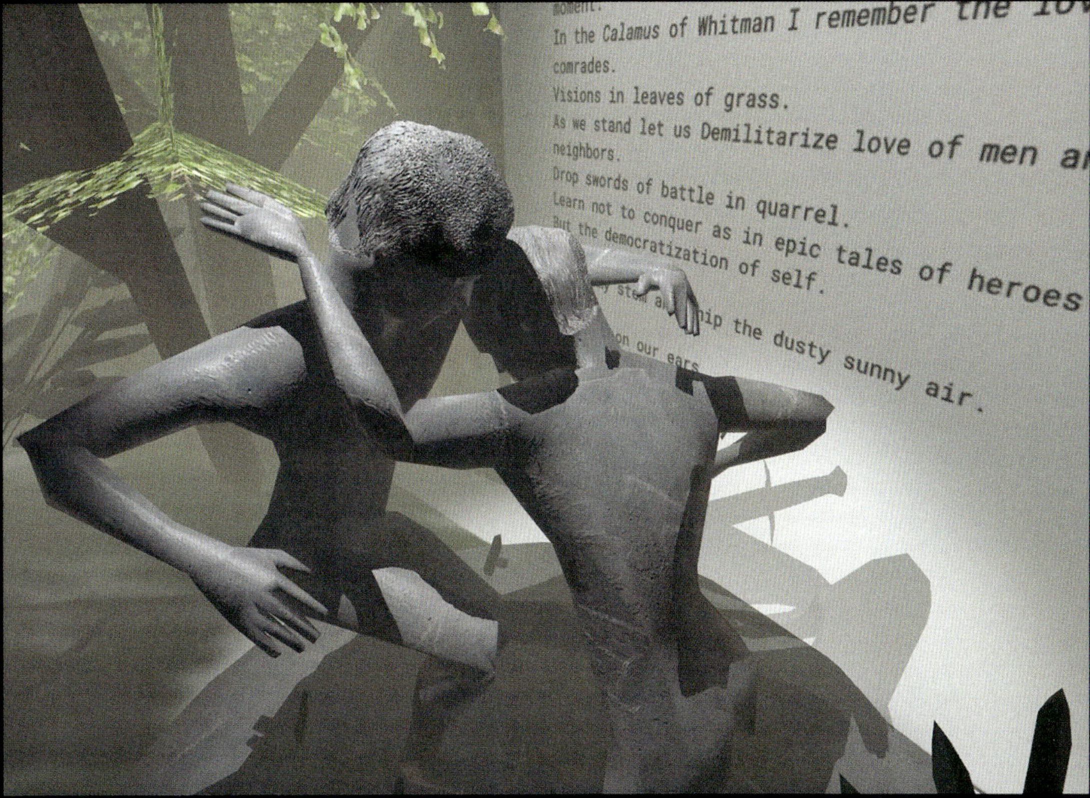

p. · S. 138/139

DROPPING SWORDS IN PATHS UNTRODDEN

2022 · 200 × 300 (150) × 10 cm (diptych · Diptychon)

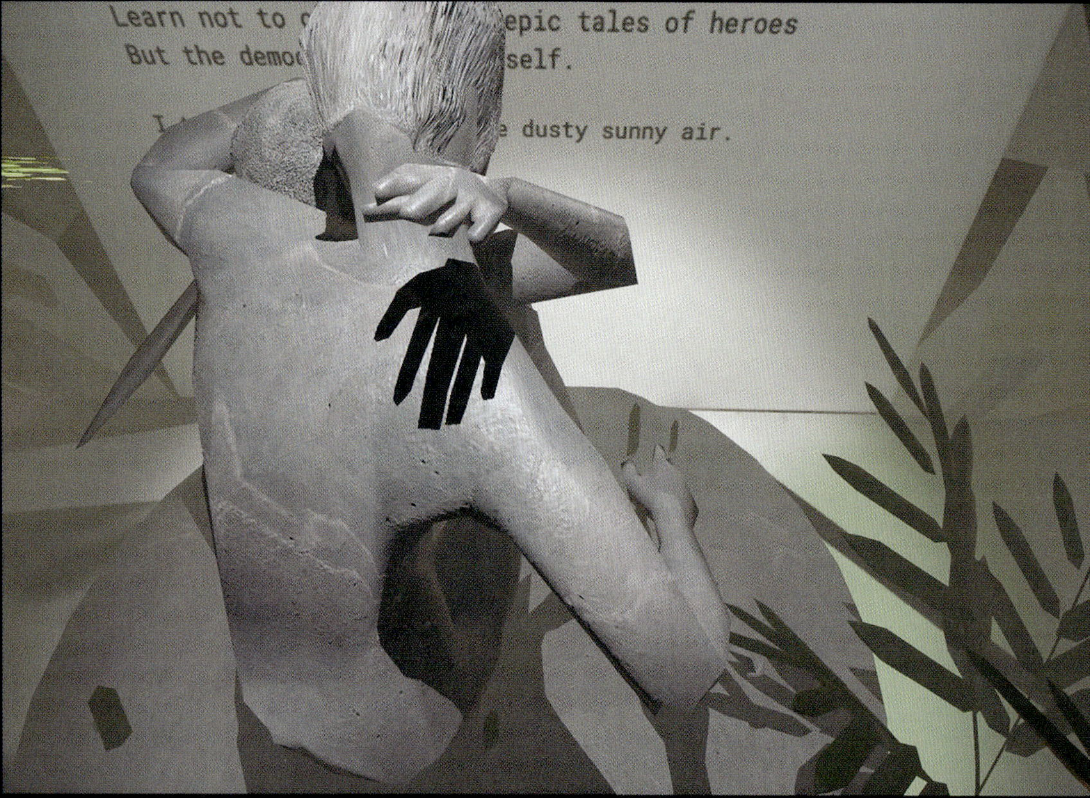

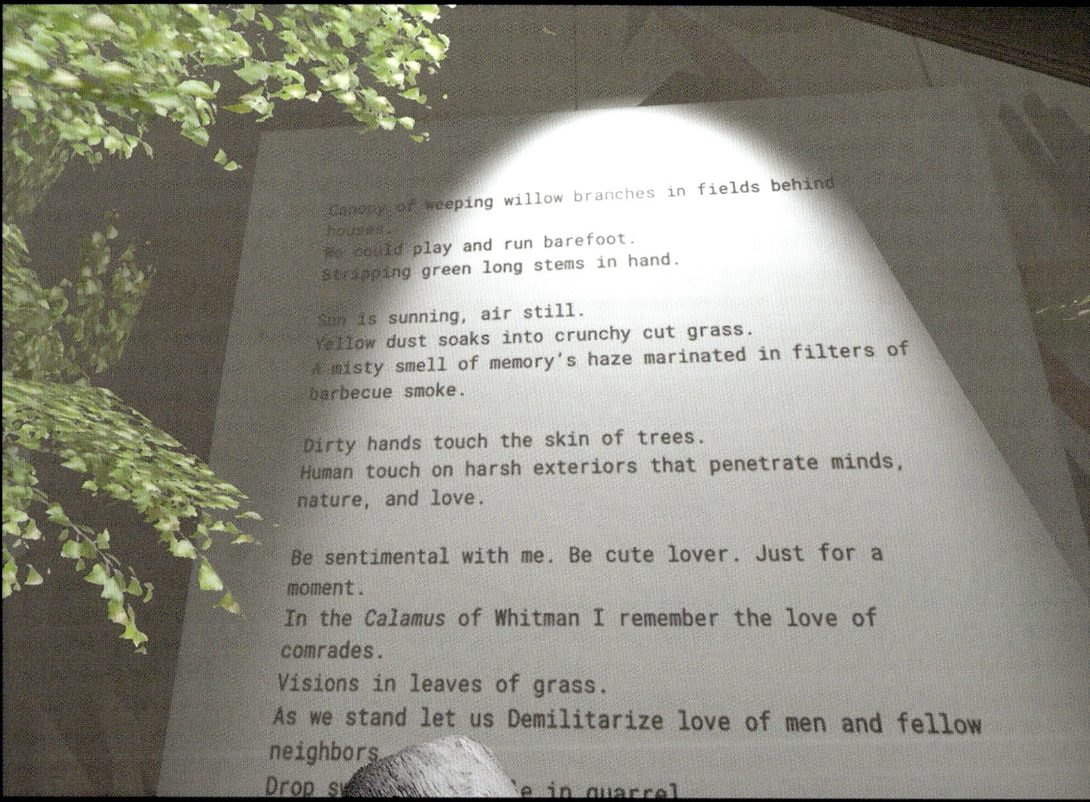

Learn not to c epic tales of *heroes*
But the democ self.

I e dusty sunny air.

Canopy of weeping willow branches in fields behind houses.
We could play and run barefoot.
Stripping green long stems in hand.

Sun is sunning, air still.
Yellow dust soaks into crunchy cut grass.
A misty smell of memory's haze marinated in filters of barbecue smoke.

Dirty hands touch the skin of trees.
Human touch on harsh exteriors that penetrate minds, nature, and love.

Be sentimental with me. Be cute lover. Just for a moment.
In the *Calamus* of Whitman I remember the love of comrades.
Visions in leaves of grass.
As we stand let us Demilitarize love of men and fellow neighbors
Drop s e in quarrel

p. · S. 141–143
MONUMENT OF DROPPED SWORDS IN PATHS UNTRODDEN
2020 · Render Stills of Virtual Reality

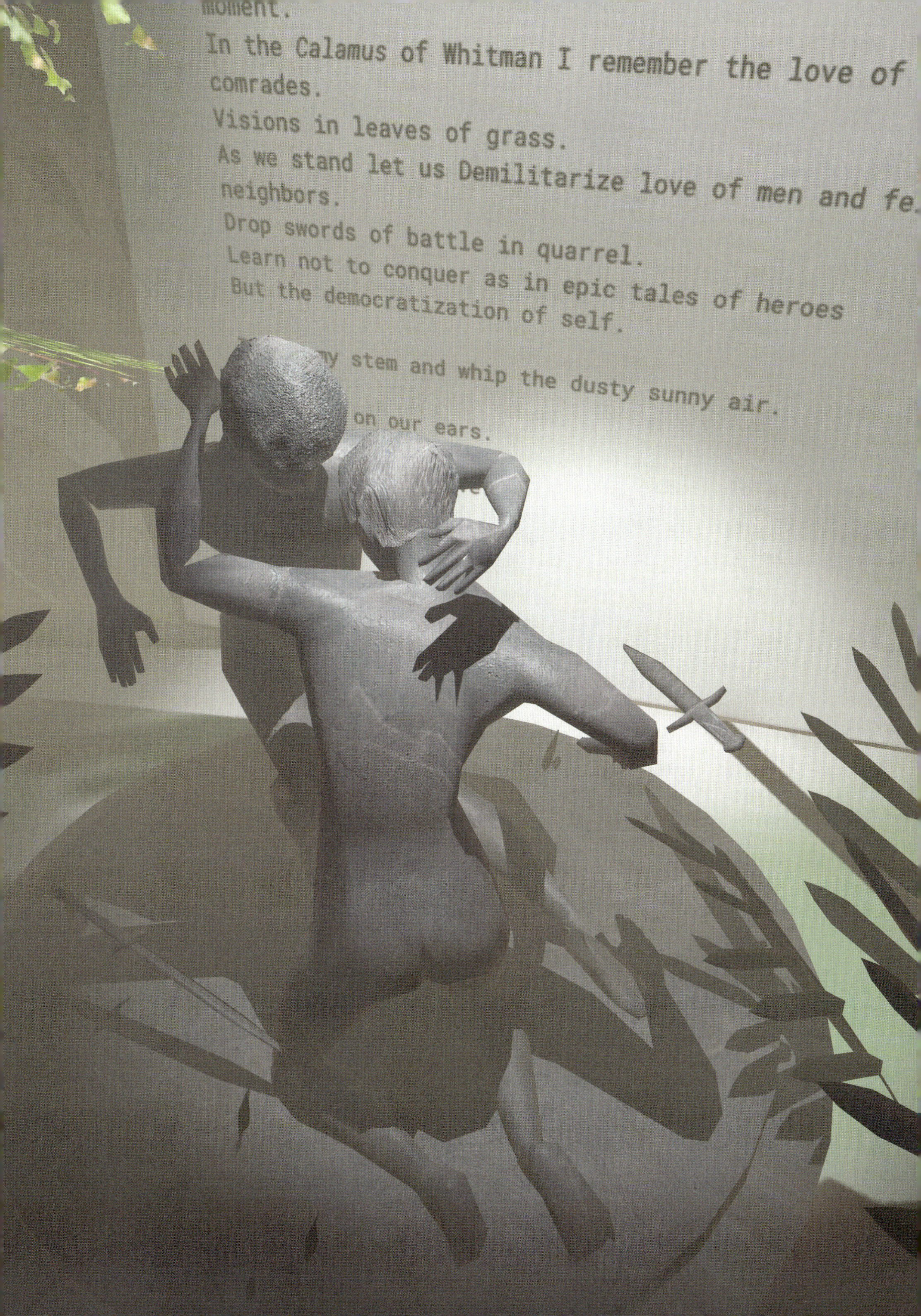
moment.
In the Calamus of Whitman I remember the love of
comrades.
Visions in leaves of grass.
As we stand let us Demilitarize love of men and fe
neighbors.
Drop swords of battle in quarrel.
Learn not to conquer as in epic tales of heroes
But the democratization of self.
stem and whip the dusty sunny air.
on our ears.

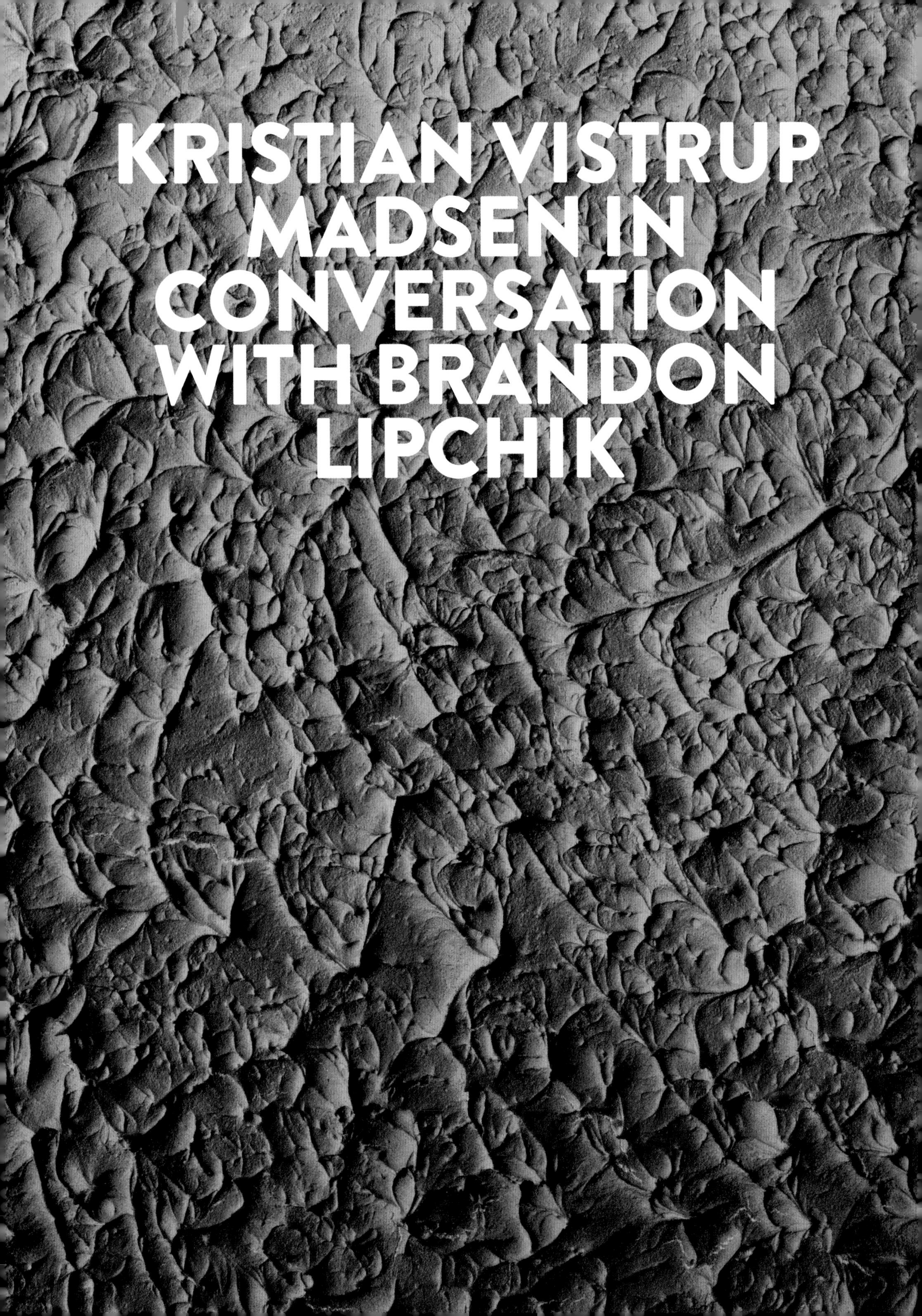

KRISTIAN VISTRUP MADSEN IN CONVERSATION WITH BRANDON LIPCHIK

FROM E(E)RIE TO BERLIN

Brandon Lipchik has lived in Berlin for about a year. We met in his studio in a sunny and idyllic backyard in Kreuzberg, a far cry from the dance floors of the city's techno clubs, but also from the relentless grayness of the winters here, the first of which poses a cruel rite of passage to every new Berliner. Open and unjaded, Lipchik seems to have emerged on the other side of it unscathed. He appears to fit the perfect image of the American youth: someone you could imagine catching a football in slow-motion on a beach in California or driving a red pickup truck through a cornfield in Iowa. Actually, his story is a different one, and the paintings he has made during his first year in Germany—more sinister and violent than his earlier work—suggests this time away from his homeland might have altered his perspective. We had a conversation about how escapism and loneliness settle on a canvas, and whether it's true that what you learn about America from leaving it, is that it was always at a distance, even from up close.

KRISTIAN VISTRUP MADSEN **You studied at the Rhode Island School of Design, and then you moved to New York?**

BRANDON LIPCHIK Yes, I was in New York for five years. I liked living there, but it was hard. I didn't really know anything else because I moved there straight out of school, so it was my first adult decision. Obviously, New York is wonderful, and there's so much to see and do there—art, especially. But sometimes when you're living somewhere, you don't take advantage of that. I think, overall, it has a lot of benefits, but… it's intense.

K **I sense some ambivalence. I lived in London for five years in my early twenties, and of course New York has a different kind of energy, but it does share some of the same sense that everything is a promise of something to come, and the stress of disappointment that comes with that.**

B Definitely. There are obviously a lot of opportunities in New York, a lot of stuff happening in Brooklyn and all that. But I found that there are more opportunities for young artists in Europe. New York is getting bigger and bigger, more and more expensive every year, and that's not good for artists.

K **Where did you grow up?**

B Erie, Pennsylvania.

K **I once went swimming in Lake Erie, and I was struck by how wild it was to be among such great waves, like an ocean, and for it to not be salty. That's a mindfuck. Erie doesn't have three Es, but is it also kind of eerie?**

B Yes, the fresh water is weird! Of course, growing up there, it was what I was used to. But yeah, it's a spooky place, to be honest. We always had the feeling: "We gotta get out of here. We gotta go somewhere else. There's nothing to do here." It has a population of about 100,000. It's an industrial city—or at least it was. Now it's more like the shell of an industrial city. My dad worked in car parts manufacturing. And I used to work in an automotive factory, too. Just before school, moving stuff around on an assembly line—it was horrible.

K **How did you become interested in art?**

B That's a good question, because art wasn't something that was necessarily appreciated. Art is very much an upper-class privilege, and it wasn't like my parents or anyone around me was interested in that. I just really loved it. I was obsessed. Just naturally, I was like that. I remember watching Bob Ross, this painter guy with an afro, painting landscapes on PBS. Bizarre to be thinking about him again …

K **Was it for the beauty? Or for the calm?**

B Probably the beauty. I think there was always a certain level of escapism, and something that I was trying to work through.

K **Art is often derided as elitist, but it's easy to forget that its special status in the culture industry is also what makes it an important escape route for a lot of people. I certainly feel like that. Your work shows an interest in suburban American pop culture: swimming pools and front lawns—things I wouldn't associate with ex-industrial towns and assembly lines. It makes me think about high school TV shows, and how in small towns in America it feels like you are living in this constant projection of "American Life" that's composed of the same props and backdrops everywhere.**

B Yeah, there's some truth to that. If you're a young painter, and you're trying to figure out what you're about and what drives your work, I think it can be good to start with what you've done, where you have lived, and how you identify with the context of everyone around you. After I started doing some small shows in Europe, and began spending more time here, when I went back to the US, I was so hypersensitive to Americana, this simulation of American life. It has a real flavor to it that you get so used to when you are surrounded by it—you don't even notice.

K **Like ocean waves in fresh water. It's often the case that you start being able to make work about the place you came from only once you move away, because you can see it more clearly.**

B Yeah, and with a different set of eyes. I think I'm definitely more and more interested in Americana and this space of the backyard.

K Seeing your portfolio from the last years, and then looking around the room at your recent works, the color palette has gotten a lot darker. Do you think that has to do with this distance you've gained from America, this different set of eyes?

B Probably. That's a good observation. I started making more nocturne paintings in the last year. I became fascinated with this metaphor of nighttime or darkness, and how it can be a kind of mask. It could also be because of my environment. I came to Berlin, and, you know, the darkness is real here in the winter, you don't get much light, and there was definitely a point where it kind of shifted my psychology.

K Interesting that the nighttime is both a space for performance of outward identity—what you say about the mask—and a psychological space. Since you mentioned going to the Magritte Museum in Brussels recently, I thought about this painting of his, *La Carte Blanche*, of a woman riding through the forest. She is obscured by the trees, but not in the right places. It's like a technological glitch, which also speaks to a psychological or subconscious one. In some of your paintings, you also use these glitch-like obfuscations. It makes me think that what in Magritte is a surreality could be close to a kind of meta-reality, what we now know as virtual or digital space.

B Yeah. I've been thinking a lot about what it is that makes the virtual space so attractive. For me, it's associated with searching for a certain sense of spirituality, or something that transcends the reality we live in. When I'm constructing a digital image, say, in preparing for a painting, there's a certain freedom to transcend the body or gender or anything at all. Like when you're playing video games, and you can just pick a different character, or construct an avatar just as you want them.

K It's also definitely a kind of escapism. Did you play a lot of video games when you were growing up?

B I did. I grew up with the Nintendo and all these old Mario games, and Gamecube, and *The Sims*. The games that were most interesting to me were the ones where you simulate reality and build worlds, and you can just keep going. They're open-ended. Like farming games or games about building a house and then paying off your debt.

K When you're a teenager, maybe because you feel so trapped, time has a different substance. I think playing video games is something that can make hours pass by without you realizing. Maybe painting is a bit similar in offering this sort of hermetic, amorphous time-space?

B Yeah, absolutely. I spend so much time alone in the studio working on these illusory objects that transport you into another kind of space, but it's still tactile and material, which is something that has become very important to me. When I was in college, I stopped painting for a while because I didn't feel like I could make anything, given the history and all that. I was only building virtual reality spaces. But after this one really horrible day—you know, where you are faced with your own existence in a way—I had this great urge to just create something with my hands. I realized that I can't have a practice that only exists digitally. That wasn't right for me.

K VR works often produce an experience of being alone inside of a world without tactility. Especially when you're wearing the goggles. Normally, it would take a really long time to get into a zone intensely severed from material surroundings like that—you'd have to be playing a video game for hours, alone, in the middle of the night—but with virtual reality, you get there very fast. In a way, I understand your work as a fantasy of being able to give material form to something usually reserved for a really particular kind of loneliness, so that it can be shared with other people.

B That's an interesting point. Recently, I've been asked a lot to open up my studio and talk about everything … Sometimes that can feel hard, I think, as an artist, to constantly be putting yourself out there. I mean, not just your work, but you.

K There's a real tension between the intimate space of the virtual and the publicness of a painting.

B But if that tension wasn't there, that would also be horrible.

K An artist needs an audience …

B Of course! But it's a point of struggle.

K Paintings are so strong as objects, and carry themselves so well, you don't have to worry about accompanying them, or saying so much about them. It's partly to do with the history of the medium, but also with why people started to paint in the first place: this potential of auratic presence that comes with a painting being both an illusion of space *and* a body. This is more difficult to achieve in other media, I think. You work a lot with different textures in your paintings, from the flatness of the airbrush to these parts where the paint is caked on so thick, they're set into relief.
B I always try to leave a little bit of space to dream inside the painting, and for someone else to engage with it. These dissonances in texture and material help create that space.

K The more I look at the ones you have here in the studio, the more I just see the moon. Even though they're so full of content, the moon becomes this point of fixation, like a red thread.
B Yeah, it's a character that crops up in all the pieces. I think it figures as a kind of romantic symbol in the works, a sense of longing, or that there's something greater than the narrative being shown.

K Given its prominent place in the history of painting, the moon is a very strong symbol to pick up. A symbol of both transformation and contemplation, even a kind of romantic melancholy. It's interesting that the moon is never a source of light in your pictures, but just hangs there like a dead sign. Meanwhile, you have these stage lights that make it clear that we are in a contrived space. Sometimes we can even see them, like in a theater.
B Yeah, I've been thinking a lot about artifice, and how literal the idea of staging becomes when I'm rendering the 3D mockups for the paintings. I am interested in how that conceptual idea can be carried through in the works themselves.

K It reminds me of all those Hollywood films that are about Hollywood, like *Sunset Boulevard*, *Whatever Happened to Baby Jane?*, or *Mulholland Drive*—Hollywood eating itself. In *Moongazing with Garden Hose* (2021) [▶ P. 60] you don't have the stage lights, but the picture creates a sense of horror and claustrophobia in a highly cinematic way, by a bird's-eye view and a close crop.

B For me it's also about breaking the fourth wall and revealing the seams of the narrative. That's how the moon becomes a set piece, and the horizon and the sky are just features on a wall. I also like how, by installing artificial light in the paintings, you play with the viewer's curiosity. There's a sense of drama that comes from the uncertainty; it makes you wonder what else could be happening.

K It brings me back to this idea of American culture as a projection that can be cast onto every small town, like in a cinema. Everything is already bathed in stage lights, and seen as if through a camera lens. In the end, it produces its own kind of authenticity. Like in *Mulholland Drive*, it is an infinity mirror of fictions, but the emotion is real, so it doesn't matter.
B Often when I'm working on a piece, I'll be inspired by a painting or a film, and then work it through the digital rendering to create my own picture. Like with this piece *A beauty and the beast* (2022) [▶ P. 78/79], I was looking at an old Rousseau painting. And *Elizabeth Taylor's Reflection* (2021) [▶ P. 106], which was in the exhibition at Robert Grunenberg last year, was inspired by a story about Elizabeth Taylor trying on a necklace, and when she didn't have a mirror to see herself, she bent over the pool instead, like Narcissus at the pond.

K That's such a powerful image. Also because Elizabeth Taylor is sort of beyond gender and individuality; all the hundreds of roles that she's played at once. It points to how Narcissus is also a kind of shell, or a mask; a reflection mistaken for a self. In Freud, autism is short for autoeroticism, and understood as a short-circuiting of the sexual drive, so that instead of going outward, it goes back to the self and closes it off from the world. I think this painting, and your work more generally, really brings the concepts of narcissism, autism, and the erotic together through the lens of virtual space in a way that's very poignant to our time. The rubies on her necklace look like blood dripping into the pool.
B For me, it's related to why I became fascinated with the nocturnal: the liquid of nighttime as a kind of mask, but one that actually reveals something rather than concealing it. In a way, I think that the mask you put on can be more reflective of who you are.

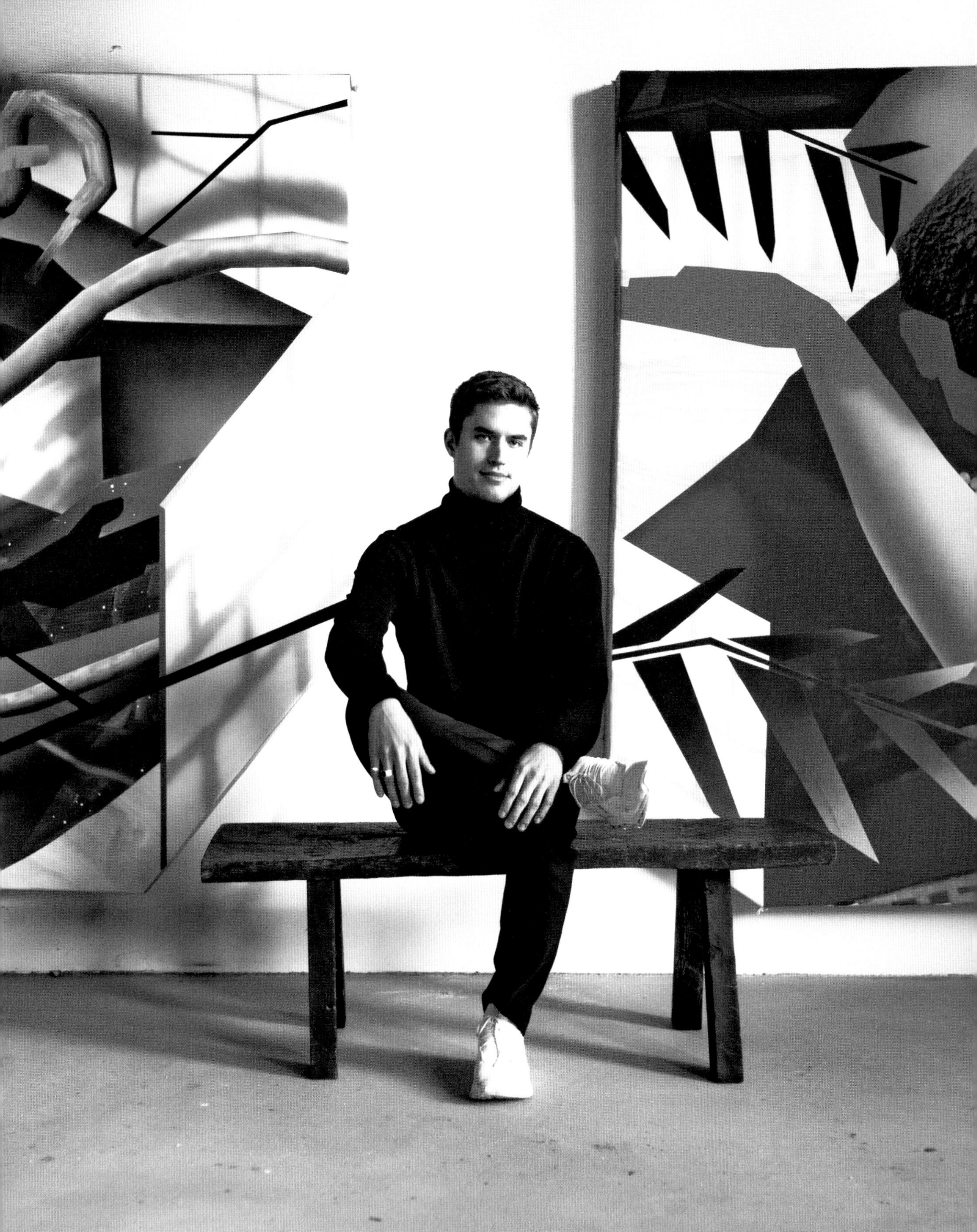

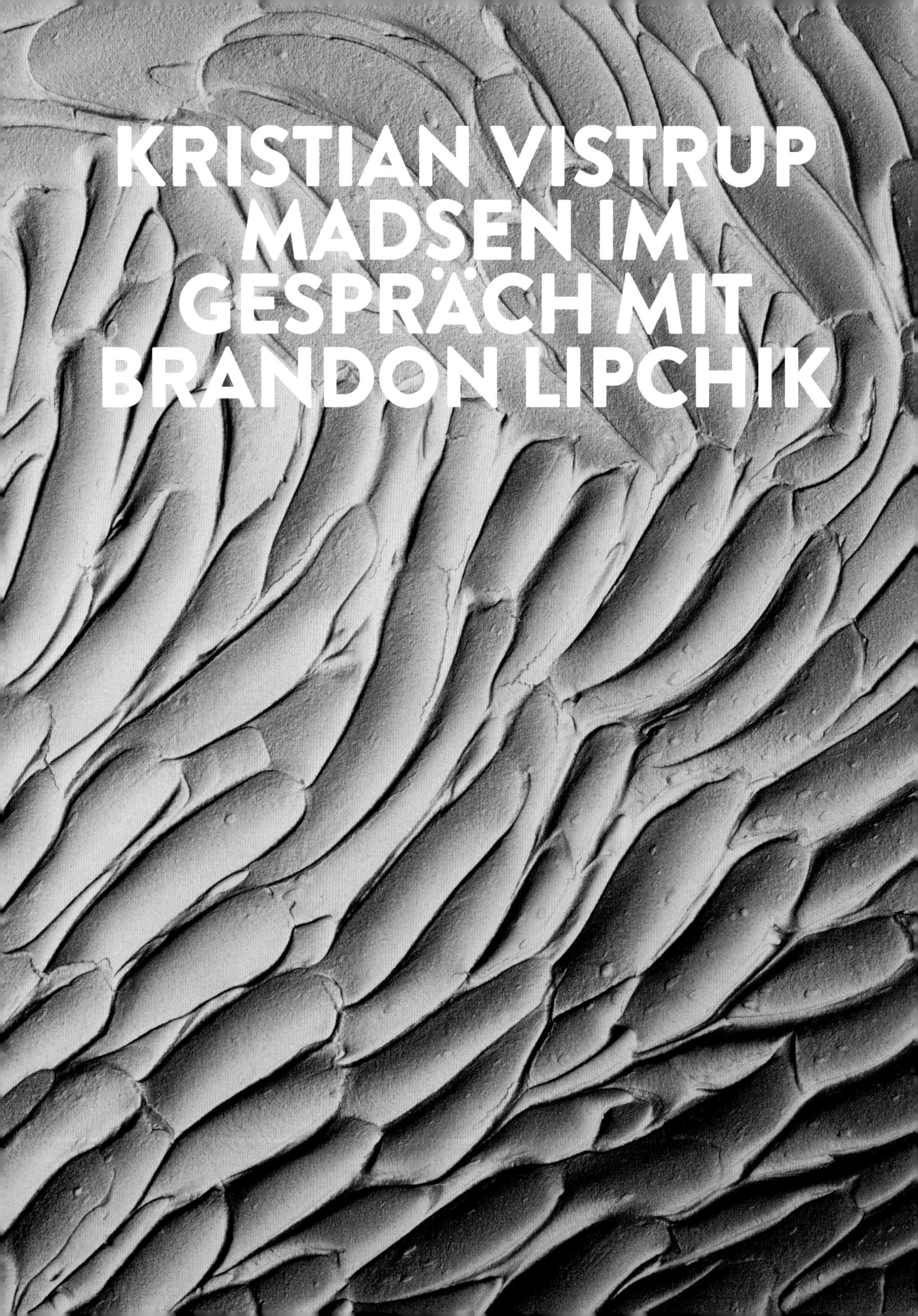
KRISTIAN VISTRUP
MADSEN IM
GESPRÄCH MIT
BRANDON LIPCHIK

VON E(E)RIE NACH BERLIN

Brandon Lipchik lebt seit etwa einem Jahr in Berlin. Wir haben uns in seinem Atelier getroffen, das in einem sonnigen, idyllischen Hinterhof in Kreuzberg liegt, weitab der Tanzflächen der hiesigen Techno-Clubs, aber auch fern vom unerbittlichen Grau des Berliner Winters – ein grausamer Initiationsritus für alle Neuberliner*innen, wenn sie ihn zum ersten Mal durchleben. Lipchik wirkt offen und unverbraucht, er scheint den Winter gut überstanden zu haben. Äußerlich entspricht er dem perfekten Bild der amerikanischen Jugend: Jemand, von dem man sich vorstellen kann, dass er am Strand in Kalifornien einen Football in Zeitlupe fängt oder in einem roten Pick-up durch ein Maisfeld in Iowa fährt. Doch in Wahrheit ist seine Story eine ganz andere. Die Malereien, an denen er in seinem ersten Jahr in Deutschland gearbeitet hat und die düsterer und gewaltsamer wirken als seine früheren Arbeiten, legen nahe, dass die Zeit in der Fremde möglicherweise mit einer Veränderung seiner Sichtweisen einhergegangen ist. Wir haben uns darüber unterhalten, wie Eskapismus und Einsamkeit auf der Leinwand zum Ausdruck kommen, und darüber, ob es stimmt, dass man, wenn man die USA verlässt, über dieses Land lernt, dass schon immer eine Distanz dazu bestand, auch wenn man ganz nahe dran war.

KRISTIAN VISTRUP MADSEN Du hast an der Rhode Island School of Design studiert und bist dann nach New York übersiedelt?
BRANDON LIPCHIK Ja, ich habe fünf Jahre lang in New York gelebt. Ich mochte es dort gerne, aber es war schon hart. Ich kannte nicht wirklich etwas anderes, weil ich direkt nach meinem Abschluss dorthin gezogen bin. Das war also meine erste eigenständige Entscheidung. New York ist natürlich toll, es gibt so viel zu sehen und zu tun – insbesondere was die Kunst angeht. Aber wenn man irgendwo lebt, nutzt man das manchmal gar nicht so richtig aus. Insgesamt bietet New York schon viele Vorteile, aber ... es ist ganz schön intensiv.

K Ich spüre da eine gewisse Ambivalenz. Ich habe in meinen frühen Zwanzigern fünf Jahre in London gelebt. Natürlich hat New York eine ganz andere Energie, aber beide teilen sich irgendwie das Gefühl, dass alles ein Versprechen auf etwas Kommendes ist, und den Stress der Enttäuschung, der damit einhergeht.
B Genau. New York bietet natürlich zahllose Möglichkeiten, in Brooklyn passiert eine Menge usw. Aber ich habe den Eindruck, dass es in Europa mehr Möglichkeiten gibt für junge Künstler*innen. New York wird jedes Jahr größer und teurer, und das ist nicht gut für Künstler*innen.

K Wo bist du aufgewachsen?
B In Erie, Pennsylvania.

K Ich war einmal schwimmen im Lake Erie und war erstaunt, wie abgefahren es sich anfühlte, zwischen so hohen Wellen zu sein, wie in einem Meer, das aber nicht salzig ist. Das ist ein Wahnsinnsgefühl. Erie schreibt man zwar nicht mit drei E, aber ist es nicht auch irgendwie unheimlich [eerie]?
B Ja, das Süßwasser ist schon komisch! Aber da ich dort aufgewachsen bin, war das für mich natürlich ganz normal. Aber ja, es ist ehrlich gesagt ein gespenstischer Ort. Wir hatten immer das Gefühl: „Wir müssen hier weg. Wir müssen woanders hin. Es gibt hier nichts zu tun." In Erie leben ca. 100.000 Menschen. Es ist eine Industriestadt – oder zumindest war sie das einmal. Jetzt ist sie nur noch der Schatten einer Industriestadt. Mein Vater hat bei einem Autoteilezulieferer gearbeitet. Und ich habe auch in einer Autofabrik gearbeitet. Noch vor der Schule am Fließband Sachen herumschieben – es war furchtbar.

K Wie kamst du zur Kunst?
B Das ist eine gute Frage, denn Kunst war nicht unbedingt etwas, das man zu schätzen wusste. Kunst ist ein Privileg der Oberschicht, und es war nicht so, dass meine Eltern oder irgendjemand sonst in meinem Umfeld sich dafür interessiert hätte. Ich liebte sie einfach. Ich war von ihr besessen. Ich war einfach so, von Natur aus. Ich erinnere mich, dass ich mir die Fernsehsendung von Bob Ross angesehen habe, diesem Maler mit dem Afro, der auf PBS Landschaften gemalt hat. Es fühlt sich seltsam an, jetzt wieder an ihn zu denken ...

K Ging es dir um Schönheit? Oder um Ruhe?
B Wahrscheinlich Schönheit. Ich glaube, es gab immer einen gewissen Eskapismus und irgendetwas, das ich verarbeiten wollte.

K Kunst wird oft als elitär verspottet, dabei wird manchmal vergessen, dass sie aufgrund ihres Sonderstatus innerhalb der Kulturindustrie auch eine Exit-Strategie bietet für viele Menschen. Davon bin ich überzeugt. In deiner Arbeit geht es oft um die suburbane amerikanische Popkultur: Swimmingpools und der Rasen vor dem Haus – Dinge, die ich nicht mit ehemaligen Industriestädten und Fließbändern in Verbindung bringen würde. Ich muss dabei an Highschool-Fernsehsendungen denken, und daran, dass man in amerikanischen Kleinstädten das Gefühl hat, in dieser dauerhaften Projektion des „American Life" zu leben, das sich aus den immer gleichen Requisiten und Kulissen zusammensetzt.
B Ja, da ist was Wahres dran. Wenn du ein*e junge*r Maler*in bist und herauszufinden versuchst, was du da machst und was dich in deiner Arbeit voranbringt, ist es meines Erachtens sinnvoll, mit dem zu beginnen, was man bislang getan hat, wo man gelebt hat und wie man sich mit seinem Umfeld identifiziert. Nachdem ich begonnen hatte, ein paar Ausstellungen in Europa zu machen und mehr Zeit hier zu verbringen, reagierte ich, wenn ich in die USA zurückkam, überempfindlich auf jegliche Americana, auf diese Simulation des amerikanischen Lebens.

Es hat einen ganz eigenen Charakter, an den man sich so sehr gewöhnt, wenn man von ihm umgeben ist, dass man ihn gar nicht mehr wahrnimmt.

K Wie Süßwasser-Ozeanwellen. Es ist oft so, dass man erst eine Arbeit über seinen eigenen Heimatort machen kann, wenn man weggezogen ist, da man ihn dann deutlicher erkennt.
B Ja, und ihn mit anderen Augen sieht. Ich denke, ich interessiere mich definitiv immer mehr für Americana und für diese Hinterhöfe.

K Wenn man dein Portfolio der letzten Jahre durchgeht und sich dann in diesem Raum mit deinen aktuellen Arbeiten umsieht, wird deutlich, dass die Farbpalette entschieden dunkler geworden ist. Glaubst du, dass das mit der Distanz zu tun hat, die du zu Amerika gewonnen hast, mit diesen anderen Augen, mit denen du auf dieses Land blickst?
B Ja, wahrscheinlich. Das ist eine gute Beobachtung. Ich habe im vergangenen Jahr begonnen, mehr Nachtstücke zu malen. Ich habe eine Faszination entwickelt für diese Metapher des Nächtlichen oder der Dunkelheit, und wie sie eine Art Maske sein können. Vielleicht liegt das auch an meinem Umfeld. Ich kam nach Berlin, und es gibt hier echte Dunkelheit im Winter, man bekommt nicht viel Licht ab, und es gab definitiv einen Punkt, an dem das meine Psyche veränderte.

K Es ist interessant, dass die Nacht sowohl ein Raum für die Darstellung der äußerlichen Identität ist – was du über die Maske sagst – als auch ein psychologischer Raum. Weil du erwähnt hast, dass du kürzlich im Magritte Museum in Brüssel warst, habe ich an seine Malerei *La Carte Blanche* gedacht, in der eine Frau durch den Wald reitet. Sie wird durch die Bäume verdeckt, aber nicht an den richtigen Stellen. Es ist wie eine technische Störung, die auch auf eine psychologische oder unterbewusste Störung verweist. In manchen deiner Bilder greifst du ebenfalls auf solche störungsähnlichen Unschärfen zurück. Das bringt mich auf den Gedanken, dass das, was bei Magritte eine Sur-Realität ist, jener Art Meta-Realität nahekommen könnte, die wir heute als virtuellen oder digitalen Raum kennen.
B Ja. Ich habe viel darüber nachgedacht, was den virtuellen Raum so attraktiv macht. Für mich ist er mit der Suche nach einer gewissen Art von Spiritualität verbunden, oder nach etwas, das die Realität, in der wir leben, transzendiert. Wenn ich ein digitales Bild generiere, zum Beispiel um mich auf die Arbeit an einer neuen Malerei vorzubereiten, habe ich eine gewisse Freiheit, Körper oder Geschlecht oder was auch immer zu transzendieren. Wie bei einem Videospiel, bei dem man einfach einen anderen Charakter auswählen oder einen Avatar nach eigenen Vorstellungen gestalten kann.

K Es ist definitiv auch eine Art von Eskapismus. Hast du in deiner Kindheit viele Videospiele gespielt?
B Ja. Ich bin mit dem Nintendo und diesen ganzen alten Super-Mario-Spielen aufgewachsen, mit dem Gamecube und mit *The Sims*. Die Spiele, die mich am meisten interessiert haben, waren jene, in denen man die Realität simuliert und Welten erschafft. Solche mit einem offenen Ende, bei denen man immer weitermachen kann. Zum Beispiel Spiele, in denen man einen Bauernhof bewirtschaften oder ein Haus bauen und dann seine Schulden abbezahlen muss.

K Als Teenager hat Zeit eine andere Bedeutung, vielleicht weil man sich so gefangen fühlt. Ich denke, wenn man Videospiele spielt, verfliegen die Stunden, ohne dass man es mitbekommt. Vielleicht ist das beim Malen ein bisschen ähnlich, weil es diese Art von hermetischem, formlosem Zeit-Raum bietet?
B Auf jeden Fall. Ich verbringe so viel Zeit alleine im Atelier, um an diesen illusionären Objekten zu arbeiten, die dich in einen anderen Raum versetzen, die aber immer noch haptisch und materiell sind, was mir sehr wichtig geworden ist. Auf dem College habe ich eine Weile nicht gemalt, weil ich glaubte, nichts machen zu können angesichts der Geschichte und all dem. Ich habe ausschließlich virtuelle Räume konstruiert. Aber nach diesem einen wirklich schlimmen Tag – an dem du gewissermaßen mit deiner eigenen Existenz konfrontiert wirst – hatte ich das große Verlangen, einfach etwas mit meinen Händen zu erschaffen. Mir wurde klar, dass ich nicht ausschließlich digital arbeiten kann. Das ist nicht das Richtige für mich.

K **Bei VR-Arbeiten hat man oft das Gefühl, alleine in einer nicht-taktilen Welt zu sein. Vor allem, wenn man die VR-Brille trägt. Normalerweise würde es sehr lange dauern, in einen Bereich vorzustoßen, der derartig hermetisch abgetrennt ist von unserem materiellen Umfeld. Man müsste stundenlang Computerspiele spielen, alleine, mitten in der Nacht. Dank virtueller Realität gelangt man aber sehr schnell dorthin. Ich verstehe deine Arbeit gewissermaßen als eine Vision, etwas in eine materielle Form zu bringen, das normalerweise einer ganz bestimmten Art von Einsamkeit vorbehalten ist – um das dann mit anderen Menschen teilen zu können.**

B Das ist ein interessanter Punkt. Ich wurde kürzlich wiederholt gebeten, mein Atelier für Besucher*innen zu öffnen und über alles zu sprechen … Ich denke, es ist manchmal ganz schön hart, dass du als Künstler dauernd im Rampenlicht stehst. Ich meine: nicht nur deine Arbeit, sondern du als Person.

K **Es besteht eine Spannung zwischen dem intimen Raum des Virtuellen und dem öffentlichen Charakter einer Malerei.**

B Aber wenn es diese Spannung nicht gäbe, wäre das auch schrecklich.

K **Künstler*innen brauchen ein Publikum …**

B Selbstverständlich! Aber das birgt auch Konfliktpotenzial.

K **Malereien sind als Objekte so stark und können sich selbst so gut behaupten, dass man sie nicht begleiten oder viel über sie sagen muss. Das hat zum Teil mit der Geschichte des Mediums zu tun, aber auch damit, warum Leute überhaupt mit dem Malen angefangen haben: dieses Potenzial einer auratischen Präsenz, die sich daraus ergibt, dass ein Gemälde die Illusion von Raum *und* ein Körper ist. Das lässt sich meiner Meinung nach mit anderen Medien viel schwieriger erreichen. Du arbeitest in deinen Malereien viel mit unterschiedlichen Texturen, von der Flächigkeit des Airbrush hin zu den Stellen, an denen die Farbe so dick aufgetragen ist, dass sie reliefartig wirkt.**

B Ich versuche immer, im Bild ein wenig Raum zum Träumen zu lassen, damit sich andere darauf einlassen können. Diese Dissonanzen in Textur und Material helfen dabei, diesen Raum zu kreieren.

K **Je länger ich die Bilder in deinem Atelier betrachte, desto mehr sehe ich bloß den Mond. Obwohl sie so voller Inhalt sind, wird der Mond zum Fixpunkt, wie ein roter Faden.**

B Ja, er ist eine Figur, die in allen Arbeiten auftaucht. Ich glaube, er funktioniert in den Arbeiten als eine Art romantisches Symbol, als eine Sehnsucht, oder er steht dafür, dass es da noch etwas Größeres gibt als das dargestellte Narrativ.

K **In Anbetracht seiner prominenten Rolle in der Geschichte der Malerei ist der Mond ein sehr starkes Symbol. Ein Symbol für Transformation und für Kontemplation, sogar für eine Art romantische Melancholie. Es ist interessant, dass der Mond in deinen Bildern nie als Lichtquelle dient, sondern wie ein totes Zeichen darin schwebt. Gleichzeitig hast du diese Bühnenleuchten, die verdeutlichen, dass wir uns in einem künstlichen Raum befinden. Manchmal zeigst du sie uns sogar, als wären wir im Theater.**

B Ja, ich habe viel über Kunstgriffe nachgedacht, und wie wörtlich die Idee der Inszenierung umgesetzt wird, wenn ich die 3D-Modelle für die Malereien erstelle. Ich interessiere mich dafür, wie diese konzeptuelle Idee in den Arbeiten umgesetzt werden kann.

K **Das lässt mich an all die Hollywoodfilme denken, in denen es um Hollywood geht, wie etwa *Sunset Boulevard*, *Whatever Happened to Baby Jane*? oder *Mulholland Drive* – Hollywood verspeist sich selbst. In *Moongazing with Garden Hose* (2021)** **[▶ S. 60]** **gibt es keine Bühnenlichter, aber das Bild verursacht ein Gefühl des Grauens und der Klaustrophobie, und zwar auf eine sehr cineastische Art und Weise, durch die Vogelperspektive und den engen Ausschnitt.**

B Für mich geht es auch darum, die „vierte Wand“ zu durchbrechen und die Struktur des Narrativs offenzulegen. So wird der Mond zu einer Requisite und Horizont und Himmel sind bloß noch Elemente an einer Wand. Mir gefällt auch, wie man durch das Einbringen von künstlichem Licht in den Bildern mit der Neugier der Betrachter*innen spielen kann. Da ist dieser Anflug von Drama, der vom Ungewissen herrührt; man fragt sich, was sonst noch passieren könnte.

K Das bringt mich zurück zu dieser Idee von der US-amerikanischen Kultur als einer Projektion, die jeder Kleinstadt übergestülpt werden kann, als wäre man im Kino. Alles ist bereits in das Licht der Bühnenbeleuchtung getaucht und sieht aus, als würde man es durch ein Kameraobjektiv betrachten. Am Ende bringt es seine eigene Form von Authentizität hervor. Wie in *Mulholland Drive* ist es ein unendlicher Spiegel der Fiktionen, aber die Emotion ist real, also ist das egal.

B Wenn ich an einem Bild arbeite, lasse ich mich oft von einer Malerei oder von einem Film inspirieren, die oder den ich dann digital überarbeite, um mein eigenes Bild zu erschaffen. So war das auch bei der Arbeit *A beauty and the beast* (2022) **[▸ S. 78/79]**, die in Anlehnung an ein altes Gemälde von Rousseau entstanden ist. Und *Elizabeth Taylor's Reflection* (2021) **[▸ S. 106]**, das letztes Jahr in der Ausstellung bei Robert Grunenberg zu sehen war, ist von einer Geschichte über Elizabeth Taylor inspiriert. Sie probierte eine Halskette an und beugte sich dabei – weil sie keinen Spiegel hatte – über einen Pool, so wie Narziss am Teich.

K Das ist so ein starkes Bild. Auch weil Elizabeth Taylor auf eine Art jenseits von Gender und Individualität steht; bei den Hunderten Rollen, die sie gleichzeitig gespielt hat. Es verweist darauf, dass Narziss auch eine Art Hülle oder eine Maske ist; eine Spiegelung, die fälschlich für ein Selbst gehalten wird. Bei Freud ist Autismus die Kurzform von Autoerotismus und wird als ein Kurzschluss des Sexualtriebs verstanden. Anstatt nach außen zu treten, zieht er sich in das Selbst zurück und schottet es von der Welt ab. Ich denke, dass dieses Bild – so wie deine Arbeit im Allgemeinen – die Konzepte Narzissmus, Autismus und Erotik durch die Linse des virtuellen Raums auf eine Art und Weise zusammenbringt, die in der heutigen Zeit sehr treffend ist. Die Rubine an ihrer Halskette sehen aus wie Blut, das in den Pool tröpfelt.

B Das steht für mich in Verbindung mit dem Grund dafür, dass mich das Nächtliche zu faszinieren begann: Der Sud der Nacht als eine Art Maske, die in Wirklichkeit etwas offenbart, anstatt es zu verbergen. Ich glaube, dass die Maske, die man aufsetzt, in gewisser Weise viel darüber aussagt, wer man ist.

AMELY DEISS has been director of Kunstpalais in Erlangen since 2015. She studied art history and German studies in Berlin, Heidelberg, and Rome. From 2009 to 2013 she was the curator of the Stiftung für Konkrete Kunst und Design Ingolstadt, and from 2013 she was the deputy director of the Museum für Konkrete Kunst. She has curated numerous exhibitions, including solo shows by artists such as Sol Calero, Julian Charrière and Julius von Bismarck, Juergen Teller, Timm Ulrichs, Devan Shimoyama and Mary Sibande, as well as thematic exhibitions such as *neon: vom Leuchten der Kunst*, or *Save the Data! Von Kunst und Datenträgern*. In the city of Erlangen she is also responsible for Art in Architecture and Art in Public Spaces.

TAMARA REITZ has been curator at Kunstpalais since 2022. From 2020 to 2022 she worked there as a scientific trainee. She studied art history, cultural heritage preservation and sociology in Bamberg and Leipzig.

OLIVER KOERNER VON GUSTORF is a freelance writer. He lives in Berlin and the Uckermark and writes for Monopol, BLAU, Weltkunst, 032c, Welt, taz, Freitag. From 2007 to 2014 he ran the gallery SEPTEMBER in Berlin. Recent catalog publications: Soufiane Ababri, *Something New Under The Little Prince's Body*, Dittrich & Schlechtriem, Berlin 2019; *Fantastic Failure—An Excursion into Non-Objective Art*, in: *Ways of Seeing Abstraction*, Kerber Verlag, Bielefeld 2021; Marc Brandenburg, *Hirnsturm II*, PalaisPopulaire, Kerber Verlag, Bielefeld 2021; Carsten Fock, *Vejby*, Galerie Jochen Hempel, Berlin 2021; *SKIN (Anton im Bastrock)* in Werkverzeichnis Michael Müller, 2022. He is currently working on a novel about AIDS, end times and the Berlin art scene.

KRISTIAN VISTRUP MADSEN is a writer based in Berlin. His art criticism has been published in magazines such as Artforum, Frieze, and Mousse. He is the author of *Doing Time: Essays on Using People* (2021), and a novel forthcoming from Broken Dimanche Press in 2022. In 2021, he curated exhibitions at Futura in Prague and Arthub in Copenhagen.

AMELY DEISS ist seit 2015 Leiterin des Kunstpalais in Erlangen. Sie studierte Kunstgeschichte und Germanistik in Berlin, Heidelberg und Rom. Von 2009 bis 2013 war sie Kuratorin der Stiftung für Konkrete Kunst und Design Ingolstadt, seit 2013 stellvertretende Direktorin des Museums für Konkrete Kunst. Sie kuratierte zahlreiche Ausstellungen, darunter Soloshows von Künstler*innen wie Sol Calero, Julian Charrière und Julius von Bismarck, Juergen Teller, Timm Ulrichs, Devan Shimoyama und Mary Sibande und Themenausstellungen wie *neon: vom Leuchten der Kunst* oder *Save the Data! Von Kunst und Datenträgern*. In der Stadt Erlangen ist sie zudem verantwortlich für Kunst am Bau und Kunst im öffentlichen Raum.

TAMARA REITZ ist seit 2022 Kuratorin am Kunstpalais in Erlangen. Von 2020 bis 2022 war sie dort als wissenschaftliche Volontärin tätig. Sie studierte Kunstgeschichte, Kulturgutsicherung und Soziologie in Bamberg und Leipzig.

OLIVER KOERNER VON GUSTORF ist freier Autor. Er lebt in Berlin und der Uckermark und schreibt für Monopol, BLAU, Weltkunst, 032c, Welt, taz, Freitag. Von 2007 bis 2014 betrieb er in Berlin die Galerie SEPTEMBER. Jüngste Katalogpublikationen: Soufiane Ababri, *Something New Under The Little Prince's Body*, Dittrich & Schlechtriem, Berlin 2019; *Fantastisches Scheitern – Ein Exkurs in die gegenstandslose Kunst*, in: *Ways of Seeing Abstraction*, Kerber Verlag, Bielefeld 2021; Marc Brandenburg, *Hirnsturm II*, PalaisPopulaire, Kerber Verlag, Bielefeld 2021; Carsten Fock, *Vejby*, Galerie Jochen Hempel, Berlin 2021; *SKIN (Anton im Bastrock)* in Werkverzeichnis Michael Müller, 2022. Zurzeit arbeitet er an einem Roman über Aids, Endzeiten und die Berliner Kunstszene.

KRISTIAN VISTRUP MADSEN ist Schriftsteller und lebt und arbeitet in Berlin. Seine Kunstkritiken wurden in Zeitschriften wie Artforum, Frieze und Mousse veröffentlicht. Er ist der Autor von *Doing Time: Essays on Using People* (2021) und eines Romans, der 2022 bei Broken Dimanche Press erscheint. Im Jahr 2021 kuratierte er Ausstellungen im Futura in Prag und im Arthub in Kopenhagen.

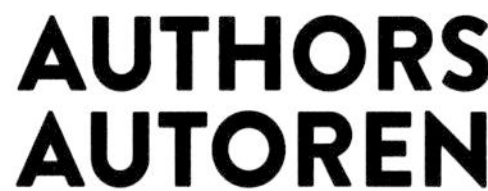

BRANDON LIPCHIK

** 1993 in Erie, Pennsylvania (US)*
Lives and works · lebt und arbeitet in New York City, NY (US) and · und Berlin (DE)

EDUCATION · AUSBILDUNG

- Rhode Island School of Design, RISD, Providence, RI (US) – Bachelor of Fine Arts, Painting
- 2016 Brown University, Providence, RI (US) – Digital Language Art

SOLO EXHIBITIONS · EINZELAUSSTELLUNGEN

2022
- *Brandon Lipchik. Moonbeams of Allegory*, Kunstpalais, Erlangen (DE)

2021
- *Above the Surface*, Robert Grunenberg, Berlin (DE)
- *Inground*, Richard Heller, Santa Monica, CA (US)

2020
- *Visions of Song*, Robert Grunenberg, Berlin (DE)
- *Upcoming Fall Residency Show*, The Garage, Amsterdam (NL)
- Galerie Julien Cadet, Paris (FR)

2019
- *Windows Into Exile*, Miettinen Collection with Robert Grunenberg Gallery, Berlin (DE)

2018
- *Nu Digital*, Galerie Julien Cadet, Paris (FR)
- *The Garden*, At Large Gallery, Brooklyn, NY (US)

GROUP EXHIBITIONS · GRUPPENAUSSTELLUNGEN

2022
- *In Search of the Present*, EMMA, Espoo (FI)

2021
- *THE ARTIST IS ONLINE*, König Galerie, Berlin (DE)

2020
- *Friends and Friends of Friends*, Schloss Museum, Linz (AT)
- *Sincere Intentions*, Robert Grunenberg, Berlin (DE)
- *Arena*, East Projects, New York City, NY (US)

2019
- *Link in Bio. Art after Social Media · Kunst nach den Sozialen Medien*, MdBK, Leipzig (DE)
- Massimo Minini, Brescia (IT)
- Expo Chicago, Richard Heller Gallery, Chicago, IL (US)
- Group Show, Galerie Julien Cadet, Montpellier (FR)
- *Post Digital Pop*, The Garage, Amsterdam (NL)
- *Something New, Something Borrowed*, Plastic Murs, Valencia (ES)
- *Time Bomb*, Wadstrom Tonnheim Gallery, Marbella (ES)
- *Ultra Light Beams*, Mount Analogue, Seattle, WA (US)

2018
- *Last Minute*, Art Haps Gallery, Bronx, NY (US)
- *While Supplies Last*, Seattle, WA (US)

2016
- *Public Park*, RISD Expose Show, Providence, RI (US)
- Senior Invitational Exhibition, Woods Gerry Gallery, Providence, RI (US)
- RISD Annual Senior Thesis Show, Providence, RI (US)

2015
- Erie Art Museum's 92nd Annual Spring Show, Erie, PA (US)

2014
- RISD Painting Department Show, Woods Gerry Gallery, Providence, RI (US)

AWARDS AND · UND RESIDENCIES

2019
- 2019 Palazzo Monti Residency, Brescia (IT)

2018
- 2018 So Far Residency, Montpellier (FR)
- 2018 Oli Epp's Summer Residency, The Koppel Project Hive, London (UK)

2014
- 2014 Anderson Ranch Arts Center, Snowmass Village, CO (US)
- 2014 Brooks Fellowship Award Winner, Snowmass Village, CO (US)

2011
- 2011 Northwestern Pennsylvania Artists Association Scholar, Erie, PA (US)
- 2011 Rhode Island School of Design Scholarship, Providence, RI (US)

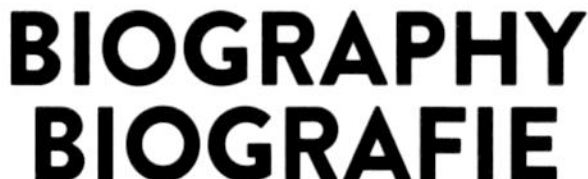

LIST OF WORKS
WERKVERZEICHNIS

COVER, P. · S. 43–45 *Forest Stage*, 2022 · Oil and acrylic paint on canvas · Öl und Acryl auf Leinwand · 175 × 250 cm · Private collection, Brussels · Privatsammlung, Brüssel · **RG**

FRONTISPIZ · FRONTISPIECE, P. · S. 108–111 *Moongazing with Garden Hose*, 2021 · Oil and acrylic paint on canvas · Öl und Acryl auf Leinwand · 195 × 219 cm · Collection · Sammlung Alexejew-Brandl, Berlin · **RG**

P. · S. 4, 20, 25, 26, 122–125 *Fallen Angel*, 2021 · Oil and acrylic paint on canvas · Öl und Acryl auf Leinwand · 197 × 200 cm · Miettinen Collection · **RG**

P. · S. 6, 9, 100/101 *Makeup Brush*, 2021 · Oil and acrylic paint on canvas · Öl und Acryl auf Leinwand · 120 × 100 cm · **RG**

P. · S. 10, 13, 116–119 *Boy with Pearl Necklace*, 2021 · Oil and acrylic paint on canvas · Öl und Acryl auf Leinwand · 198,5 × 211 cm · **RG**

P. · S. 14, 19, 48–51 *Pool Shot*, 2021 · Oil and acrylic paint on canvas · Öl und Acryl auf Leinwand · 200 × 301 cm · **RG**

P. · S. 34 *Untitled*, 2021 · Oil and acrylic paint on canvas · Öl und Acryl auf Leinwand · 120 × 100 cm · **RG**

P. · S. 46 *Bird Attack*, 2022 · Oil and acrylic paint on canvas · Öl und Acryl auf Leinwand · 170 × 158 cm · Private collection · Privatsammlung · **RG**

P. · S. 47 *Walk in the Woods*, 2022 · Oil and acrylic paint on canvas · Öl und Acryl auf Leinwand · 170 × 158 cm · **RG**

P. · S. 52 *Campfire*, 2020 · Acrylic and mixed media on canvas · Acryl und Mixed Media auf Leinwand · 120 × 100 cm · **JC**

P. · S. 53 *Cuddle*, 2020 · Acrylic and mixed media on canvas · Acryl und Mixed Media auf Leinwand · 120 × 100 cm · **JC**

P. · S. 54/55 *Rainshower Tree*, 2022 · Oil and acrylic paint on canvas · Öl und Acryl auf Leinwand · 117,5 × 100,5 · Private collection · Privatsammlung, Dr. Peter J. Henssen · **RG**

P. · S. 56–59 *Hot Tub Watch*, 2021 · Oil and acrylic paint on canvas · Öl und Acryl auf Leinwand · 175 × 223,5 cm · **RG**

P. · S. 60 *Garden Hose*, 2019 · Oil and acrylic paint on canvas · Öl und Acryl auf Leinwand · 120 × 100 cm · **RG**

P. · S. 61 *Water Hose*, 2020 · Acrylic and mixed media on canvas · Acryl und Mixed Media auf Leinwand · 120 × 100 cm · **JC**

P. · S. 62 *Sprinklers*, 2021 · Oil and acrylic paint on canvas · Öl und Acryl auf Leinwand · 185 × 200 cm · **RH**

P. · S. 63 *Pool Boy*, 2021 · Oil and acrylic paint on canvas · Öl und Acryl auf Leinwand · 120 × 120 cm · **RH**

P. · S. 64/65 *Submerge*, 2021 · Oil and acrylic paint on canvas · Öl und Acryl auf Leinwand · 120 × 120 cm · **RH**

P. · S. 66/67 *Looking through yellow light*, 2022 · Oil and acrylic paint on canvas · Öl und Acryl auf Leinwand · 101 × 117 cm · Private collection · Privatsammlung · **RG**

P. · S. 68 *Chemtrail Sky*, 2021 · Oil and acrylic paint on canvas · Öl und Acryl auf Leinwand · 140 × 150 cm · **RH**

P. · S. 69 *Abduction*, 2021 · Oil and acrylic paint on canvas · Öl und Acryl auf Leinwand · 138 × 150 cm · **RH**

P. · S. 70–73 *Rainshower*, 2021 · Oil and acrylic paint on canvas · Öl und Acryl auf Leinwand · 198,5 × 236 cm · **RG**

P. · S. 74 *Moon Swim*, 2021 · Oil and acrylic paint on canvas · Öl und Acryl auf Leinwand · 120 × 120 cm · **RH**

P. · S. 75 *Tire Swings*, 2021 · Oil and acrylic paint on canvas · Öl und Acryl auf Leinwand · 138 × 150 cm · **RH**

P. · S. 76 *The Audience*, 2022 · Oil and acrylic paint on canvas · Öl und Acryl auf Leinwand · 140 × 150 cm · **RG**

P. · S. 77 *Sebastian's revenge*, 2022 · Oil and acrylic paint on canvas · Öl und Acryl auf Leinwand · 200 × 186 cm · Private collection, Swizterland · Privatsammlung, Schweiz · **RG**

P. · S. 78/79 *A beauty and the beast*, 2022 · Oil and acrylic paint on canvas · Öl und Acryl auf Leinwand · 175 × 250 cm · Private collection · Privatsammlung, Hong Kong · **RG**

P. · S. 81–89 *Fear and Fantasy*, 2022 · Render Stills of Virtual Reality · **RG**

P. · S. 90–96 *La Guerre des Chiens*, 2022 · Render Stills of Virtual Reality · **RG**

P. · S. 98/99 *La Guerre des Chiens*, 2022 · Oil and acrylic paint on canvas · Öl und Acryl auf Leinwand · 175 × 250 cm · **RG**

P. · S. 102 *Dog Fight*, 2021 · Acrylic airbrush, oil and mixed media on canvas · Acryl-Airbrush, Öl und Mixed Media auf Leinwand · 110 × 110 cm · **RG**

P. · S. 103 *Snake Puddle*, 2021 · Oil and acrylic paint on canvas · Öl und Acryl auf Leinwand · 160 × 148 cm · **RH**

P. · S. 104 *Biker*, 2019 · Acrylic airbrush and mixed media on canvas · Acryl-Airbrush und Mixed Media auf Leinwand · 77 × 60 cm · **RG**

P. · S. 105 *Poolside*, 2019 · Acrylic airbrush and mixed media on canvas · Acryl-Airbrush und Mixed Media auf Leinwand · 75 × 60 cm · **RG**

P. · S. 106/107 *Elizabeth Taylor's Reflection*, 2021 · Oil and acrylic paint on canvas · Öl und Acryl auf Leinwand · 120 × 100 cm · **RG**

P. · S. 112 *Photographer in dark pool*, 2020 · Oil and acrylic paint on canvas · Öl und Acryl auf Leinwand · 74 × 80 cm · **JC**

P. · S. 113 *Swimming Pool*, 2020 · Acrylic paint and mixed media on canvas · Acryl und Mixed Media auf Leinwand · 200 × 185 cm · **JC**

P. · S. 114 *Howling Snake*, 2020 · Acrylic airbrush, oil and mixed media on canvas · Acryl-Airbrush, Öl und Mixed Media auf Leinwand · 200 × 185 cm · **RG**

P. · S. 115 *Vision of Monument Aflame*, 2020 · Acrylic airbrush, oil and mixed media on canvas · Acryl-Airbrush, Öl und Mixed Media auf Leinwand · 200 × 185 cm · **RG**

P. · S. 120 *Building Rooms Yet to Come*, 2020 · Acrylic airbrush, oil and mixed media on canvas · Acryl-Airbrush, Öl und Mixed Media auf Leinwand · 122 × 107 cm · **RG**

P. · S. 121 *Growth In Pond Waters*, 2020 · Acrylic airbrush, oil and mixed media on canvas · Acryl-Airbrush, Öl und Mixed Media auf Leinwand · 60 × 65 cm · **RG**

P. · S. 126 *Moonrise*, 2021 · Acrylic airbrush and mixed media on canvas · Acryl-Airbrush und Mixed Media auf Leinwand · 200 × 180 cm · **RG**

P. · S. 127 *Moonlit Lake*, 2020 · Acrylic airbrush and mixed media on canvas · Acryl-Airbrush und Mixed Media auf Leinwand · 90 × 83 cm · **RG**

P. · S. 128 *Red Wagon*, 2020 · Acrylic and mixed media on canvas · Acryl und Mixed Media auf Leinwand · 80 × 74 cm · **JC**

P. · S. 129 *Wash line*, 2020 · Acrylic and mixed media on canvas · Acryl und Mixed Media auf Leinwand · 180 × 150 cm · **JC**

P. · S. 130–133 *Poolside Cocktail*, 2021 · Oil and acrylic paint on canvas · Öl und Acryl auf Leinwand · 183,5 × 218 cm · **RG**

P. · S. 134 *Gardener*, 2019 · Acrylic airbrush and mixed media on canvas · Acryl-Airbrush und Mixed Media auf Leinwand · 75 × 60 cm · **RG**

P. · S. 135 *Under the Hood*, 2019 · Acrylic airbrush and mixed media on canvas · Acryl-Airbrush und Mixed Media auf Leinwand · 76 × 60 cm · **RG**

P. · S. 136 *Lap Dance*, 2020 · Acrylic airbrush and mixed media on canvas · Acryl-Airbrush und Mixed Media auf Leinwand · 120 × 110 cm · **RG**

P. · S. 137 *Snake Pool*, 2021 · Oil and acrylic paint on canvas · Öl und Acryl auf Leinwand · 200 × 185 cm · **RH**

P. · S. 138/139 *Dropping Swords in Paths Untrodden*, 2022 · Acrylic airbrush, oil and mixed media on canvas · Acryl-Airbrush, Öl und Mixed Media auf Leinwand · 200 × 300 (150) cm (diptych · Diptychon) · **RG**

P. · S. 141–143 *Monument of Dropped Swords in Paths Untrodden*, 2020 · Render Stills of Virtual Reality · **RG**

All · Alle: Courtesy the artist and · und
JC Galerie Julian Cadet **RG** Robert Grunenberg **RH** Richard Heller Gallery

This publication was published on occasion of the exhibition *Brandon Lipchik. Moonbeams of Allegory* · July 30, 2022 to October 23, 2022 at Kunstpalais, Erlangen, curated by Tamara Reitz

Diese Publikation erscheint anlässlich der Ausstellung *Brandon Lipchik. Moonbeams of Allegory* · 30. Juli 2022 bis 23. Oktober 2022 im Kunstpalais, Erlangen, kuratiert von Tamara Reitz

CATALOG · KATALOG

Editors · Herausgeberinnen
Amely Deiss and · und Tamara Reitz

*Authors · Autor*innen*
Amely Deiss, Oliver Körner von Gustorf, Tamara Reitz, Kristian Vistrup Madsen

Managing editor · Redaktion
Tamara Reitz

Project management · Projektmanagement
Fabian Reichel

Translation · Übersetzung
B Connects. Barbara Geier Content Services, Good & Cheap Art Translators

Copyediting · Lektorat
Kristina Becker (Deutsch · German), B Connects. Barbara Geier Content Services, Good & Cheap Art Translators, (English · Englisch)

Design · Gestaltung
Sofarobotnik, Augsburg & München

Typefaces · Schriften
Brandon Grotesque & Freight Text

Production · Verlagsherstellung
Alise Ausmane

Printing and binding · Druck und Bindung
Livonia Print Ltd., Riga

Paper · Papier
G-Print, 170 g/m²
Magno Gloss, 130 g/m²

Photography · Fotografie
Nick Ash: 60, 104, 105, 114, 115, 120, 121, 134–136; Hubertus Bessau: 149; Roman März: 2, 4, 6, 9, 10, 13, 14, 19, 20, 25, 26, 34, 43–51, 54–59, 66/67, 70–73, 76–79, 98–102, 106–111, 116–119, 122–125, 127, 130–133, 138–140; Thomas Marroni: 52, 53, 61, 112, 113, 126, 128, 129; Alan Shaffer Photography: 62–65, 68, 69, 74, 75, 103, 137

Published by · Erschienen im
Hatje Cantz Verlag GmbH
Mommsenstraße 27
10629 Berlin
Germany · Deutschland

www.hatjecantz.com
A Ganske Publishing Group Company · Ein Unternehmen der Ganske Verlagsgruppe

ISBN 978-3-7757-5346-3
Printed in Latvia

EXHIBITION · AUSSTELLUNG

Kunstpalais
Marktplatz 1, 91054 Erlangen
info@kunstpalais.de
www.kunstpalais.de

Director · Leitung
Amely Deiss

Curator of Collection · Sammlungskurator
Malte Lin-Kröger

Head of Art Education · Leitung Kunstvermittlung
Laura Capalbo, Johanna Berges-Grunert

Art in Architecture and Art Education · Kunst am Bau und Kunstvermittlung
Hannah Straub

Scientific Trainee · Wissenschaftliches Volontariat
Jacqueline Gwiasdowski

Administration and Finances · Verwaltung und Finanzen
Ilse Wittmann

Technical Staff and Exhibition Setup · Ausstellungstechnik und -aufbau
Ian Genocchi

Voluntary Social Year · FSJ Kultur
Lilly Mosig

Internship · Praktikum
Clara-Maria Habiger, Julius Jurkiewitsch, Julia Keinath, Nathifa Sucipto

Kindly supported by · Mit freundlicher Unterstützung von
Galerie Robert Grunenberg · www.robertgrunenberg.com

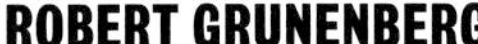

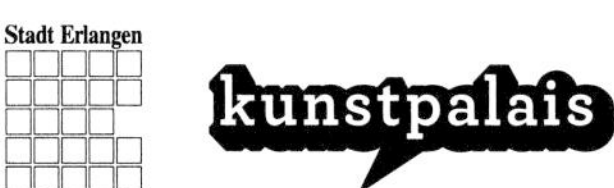